Living by the Light of the Moon
2016 Moon Book
Beatrex Quntanna

Acknowledgments

This book would never have come about without the inspiration and encouragement of Nancy Tappe, my friend, mentor, master-teacher, and mystic.

I also wish to acknowledge…

Jennifer Masters for the cover art and her ability to capture the nature of generosity with her magical painting. Thank you, Jennifer! Violet Green for her enthusiasm, teamwork, endless nights editing, and keeping me consistent. Michelenne Crab for her tech-support and personal support for the last 15 years. Michael Makay for the daily Tibetan Numerology intentions that inspire and direct us to make the most of our day. Jaime Lyerly for her research and attention to detail.

Special thanks to…

Katherine Sale for the astrological calculations for the entire year. Kaliani Devinne for contributing new goddess profiles corresponding to each moon cycle, and the moon charts. Jill Estensen for sharing aspects from her *Dimensional Astrology* system, that add an innovative approach to experiencing the degrees and the polarity they create for each moon phase. Candice Covingtion for her approach to the elements. Ann Meyer for the freedom affirmations, from Teaching of the Inner Christ. Last, but not least, deep gratitude to the countless students who come to Moon Class; without you guys this teaching would not exist!

Book Cover Art

Generosity by Jennifer Masters

Book Design & Art Direction

Jennifer Masters, artist and illustrator
www.JenniferMastersCreative.com

Tibetan Numerology of the Day

Michael Makay
mbmakay@gmail.com

Dimensional Astrology

Jill Estensen's innovative translation for the Sabian Symbols
intuvision@roadrunner.com

Astrological Calculations

Katherine Sale, MSW, MAc, is an Intuitive Astrologer with a psycho-spiritual approach to counseling, focusing on Soul-Centered Astrology, with an emphasis on the integration of the Soul through the personality.
StargazerKat@gmail.com

Copyright ©2015 by Beatrex Quntanna
All Rights Reserved. No part of this book may be reproduced or transmitted in any form or by any means without the written permission of the publisher, except for the inclusion of brief quotations in a review.

ISBN 978-0-9625292-6-9

Printed in the United States of America

ART ALA CARTE PUBLISHING
760-944-6020
beatrex@cox.net
www.mymoonbook.com
www.beatrex.com

This book is dedicated to the Generosity Buddha
who opens the pathways for prosperity so
all sentient beings may live in bliss.

Table of Contents

The Importance of Cycles __ 6

How to Use This Book _____ 7

January _____ 12
Capricorn New Moon   14
Leo Full Moon   22

February _____ 30
Aquarius New Moon   32
Virgo Full Moon   40

March _____ 48
Pisces New Moon – Solar Eclipse   50
Libra Full Moon – Lunar Eclipse   58

April _____ 66
Aries New Moon   68
Scorpio Full Moon   76

May _____ 84
Taurus New Moon   86
Sagittarius Full Moon   94

June _____ 102
Gemini New Moon   104
Sagittarius Full Moon   112

July _____ 120
Cancer New Moon   122
Capricorn Full Moon   130

August _____ 138
Leo New Moon   140
Aquarius Full Moon   148

September _____ 156
Virgo New Moon – Solar Eclipse   158
Pisces Full Moon – Lunar Eclipse   166
Libra New Moon   174

October _____ 182
Aries Full Moon   184
Scorpio New Moon   192

November _____ 200
Taurus Full Moon   202
Sagittarius New Moon   210

December _____ 218
Gemini Full Moon   220
Capricorn New Moon   228

About the Author _____ 236
Other Works by This Author   237

The Importance of Cycles

Each moon cycle offers a different combination of energies. These energies pour down to the Earth, giving us a chance to grow harmoniously into wholeness. The key is to remember that this is a study in light. Following the luminaries, the Sun and the Moon, through the zodiac and noting the cycles of illumination and reflection can bring you to a deeper creative experience of life. The Moon is the great cosmic architect, the builder and dissolver of form and foundation. The full moon is about dissolving, and the new moon is about building. The *2016 Moon Book* is a workbook that will assist you in knowing what to build and when, and what to dissolve and when.

Over the years Beatrex has developed a valuable collection of knowledge about how to use the moon cycles to enhance the quality of your life. This workbook is filled with activities to do during each moon cycle, in its specific zodiac sign and time, for the entire year. Life, at the highest spiritual level, moves beyond time and uses cycles to increase your ability to actualize your full potential for living. Cycles are in charge of your personal development; while time is in charge of the change in direction that happens when you take the risk to grow and begin to trust in Divine Timing. The *2016 Moon Book* synthesizes techniques that allow for the power of development and direction to occur in the entire spectrum of wholeness. Each zodiac sign holds the knowledge necessary to integrate an aspect of yourself in order to become whole. As the Moon and Sun travel around our planet each month, a different aspect of self-development is presented to you via the constellation (zodiac sign) it is visiting. For centuries, the Moon has been the keeper of the secrets of life. If used appropriately, the Moon sets the stage for successful living. This workbook reveals those secrets and supports you in learning them.

The Year of Generosity keeps our manifesting ability readily available to us in the moment. The more we manifest, the less we suffer and allow the bliss from our spiritual essence to come forward. Give up being devoted to the past in order to embark on new frontiers. Expect and adjustment and recalibration down to the core of your being. This workbook is set up with a support structure that easily guides you towards manifestation and recalibration so that the power of acceptance can become your reality in 2016.

When the Moon is Full

When the Moon is full, it's in direct opposition to the Sun and it's time to set yourself free. This polarity provides a disintegrating effect that presents the best possible opportunity to dissolve anything that stands in the way of your personal recalibration. Several hours before a full moon you may experience a tension that happens when the Sun and Moon come into an opposing position. This aspect asks you to learn to understand opposite natures without feeling the need to separate them. As a matter of fact, they are designed to teach you how to find the middle ground and integrate these opposites so that you cannot be manipulated by polarity. Integration creates unity, which then creates harmony. The identifying polarity themes are provided for you on the appropriate full moon pages. Use the astrological theme and recalibrating ideas as inspiration to write your list of ways to renew your life.

Once your list is written, light a candle, and read your list out loud. Then, place it under a circle-shaped mirror, and put your candle on top of the mirror. You might put the candle, wishes, and mirror outside in the moonlight or in a special place in your home. Let the candle burn out. For your protection, make sure to use a candle that is in glass, such as a votive or seven-day candle. When your candle has finished burning, your recalibrating list will be in operation. It is the empty space that makes room for manifestation to occur. Before writing your recalibrating list you might want to look over the trigger points on the previous page to see if there is anything you might want to let go of first. Remember recalibration allows you to live without resistance.

Please note: All times listed in the book are local to the Pacific time zone. Add or subtract hours accordingly to adjust times for your time zone. It is best to do your manifesting and recalibrating ceremonies at the specific time noted. Visit www.mymoonbook.com for mirrors

When the Moon is New

When the Moon is new, it is in the same sign as the Sun. This unites the power of the magnetic and dynamic fields that are in perfect resonance for manifesting. This is a potent time to make your desires known to yourself and to the Universe by writing a personal manifesting list. Use the astrological theme and manifesting ideas to write your list. Think about your list like a kid does when writing to Santa Claus. Let yourself become comfortable, while extending the boundaries beyond what you believe is possible. You might consider writing the following words at the end of your manifesting list, "This, or something better than this, comes to me in an easy and pleasurable way for the good of all concerned."

Once your list is written, light a candle, and read your list out loud. Then, place it under an eight-sided mirror, and put your candle on top of the mirror. You might put the candle, wishes, and mirror outside in the moonlight or in a special place in your home. For your protection, make sure to use a candle that is in glass, such as a votive or seven-day candle. Let the candle burn out. By the time the candle burns out, your manifestations are in place and ready to come true.

Please note: All times listed in the book are local to the Pacific time zone. Add or subtract hours accordingly to adjust times for your time zone. It is best to do your manifesting and recalibrating ceremonies at the specific time noted. Visit www.mymoonbook.com for mirrors.

How to Use This Book

These Sections Will Help You to Live by the Light of the Moon

Planetary Highlights

This section explains the planets and how they will affect your life each month. It does not contain all of the aspects; it simply highlights points of interest that promote personal growth during each month. If you are interested in more study, take an astrology class. If you are an astrologer and want more information, we have provided a chart for each moon phase for your convenience.

The Monthly Calendar

This section provides you with a monthly overview and keeps you connected to the lunar, solar, and planetary cycles. It lets you know when the Moon is void-of-course, when it moves into a new sign, when the Sun and planets change signs, and when a planet goes retrograde or stationary direct (shown by the $\frac{S}{D}$ symbol). The calendar also has the Tibetan Numerology of the Day, along with an affirmation, to help you align with the energy and set your intentions for the day.

Void Moon

When the Moon is void-of-course, it has made its last major aspect in a sign and stays void until it enters the next sign. When the Moon is void-of-course, you will see the icon V/C on the calendar. This is not a good time to start new projects, relationships, or to take trips, unless you intend to never follow through. When the Moon ☽ enters a new sign, you will see this arrow ➡ It will be followed by the symbol for the new sign and the time that the Moon enters it.

Super-Sensitivity ▲

This happens when the Moon travels across the sky, hits the center of the galaxy, and connects with a fixed star. When this happens the atmosphere becomes chaotic. An extra amount of energy pours down in a spiral at a very fast speed making it difficult to focus. This fragility can make you depressed, anxious, dizzy, and accident-prone. It is a good idea to keep your thought process away from this energy. This is global, not personal.

Low-Vitality ▼

This happens when the Moon is directly opposite the center of the galaxy. When this fixed-star opposition occurs, the Earth becomes very fragile and gets depleted. This leads to exhaustion in our physical bodies and is a sign for us to nurture ourselves by resting. The depletion can create Earth changes. Endings can also happen and resistance to these completions will bring on exhaustion. Best to detach and let go.

The Sun

Each month you will see the icon for the Sun ☉ with an arrow ➡ indicating when the Sun enters a new sign. When the Sun changes signs, the climate of energy takes on a new theme for your personal development. Look for the Sun icon, with an arrow followed by an astrological sign, to indicate sign change and time.

Planets

Planets also change signs and move in retrograde and direct motions. Retrograde planets are next to the date in each day's box followed by retrograde icon ℞. In the middle of each box is information about planetary changes of time and direction.

Please note: All times are given for the Pacific time zone. Add or subtract hours accordingly to adjust times for your time zone.

Choice Points: Light – Shadow – Wisdom

Dimensional Astrology presents us with a prescribed action for each of the 360-degrees on the astrology wheel. The object of Dimensional Astrology is to depolarize and neutralize. Each degree for the Moon and its house are described to better enhance your understanding of the phase and its effects on you and your world. The wisdom comes when we experience and combine the motivation and the resistance without judgment. For example, in the new moon in January, the Choice Point light is about accepting praise, the shadow side is gossip. You will find yourself accepting praise, and if you resist you set yourself up for gossip. The wisdom is accepting praise and acknowledgement and in so doing others accept their own authority.

"I" Statements

These statements align the Self with the characteristics of the astrological sign and the house the sign lives in.

Body Mind Spirit

Each astrological sign rules a body part, a mental trait or attitude, and a spiritual condition. This section is provided to increase understanding of the tendencies and patterns that are activated during the moon transit.

Elements

Each moon cycle has a primary element (earth, air, fire or water), attached to the constellation to which it is assigned, that brings you more awareness of what to work on during the cycle.

House Themes

Each house the Moon lands in brings a focus for that moon as a baseline for self-development during the moon phase.

Karmic Awakenings

Every once in a while the chart for the Moon will show an intercepted astrological sign in a house on the chart. This indicates that a karmic pattern is in operation on that day.

Goddesses

When the Moon enters a new zodiac sign, a changing of guardians occurs. Deep within each sign lives a goddess who is the keeper of this cyclical domain. This archetype's assignment is to hold the space for an aspect of wholeness to actualize.

Build Your Altar

An altar is an outer focus for inner work. Esoteric coordinates such as Tarot cards, flowers, colors, gemstones, fragrances, and numerology are provided as an enhancement to better assist you in working with each moon phase. Perhaps you are working on a love theme; you might want to add six hearts, six flowers, and six gemstones on your altar with your manifesting list and candle. The coordinating tarot card can be used as a visual activation. Flowers, colors, and gemstones accent your intentions. The fragrance provides a special connection to Spirit. You may want to burn candles of this scent, spritz your aura or your altar with the fragrance, or simply sniff the fragrance to awaken your olfactory system. Visit www.mymoonbook.com for moon mists.

Manifesting List

Write down what you want to create and manifest in your life.

Recalibrating List

Write down what you want to change and recalibrate in your life.

List Ideas

Use these ideas to jump start your own lists. Let your imagination take off from here.

Clearing the Slate

This is the first step to recalibrate and release during each full moon cycle. Each section is filled with trigger points that are specific to the astrological sign where the Moon resides. See if any of them feel familiar. Acknowledge what's familiar and then follow the instructions by writing down what happened and perform Ho'oponopono, the Hawaiian forgiveness ritual. For example, a negative trigger point for Leo is impatience. When you find yourself being impatient, write down the circumstances or journal about it. Then, apologize to yourself, ask for forgiveness, have gratitude for yourself with thanks that you could see your impatience as a trigger, and then return to love.

Challenges and Victories

These are sets of affirmations designed to say out loud during a specific moon cycle to determine a motivational tone for your self-discovery. After saying all of them out loud, you will know which statement applies to you. Circle the one that is yours and use it as a personal mantra daily during the moon phase.

The Astro Wheel

Western astrological charts are placed within a circle or wheel. The wheel is a picture of the sky from a particular place and time on Earth. It is divided into 12 parts called "houses." Each house deals with a particular area of life. Key concepts for each house are written outside the wheel. Compare the wheel in the book to your very own chart and discover the theme that you will be living personally during the moon phase.

Cosmic Check-In

"I" statements are designed specifically to keep you in touch with all of the signs and their houses each time the Moon is new or full. Fill in the blanks to complete each statement during each full and new moon phase to activate all parts of your birth chart and keep you in touch with Oneness. Have fun noticing how different you are during each cycle.

Blank Pages

Between each moon phase blank pages are provided for journaling.

Heavenly Bodies

☉	Sun	Outer personality, potential, director, the most obvious traits of the consciousness projection
☽	Moon	Emotion, feelings, memory, unconsciousness, mother's influence, ancestors, home life
☿	Mercury	The way you think, the intention beneath your thoughts, communication, academia (lower mind)
♀	Venus	Beauty, value, romantic love, sensuality, creativity, being social, fun, femininity
♂	Mars	Action, change, variety, sex drive, ambition, warrior, ego, athletics, masculinity
♃	Jupiter	Benevolent, jovial, excessive, expansive, optimistic, abundant, extravagant, accepting good fortune
♄	Saturn	Teacher, karma, disciplined, restrictive, father's influence
♅	Uranus	Liberated, revolutionary, explosive, spontaneous, breakthrough, innovation, technology
♆	Neptune	Mystical, charming, sensitive, addictive, glamorous, deceptive, illusions
♇	Pluto	Money, wealth, transformation, secrets, hidden information, sexuality, psychic power
⚷	Chiron	Wounded healer, healing, holistic therapies
☊	North Node	This represents where you are headed in this lifetime. In other words, it represents the direction your life will take you, your future focus. In Eastern astrology, this is sometimes called the "head of the dragon."
☋	South Node	This represents what you brought with you this lifetime and what you are moving away from. It is sometimes called the "tail of the dragon" in Eastern astrology.

Astrological Signs

Each sign of astrology has a particular quality or tone that is described in more detail with the moons.

Sign	"I" Statement		Element	Key Words
♈ Aries	I Am	Sign of the Ram Ruled by Mars ♂ Aries begins the zodiac year with the Spring Equinox	Fire	Ego, identity, championship, leadership, action-oriented, warrior, and self-first.
♉ Taurus	I Have	Sign of the Bull Ruled by Venus ♀	Earth	Self-value, abundant, aesthetic, business, sensuous, art, beauty, flowers, gardens, collector, and shopper.
♊ Gemini	I Communicate	Sign of the Twins Ruled by Mercury ☿	Air	Versatile, expressive, restless, travel-minded, short trips, flirt, gossip, "nose for news," and messenger.
♋ Cancer	I Feel	Sign of the Crab Ruled by the Moon ☽ Cancer begins with the Summer Solstice	Water	Emotional, nurturing, family-oriented, home, mother, cooking, security-minded, ancestors, builder of form and foundation.
♌ Leo	I Love	Sign of the Lion Ruled by the Sun ☉	Fire	Willful, dramatic, loyal, children, child-ego state, love affairs, decadent, royal, show-stopper, theatre, adored and adoring.
♍ Virgo	I Heal	Sign of the Virgin Ruled by Mercury ☿	Earth	Gives birth to Divinity, perfectionist, discernment, scientific, analytical, habitual, work-oriented, body maintenance, earth connection, attention to detail, service-oriented, earth healer, herbs, and judgmental.
♎ Libra	I Relate	Sign of the Scales Ruled by Venus ♀ Libra begins with the Autumnal Equinox	Air	Relationship, social, harmony, industry, the law, diplomacy, morality, beauty, strategist, logical, and over-active mind.
♏ Scorpio	I Transform	Sign of the Scorpion Ruled by Pluto ♀ and Mars ♂	Water	Intense, passionate, sexual, powerful, focused, controlling, deep, driven, and secretive.
♐ Sagittarius	I Seek	Sign of the Archer Ruled by Jupiter ♃	Fire	Optimistic, generous, preacher-teacher, world traveler, higher knowledge, goal-oriented, philosophy, culture, publishing, extravagance, excessive, exaggerator, and good fortune.
♑ Capricorn	I Produce	Sign of the Goat Ruled by Saturn ♄ Capricorn begins at the Winter Solstice	Earth	Ambitious, concretive, responsible, achievement, business, corporate structure, world systems, and useful.
♒ Aquarius	I Know	Sign of the Water Bearer Ruled by Uranus ♅	Air	Inventive, idealistic, utopian, rebellion, innovative, technology, community, friends, synergy, group consciousness, science, magic, trendy, and future-orientation.
♓ Pisces	I Trust	Sign of the Fishes Ruled by Neptune ♆	Water	Sensitive, creative, empathetic, theatre, addiction, escape artist, glamor, secretive, Divinely guided, healer, medicine.

The Astro Wheel

Western astrological charts are placed within a circle or wheel. The wheel is a picture of the sky from a particular place and time on Earth. It is divided into 12 parts called "houses." Each house deals with a particular area of life. Below are some key concepts for each house.

	Statement	Ruling Sign		Key Notes
1st House	**I Am**	♈	Aries	Your outer appearance, the way you present yourself, the way you dress, the way you enter a room, and what you leave behind when you leave the room.
2nd House	**I Have**	♉	Taurus	The way you make your money and the way you spend your money.
3rd House	**I Communicate**	♊	Gemini	How you get the word out and the message behind the words.
4th House	**I Feel**	♋	Cancer	The way your early environmental training was and how that set your foundation for living, and why you chose your mother.
5th House	**I Love**	♌	Leo	The way you love and how you want to be loved.
6th House	**I Heal**	♍	Virgo	The way you manage your body and its appearance.
7th House	**I Relate**	♎	Libra	One-on-one relationships, defines your people attraction, and how you work in relationships with the people you attract.
8th House	**I Transform**	♏	Scorpio	How you share money and other resources, what you keep hidden regarding sex, death, real estate, and regeneration.
9th House	**I Seek**	♐	Sagittarius	The way you approach spirituality, philosophy, journeys, higher knowledge, and aspiration.
10th House	**I Produce**	♑	Capricorn	Your approach to status, career, honor, and prestige, and why you chose your Father.
11th House	**I Know**	♒	Aquarius	Your approach to friends, social consciousness, teamwork, community service, and the future.
12th House	**I Trust**	♓	Pisces	Determines how you deal with your karma, unconscious software, and what you will experience in order to attain mastery by completing your karma. It is also about the way you connect to the Divine.

Tibetan Numerology of the Day

2	**Balance**	Be decisive and move past vacillation.
3	**Fun**	Have a party. Take on a creative project. Express the "Disneyland" side of yourself.
4	**Structure**	Take the day to organize. Get the job done. Work and you will sail through the day.
5	**Action, exercise, travel**	Exercise—join a gym, take a dance class, play tennis, go for a walk. Travel—go for a drive, travel the world, visit your travel agent. Make a change.
6	**Love**	Go out for a night of romance. Work on beauty in your home. Nurture yourself and take care of your health.
7	**Research**	Read a book. Learn something new and get smart. Take a class.
8	**Money**	Have a business meeting. Meet with your accountant. Make a sales call. Start a new business.
9	**Connecting with the Divine**	Meditate. Take part in a humanitarian project. Do community service.
10	**Seeing the "big picture"**	Take an innovative idea and run with it today!
11	**Completion**	Do what it takes to be complete.

January Planetary Highlights

Mercury goes Retrograde in Aquarius on January 5 through January 25

Protect your technology, avoid travel if possible, and prepare files for the new year. Decide not to decide on anything.

Jupiter goes Retrograde in Virgo on January 7 Until May 9

An "Attitude of Gratitude" will keep you on the right side of Jupiter.

January 1 – Mercury Enters Aquarius

The mind will be very active. If you add some intention into the mix, you might come up with some great projects, programs, and inventions.

January 3 – Mars Enters Scorpio

An extra focus on sex could come forward into your experience.

January 8 – Mercury Enters Capricorn

The mind could become overburdened with details and responsible action – Make sure that this doesn't kill the magic.

January 20 – The Sun Enters Aquarius

Innovation, teamwork, group, and community-centered issues could be very rewarding at this time, especially as they relate to technology and the future. Get in the flow and you will be very surprised at where you end up.

January 23 – Venus Enters Capricorn

Resistance could become part of your experience, especially if you feel as if your fun is being blocked. Brat attacks could come into play and regrets will come later.

January 23 – The Sun, Moon, and Pluto All Tripled in Capricorn

Know that your potential for abundance is gaining more courage to move beyond fear and accept a prosperous life.

Saturn Conjunct with Venus and in Sagittarius Until the End of the Month

Time to look at being practical. Know that this is only temporary and just tell yourself that the sales will be better next month.

Jupiter is Dancing with the North Node in Virgo Ongoing

Under the umbrella of service you can shine. If attention to self is required by your ego, it won't work. All action must be based in love.

Jupiter is Opposite Chiron Ongoing

This could herald in a new miracle healing or a healer.

Mercury and Pluto Exact in Capricorn for the Entire Month

The message for the new abundance factor is clearly outlined and coming alive!

Chiron is Conjunct with the South Node in Pisces Ongoing

Unnecessary modalities for healing are washing away. Watch this happen so you can see the new healing methods clearly.

Super-Sensitivity – January 7-8

Stay out of what you consider to be chaotic.

Low-Vitality – January 20-21

Pay attention to your body.

Sunday	Monday	Tuesday	Wednesday	Thursday	Friday	Saturday
					1 New Year's Day ♀→♒ 6:21pm 11. Send love to the center of the Earth.	2 ☽ V/C 8:23am 3. Honor yourself first.
3 ♂→♏ 6:34am ☽→♏ 11:35am 4. You become what you judge.	4 5. Transform through change.	5 ☿℞ ☿ SD → 1°♒02' 5:06am ☽ V/C 9:47am ☽→♐ 10:56pm 6. "Being right" lacks enlightenment.	6 ☿℞ 7. Opposition can work as a team.	7 ☿♃℞ ▲ ♃ SR → 23°♍14' 8:41pm ☽ V/C 6:44pm 8. Abundance is your birthright.	8 ☿♃℞ ▲ ♀→♑ 11:37am ☽→♑ 7:06am 9. Truth lies in simplicity.	9 ☿♃℞ ● 19°♑13' 5:32pm 10. You create the future in the now.
10 ☿♃℞ ☽ V/C 9:39am ☽→♒ 12:22pm 2. Take action to stay balanced.	11 ☿♃℞ ☽ V/C 5:09pm 3. Make music wherever you go.	12 ☿♃℞ ☽→♓ 3:53pm 4. Follow the cycles of nature.	13 ☿♃℞ 5. Be willing to change.	14 ☿♃℞ ☽ V/C 8:31am ☽→♈ 6:48pm 6. Create beauty in your home.	15 ☿♃℞ 7. Learn something new today.	16 ☿♃℞ ☽ V/C 3:26pm ☽→♉ 9:48pm 8. Your abundance knows no limits.
17 ☿♃℞ 9. Pray from your heart not your head.	18 ☿♃℞ Martin Luther King ☽ V/C 10:49pm 10. You can change rain into sunshine.	19 ☿♃℞ ☽→♊ 1:12am 2. Look at both sides, then decide.	20 ☿♃℞ ▼ ☉→♒ 7:28am 3. Worry is the misuse of imagination.	21 ☿♃℞ ▼ ☽ V/C 12:00am ☽→♋ 5:27am 4. Ask for protection on all levels.	22 ☿♃℞ ☽ V/C 10:20pm 5. To find your path, be the path.	23 ☿♃℞ ♀→♑ 12:33pm ☽→♌ 11:20am ○ 3°♌29' 5:47pm 6. See beauty in all of nature.
24 ☿♃℞ ☽ V/C 6:51pm 7. Don't think, use thought.	25 ♃℞ ☿ SD → 14°♑55' 1:51pm ☽→♍ 7:45pm 8. Make money your friend.	26 ♃℞ 9. Silence brings the message.	27 ♃℞ ☽ V/C 4:10pm 10. Plan ahead, but live in the now.	28 ♃℞ ☽→♎ 6:59am 2. Gather opinions and then decide.	29 ♃℞ ☽ V/C 5:34pm 3. Celebrate joy with those you love.	30 ♃℞ ☽→♏ 7:50pm 4. Organize what you resist.
31 ♃℞ 5. Accept change and all will be well.						

♈ Aries	♎ Libra	☉ Sun	♄ Saturn	☊ North Node	▲ Super Sensitivity	6. Love
♉ Taurus	♏ Scorpio	☽ Moon	♅ Uranus	☋ South Node	▼ Low Vitality	7. Learning
♊ Gemini	♐ Sagittarius	☿ Mercury	♆ Neptune	➡ Enters	2. Balance	8. Money
♋ Cancer	♑ Capricorn	♀ Venus	♇ Pluto	℞ Retrograde	3. Fun	9. Spirituality
♌ Leo	♒ Aquarius	♂ Mars	⚷ Chiron	SD Stationary Direct	4. Structure	10. Visionary
♍ Virgo	♓ Pisces	♃ Jupiter		V/C Void-of-Course	5. Action	11. Completion

January 9th
5:32 PM

New Moon in Capricorn

Degree Choice Points
19° Capricorn 13'

Light Praise

Shadow Gossip

Wisdom Accept praise and acknowledgement to allow others to accept their own authority.

Statement I Produce
   Body Knees
   Mind Authority Issues
   Spirit Self-reliance

Element
Earth – Family lineage and DNA healing, knowing nutrition and abundance, body awareness, healing power from the plant kingdom, connection to small animals.

Sixth House Moon
25° Sagittarius 58'

Sixth House Umbrella Theme
I Heal/I Seek – The way you manage your body and appearance.

Light Universal Calling

Shadow Fanaticism

Wisdom Familiarize yourself with planetary, solar, and galactic law.

When the Sun is in Capricorn

When the Sun is in Capricorn, we are given opportunities to receive the blessings of abundance and prosperity on a concrete level. Material satisfaction is at the top of the priority list for Capricorns. This is why they are known to be ambitious. Let integrity and goodwill set the standard for your recognition and accomplishments. Now is the time to take advantage of the energy by being useful and productive with a higher purpose. Capricorn is going through the most difficult times right now as the "old guard" is being swept away and creating space for the opening of the human heart. The presence of Pluto in this constellation is transforming all of the systems and structures that are so familiar and placing the Capricorn on unstable ground. Authority symbols and traditions are dissolving and opening new pathways for self-reliance to emerge as a reality, so that the idea of elitism can diminish and synergy will be the new status quo.

Capricorn Goddess

Srinmo, the ancestral Earth goddess of Tibet, holds "The Great Round" or "Wheel of Life" upon which all thoughts and deeds of humankind are recorded. She represents the wild, chaotic energy of the Feminine. Her incarnation in the land of Tibet is said to be held fast by twelve geomantic templates with Lhasa, the "plain of milk," representing her pulsing heart and life-giving breasts.

Carry a round object in your pocket between now and the full moon, to remind you of cycles and how Srinmo's karmic wheel brings your words, thoughts, and deeds back to you. Cycle a positive mantra in your mind to channel and harness your underground creative energy.

Build Your Altar

Colors Forest green, tan, earth tones, deep red

Numerology 10 – You create the future in the now

Tarot Card The Devil – Being a prisoner of a choice-less reality

Gemstones Topaz, carnelian, amber, smoky quartz, jasper

Plant Remedy Rosemary – The power of memory

Fragrance Frankincense – Opens the gateway for the Soul to enter the body

Manifesting List

This or something better than this comes to me in an easy and pleasurable way, for the good of all concerned. Thank you, Universe!

Capricorn Manifesting Ideas
Now is the time to focus on manifesting flexibility, productivity, authenticity, timing, new paradigms, transmuting, transformation, and re-translating structure.

January 9th
5:32 PM

New Moon in Capricorn

Capricorn Challenges and Victories

Say all of the statements in this section out loud. Then, underline the phrase that means the most to you. Use the phrase as your special affirmation for manifesting throughout this phase of the moon.

Ultimate fulfillment is mine today! My willingness to live my life to the fullest, each day, is making all of my dreams come true. I am fulfilling the promise of my destiny, and, in so doing, I make my mark on the world. I have completed my commitment to the Earth and to the cosmos by being all that I can be in the cycles of time on the inner and outer planes of awareness. All four seasons have been activated within me, so that I am in alignment and in motion with the cycles of releasing, rebirthing, planting, and harvesting. I can now claim my citizenship in all four worlds. I am open and ready for the inspiration that the spirit world brings me. I am ready to conquer the mental world by using thought, rather than thinking. I am open to the expression of my heart and the magnetic field of love that is ever-present in my experience. I am open to receive abundance from Nature and I contribute to the physical world by actively manifesting my ideas into reality. I am in harmony with the four elements and keep them active within me, as well as contribute to them externally. The element of air is within me as I breathe in the miracle of life. The element of earth is within me as I honor my body and use all of its senses to enhance the quality of life. I honor the Earth as my home and take complete stewardship of my home and property on this Earth. I honor the water, the wellspring of life eternal, and allow for the flow of my feelings and emotions to be a creative influence on the unconscious and conscious planes. I honor the fire within me as the spark of light that is a source of inspiration in my experience, and, in so doing, I have fulfilled the promise of my destiny to live fully, freely, and passionately on all levels and on all dimensions with my Earth-Cosmos connection.

Capricorn Homework

The Capricorn moon is the reincarnation of Spirit, emerging from the dark waters of our past emotions and releasing us from our fears of change and loss. Awaken your powerful and positive spiritual connection to be open to new possibilities. Ask yourself to move beyond your emotional loyalty to the past in order to manifest. We are reminded of our need for material and emotional security at this time. In order to insure this, we must learn to build a foundation for ourselves that is lit from within, and made from the materials of love, goodwill, and intelligence. Give yourself permission to throw away your watch and celebrate living in the moment.

Without Acknowledgment Progress Cannot Occur

Acknowledgement creates space for victory and gratitude, which automatically brings you to a level of completion so a new cycle of opportunity can occur in your life. When you celebrate your wins and acknowledge your victories with gratitude, you update your cells so that your ability to move forward is not hindered by a cellular holographic pattern that is stuck in the past. Cellular lag creates resistance and makes moving forward most difficult. The key is to stay continuously updated by acknowledging yourself for what you did do at the end of each day, rather than heading off to sleep thinking about what you did not do. By acknowledging what you did not do, you play into your karmic storage bank and keep your progress at bay. When you acknowledge yourself and your manifestations you are complete, and more cycles of opportunity become available to you in each new day. Be prepared for miracles!

Victory List

When a creation result is acknowledged it seals the deal. This makes room for more magnificence to expand into your life and increases your abundance factor adding to your ability to receive. As each aspect of your manifesting list arrives in your life, spend time allowing, acknowledging, and accepting it with the true gusto of gratitude! Keep your victory list active here.

Gratitude List

This fulfills the relationship between the giver and the receiver, which completes the cycle with the Universe so that a new beginning can be established.

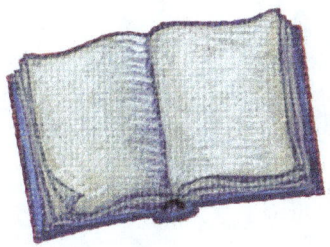

January 9th
5:32 PM

New Moon in Capricorn

How to Use the Moon Book With Your Chart

Fill in the blanks on the Cosmic Check-In page. Then look up the degree of the Moon on the chart below. Take note of the "I" statement on the outside of the wheel where the Moon is located. Now, locate the same degree on your own chart and make a note of the house and corresponding "I" statement. Go back to the Cosmic Check-In page and circle the two statements from the charts and read what you wrote. This will give you an idea about what to expect from this moon phase on a personal level.

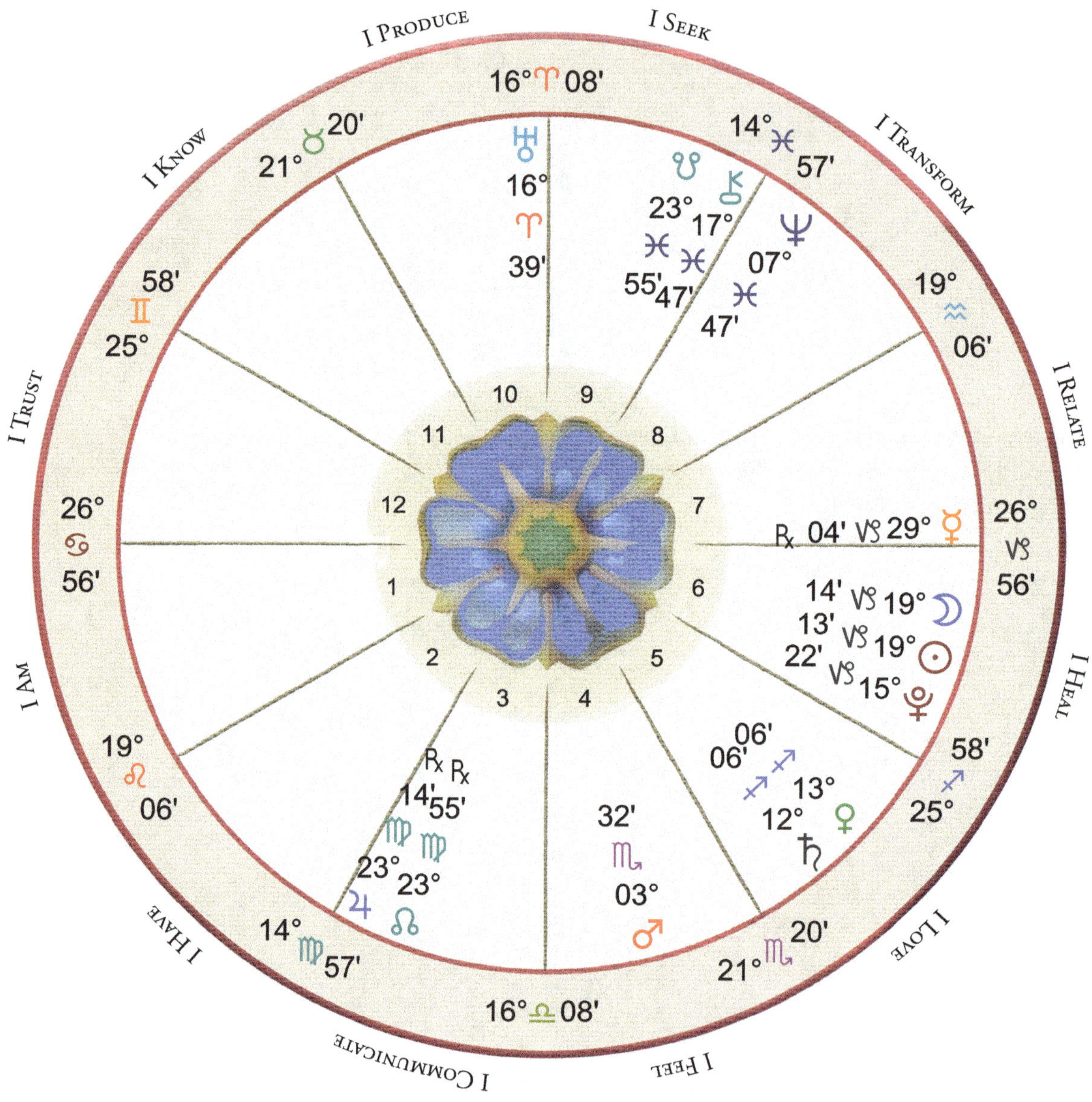

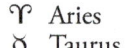

♈ Aries	♋ Cancer	♐ Sagittarius	☽ Moon	♄ Saturn	☊ North Node	V/C Void-of-Course
♉ Taurus	♌ Leo	♑ Capricorn	☿ Mercury	♅ Uranus	☋ South Node	▲ Super-Sensitivity
♊ Gemini	♍ Virgo	♒ Aquarius	♀ Venus	♆ Neptune	➔ Enters	▼ Low-Vitality
	♎ Libra	♓ Pisces	♂ Mars	♇ Pluto	℞ Retrograde	
	♏ Scorpio	☉ Sun	♃ Jupiter	⚷ Chiron	S/D Stationary Direct	

Cosmic Check-In

Take a moment to write a brief phrase for each "I" statement.
This activates all areas of your life for this creative cycle.

♑ I Produce

♒ I Know

♓ I Trust

♈ I Am

♉ I Have

♊ I Communicate

♋ I Feel

♌ I Love

♍ I Heal

♎ I Relate

♏ I Transform

♐ I Seek

January 23rd
5:47 PM

Full Moon in Leo

Degree Choice Points
3° Leo 29'

Light   Distinctions

Shadow   Generation Gaps

Wisdom   Knowledge and truth dispel fear reuniting your spirit and body.

Statement   I Love
    Body   Heart
    Mind   Self-confidence
    Spirit   Generosity

Element
Fire – Passion, enthusiasm, warmth, centered in personal identity.

Twelfth House Moon
11° Cancer 53'

Twelfth House Umbrella Theme
I Trust/I Feel – Determines how you deal with your karma, unconscious software, and what you will experience in order to attain mastery by completing your karma. It is also about the way you connect to the Divine.

Light   Recognizing Greatness

Shadow   Being Precocious

Wisdom   Your emotional responses are fuel for other entities.

The Sun is Opposite the Moon

Full moons are always in opposition to the Sun. This creates a feeling of tension between where you want to shine and how your feelings are flowing on a sensory level about the Sun's directive. The two forces seem like they are working against each other, yet they are on the same team displaying different techniques to obtain the same mission. The Leo/Aquarius polarity creates tension about the need to be adored and the need to be free.

Leo Goddess

The depth of Winter is the dreaming time, when your seed has been planted. The colder temperatures and lack of light naturally draw us inside – within. Rhiannon, the Celtic Goddess, rides her horse through your dreams by night and guides your visions as you stare into the hearth fire. She transverses the liminal space, the doorway between the worlds.

Take a ride with Rhiannon, allowing her to transport you as you do your inner work. Revel in the silence of a quiet night before the fireplace. Find comfort in a hot cup of relaxing herbal tea. Rest and allow yourself a few extra hours of well-deserved sleep!

Build Your Altar

Colors   Royal purple, gold, orange

Numerology   6 – See the beauty in all of nature

Tarot Card   Strength – Passion for all of life

Gemstones   Amber, emerald, pyrite, citrine, yellow topaz

Plant remedy   Sunflower – Standing tall in the center of life

Fragrance   Jasmine – Remembering your Soul's original intention

Clearing the Slate

Remember a time when you experienced the following trigger points.
Write down what happened and perform Ho'oponopono, the Hawaiian forgiveness ritual.

Impatience

- I'm Sorry
- Please Forgive Me
- Thank You
- I Love You

Feeling Superior

- I'm Sorry
- Please Forgive Me
- Thank You
- I Love You

Controlling

- I'm Sorry
- Please Forgive Me
- Thank You
- I Love You

"Off with their Heads" Syndrome

- I'm Sorry
- Please Forgive Me
- Thank You
- I Love You

Brat Attacks (Being Childish)

- I'm Sorry
- Please Forgive Me
- Thank You
- I Love You

January 23rd
5:47 PM

Full Moon in Leo

Leo Challenges and Victories

Say all of the statements in this section out loud. Then, underline the phrase that means the most to you. Use the phrase as your special affirmation for recalibrating throughout this phase of the moon.

I no longer feel the need to be in control and dominated by my mind telling me that it is appropriate to repress my feelings. I am going to claim my dominion today and feel the power of life running through me. I accept the privilege of being fully human and fully alive. I look to see where I lack courage to connect to what is natural for me. I see where I have been stubborn and turn to face my resistance. I become aware of when my higher self says "Go" and my lower self says "No." I am aware that my lower self (my body) is a creature of habit and will sabotage me with the idea that change takes too much energy. I take responsibility for the part of me that is a creature of habit and talk to my body about coming into alignment with my new intention to become fully passionate and fully alive. I remember today that in order to get the body to move forward with me, I need two-thirds of my cells to align with my request. First, I become aware of the part of myself that is trying to control all of my outcomes and keep me a slave to those outcomes, rather than trusting in the evolution of nature and the concept of Divine Order. I give up the fight today knowing that this struggle is dissipating all my energy and making me exhausted. In order for my body to respond, I need to awaken my cells through sound and touch. So, today I rub my body and speak out loud by sharing my request for connection, revitalization, rejuvenation, passion, and support. Today, I celebrate the idea that I can connect to my wholeness by activating my cells to support my commitment to my aliveness. I can now stand tall in the center of life and grow in self-confidence.

Leo Homework

Review your memorabilia and see what no longer matches your current love nature, your creative nature, and your loving self. Set your heart free while chanting, "Love is all you need." Become a part of the new consciousness on the Earth that brings a more abundant life when we expand the radius of our love. Live Love Every Day!

Recalibrating List

Say this statement out loud three times before writing your recalibrating list!

I am a free spiritual being and it is my desire to be free to think and to express myself fully.

From this day forward I resolve to be true – first to myself and my highest self,
and then to the highest self in me which is the Source of Love That I Am.

Leo Recalibrating Ideas

Now is the time to activate a game change in my life, and give up the need to be the center of attention, obstacles to generosity, false pride and false identity, blocks to confidence and creativity, excuses that keep me from quality time with my children, blocks to knowing that I am loved and lovable, and the idea that everyone needs to be devoted to me in all situations.

January 23rd
5:47 PM

Full Moon in Leo

How to Use the Moon Book With Your Chart

Fill in the blanks on the Cosmic Check-In page. Then look up the degree of the Moon on the chart below. Take note of the "I" statement on the outside of the wheel where the Moon is located. Now, locate the same degree on your own chart and make a note of the house and corresponding "I" statement. Go back to the Cosmic Check-In page and circle the two statements from the charts and read what you wrote. This will give you an idea about what to expect from this moon phase on a personal level.

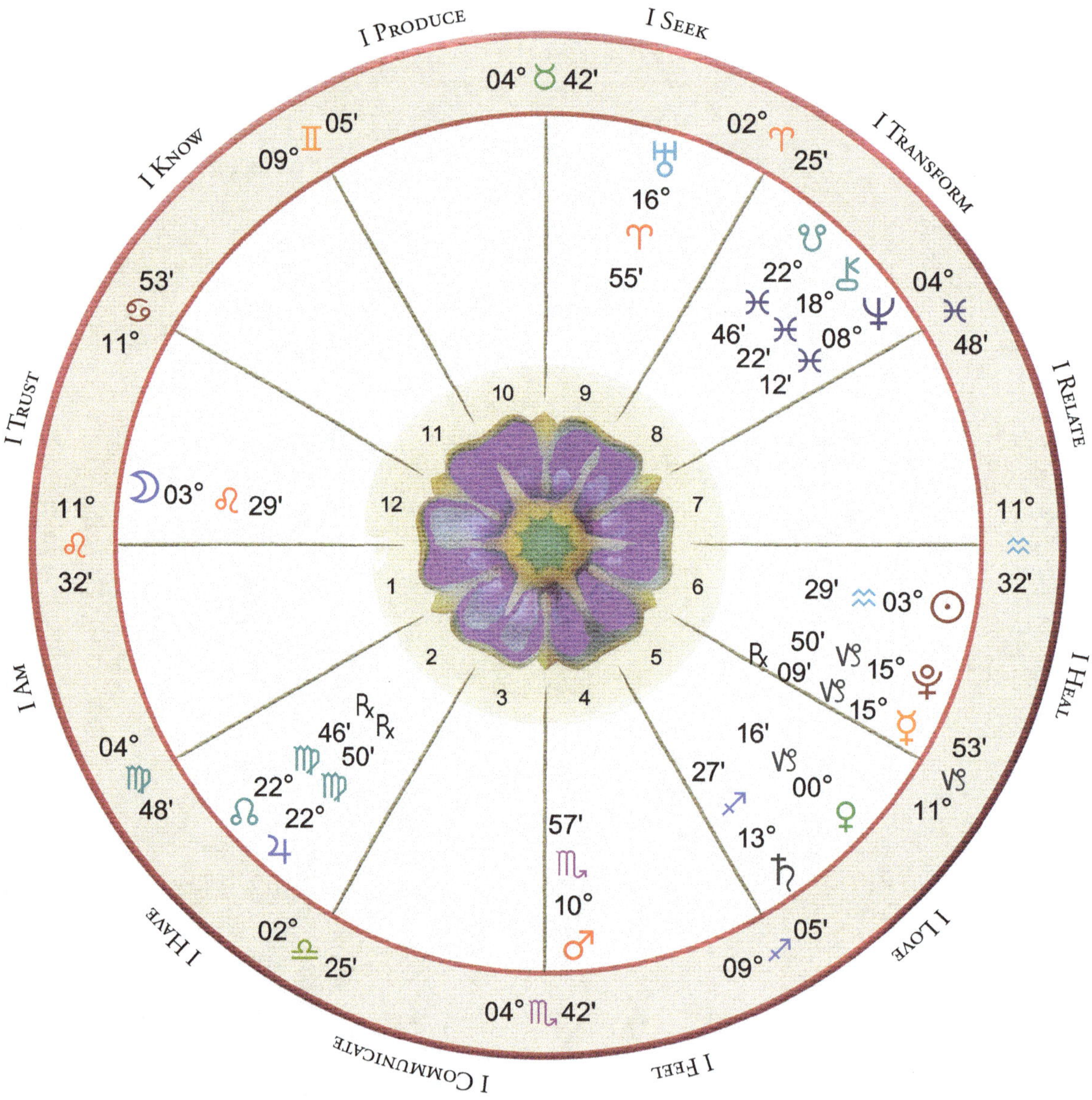

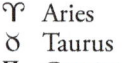

♈ Aries	♋ Cancer	♐ Sagittarius	☽ Moon	♄ Saturn	☊ North Node	V/C Void-of-Course
♉ Taurus	♌ Leo	♑ Capricorn	☿ Mercury	♅ Uranus	☋ South Node	▲ Super-Sensitivity
♊ Gemini	♍ Virgo	♒ Aquarius	♀ Venus	♆ Neptune	➡ Enters	▼ Low-Vitality
	♎ Libra	♓ Pisces	♂ Mars	♇ Pluto	℞ Retrograde	
	♏ Scorpio	☉ Sun	♃ Jupiter	⚷ Chiron	S/D Stationary Direct	

26

Cosmic Check-In

Take a moment to write a brief phrase for each "I" statement.
This activates all areas of your life for this creative cycle.

♌ I Love

♍ I Heal

♎ I Relate

♏ I Transform

♐ I Seek

♑ I Produce

♒ I Know

♓ I Trust

♈ I Am

♉ I Have

♊ I Communicate

♋ I Feel

February Planetary Highlights

Jupiter is Retrograde for the Entire Month Until May 9

Expect to recognize and integrate upgrades and recalibrations from 2004.

February 8 – Chinese New Year – Enter the Monkey

Expect to feel smart, clever, and intelligent, especially in areas like career and wealth. You will feel lively, flexible, quick-witted, and versatile. Honesty will bring an everlasting love-life and good fortune. Shortcomings could be an impetuous temper and tending to look down upon others.

February 8 – Chiron is Conjunct with the South Node in Pisces Throughout the Month

This is an important time to do a "spring cleaning" on your tools for healing. Your toolbox is filled with outdated devices and formulas that were perfect for you 10 years ago. Spend time seeing where the upgrades are needed and refill your box.

February 13 – Mercury Re-enters Aquarius

Advancement will happen in the ideas arena. Surround yourself with brilliant people and hang out with them. A higher state of intelligence is in operation and will bring forth top-of-the-line ideas.

Pluto is Dancing with Venus in Capricorn Until February 15

This is where sexuality and sensuality integrate. This meet-up could bring out amazing refinement for Venus, if she allows her deep waters to be stirred up. If Pluto can accept a creative influence, he will experience an amazing upgrade.

February 16 – Venus Enters Aquarius

Hold on to your hat – a new kind of love interest may catch your eye and you just might say yes. It will be a wild ride. Enjoy!

February 18 – The Sun Enters Pisces

It's time to upgrade your intuitive abilities. Meditation is very appealing right now. Follow your instincts – you won't regret it. Creative juices are flowing, join a theatre group and learn how to emote.

Jupiter Conjunct with the North Node in Virgo Ongoing

Jupiter takes time here to add influence to the future by updating your ability to be happy as a formula for the future. Status will also be encouraged to upgrade to a more practical process.

Super-Sensitivity – February 3-4

Chaos is in the air – keep your thoughts to yourself. Avoid rushing, get rest, stay home, and allow yourself to be slow.

Low-Vitality – February 16-17

The Earth needs you now. Have a drum circle and connect with the heartbeat of the Great Mother so she can feel supported.

Sunday	Monday	Tuesday	Wednesday	Thursday	Friday	Saturday
	1 ♃℞ ☽ V/C 4:35pm 6. Make your home your castle.	**2** ♃℞ ☽→♐ 7:49am 7. You learn when you teach.	**3** ♃℞ ▲ 8. A leader knows when to follow.	**4** ♃℞ ▲ ☽ V/C 2:03am ☽→♑ 4:43pm 9. Your heart will have the answer.	**5** ♃℞ 10. Planning is half the fun of doing.	**6** ♃℞ ☽ V/C 7:53am ☽→♒9:58pm 2. Balance is the consequence of love.
7 ♃℞ 3. Acknowledge the progress of others.	**8** ♃℞ Chinese New Year Enter the Monkey ☽ V/C 6:38am ● 19°♒16′ 6:40am 4. Let the body's knowledge speak.	**9** ♃℞ ☽→♓12:31am 5. Eliminate regret, breathe in love.	**10** ♃℞ Ash Wednesday ☽ V/C 8:24pm 6. Release limitation to find the prize.	**11** ♃℞ ☽→♈1:54am 7. Wisdom is knowing your truth.	**12** ♃℞ 8. Mastery on any level enhances life.	**13** ♃℞ ☿→♒2:44pm ☽ V/C 2:32am ☽→♉ 3:35am 9. Remember the love in your heart.
14 ♃℞ Valentine's Day 10. See each day as a new beginning.	**15** ♃℞ President's Day ☽ V/C 2:35am ☽→♊ 6:34am 2. Staying in balance requires action.	**16** ♃℞ ▼ ♀→♒8:18pm 3. Go dance now and be one with joy.	**17** ♃℞ ▼ ☽ V/C 8:36am ☽→♋11:23am 4. Be organized to stay on purpose.	**18** ♃℞ ☉→♓ 9:35pm 5. Healing happens by adapting.	**19** ♃℞ ☽ V/C 6:35am ☽→♌ 6:17pm 6. Know that you are never alone.	**20** ♃℞ 7. Knowledge is a treasure.
21 ♃℞ ☽ V/C 5:16pm 8. Wealth is fullness.	**22** ♃℞ ☽→♍ 3:24am ○ 3°♍34′ 10:21am 9. Spirit springs from your heart.	**23** ♃℞ 10. Move beyond wishing into being.	**24** ♃℞ ☽ V/C 6:22am ☽→♎ 2:41pm 2. Staying aligned creates balance.	**25** ♃℞ 3. The right to be is not being right.	**26** ♃℞ ☽ V/C 3:18am 4. Solid foundations allow life to grow.	**27** ♃℞ ☽→♏3:26am 5. Expand your generosity today.
28 ♃℞ 6. Clutter interferes with graceful living.	**29** ♃℞ ☽ V/C 11:54am ☽→♐ 3:55pm 6. Treat a friend to a home-cooked meal.					

♈ Aries	♎ Libra	☉ Sun	♄ Saturn	☊ North Node	▲ Super Sensitivity	6. Love
♉ Taurus	♏ Scorpio	☽ Moon	♅ Uranus	☋ South Node	▼ Low Vitality	7. Learning
♊ Gemini	♐ Sagittarius	☿ Mercury	♆ Neptune	➡ Enters	2. Balance	8. Money
♋ Cancer	♑ Capricorn	♀ Venus	♇ Pluto	℞ Retrograde	3. Fun	9. Spirituality
♌ Leo	♒ Aquarius	♂ Mars	⚷ Chiron	SD Stationary Direct	4. Structure	10. Visionary
♍ Virgo	♓ Pisces	♃ Jupiter		V/C Void-of-Course	5. Action	11. Completion

February 8th
6:40 AM

New Moon in Aquarius

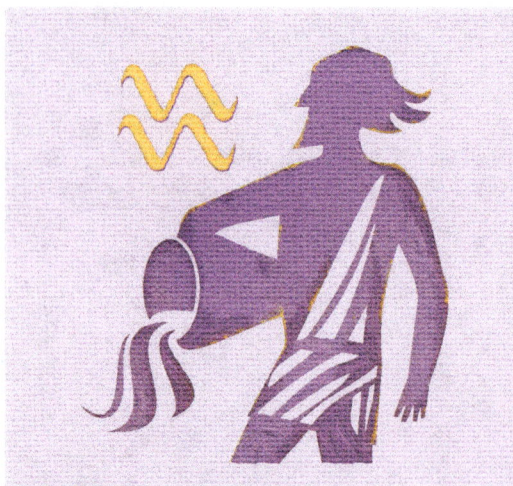

Degree Choice Points
19° Aquarius 16'

Light   Tapping the Akashic

Shadow   Holier-than-thou

Wisdom   Allow for some minor adjustments to ease discomfort.

Statement   I Know
    Body   Ankles
    Mind   True Genius
    Spirit   Vision

Element
Air – The Breath of Life that allows the mind to achieve new insights and fresh perspectives, inspiration, active and abstract dreaming, freedom from attachments.

First House Moon
18° Aquarius 26'

First House Umbrella Theme
I Am/I Know – Your outer appearance, the way you present yourself, the way you dress, the way you enter a room, and what you leave behind when you leave the room.

Light   Calm after the Storm

Shadow   Fear of Experience

Wisdom   Flexibility and diversity give you the power to communicate.

Karmic Awakening

Virgo/Pisces – The conflict here is getting lost in the vastness due to lack of boundaries or restriction due to over-analyzing details.

Karmic stress will appear when your intention is not in place to serve for the highest good. It's best to know your motives where service is concerned. Check your shadow for any fear relating to this action. The boundaries of this karmic pattern run on the razor's edge of action for others or yourself. If your intention and boundaries are correct, you will experience the calm after the storm. Then leave it alone for a few days.

When the Sun is in Aquarius

This is a time when the higher octave of the mind comes into play and one is given the power of vision. The Aquarian energies promote knowing by being a wellspring of knowledge. They expand the radius of contact by going beyond the known in areas of communication and cooperation. Now is the time to be initiated into greater awareness to serve the fields of human endeavors. Connect and combine magic with science and become a creative influence. When the sun is in Aquarius we must unify with our team players and collect innovative ideas to advance the world to a better place.

Aquarius Goddess

White Tara steps in to assist you with compassionate acceptance and healing of old, deep wounds that are now illuminated by both the Sun and the Moon. With seven eyes (one on her forehead, one on each hand and each foot), White Tara's ability to see encompasses her ability to feel and connect with others and with the Earth. Her name is derived from the root "tri," which means to cross. She has accepted the task of remaining in feminine form until all beings are enlightened, and is here to help all cross the ocean of existence and suffering.

Call upon White Tara's guidance to navigate towards self-acceptance and self-forgiveness on your path to healing.

Build Your Altar

Colors   Violet, neon, crystalline rainbow tints

Numerology   4 – Let the body's knowledge speak

Tarot Card   The Star – Golden opportunities for the future

Gemstones   Aquamarine, blue topaz, peacock pearls

Plant Remedy   Queen of the Night Cactus – Ability to see light in the dark

Fragrance   Myrrh – Healing the nervous system

Manifesting List

This or something better than this comes to me in an easy and pleasurable way, for the good of all concerned. Thank you, Universe!

Aquarius Manifesting Ideas

Now is the time to focus on manifesting vision, invention, technology, freedom, friends, community, personal genius, higher awareness, teamwork, science, and magic.

February 8th
6:40 AM

New Moon in Aquarius

Aquarius Challenges and Victories

Say all of the statements in this section out loud. Then, underline the phrase that means the most to you. Use the phrase as your special affirmation for manifesting throughout this phase of the moon.

Today, I chart my course for my new direction. My future is set on a new, fresh evolutionary course. I am guided by a higher source and trust in that guidance. I know my life has value and I am willing to contribute to the pool of consciousness by experiencing my life and living my life to the fullest view of possibility. Today, I know my possibilities are endless. My Spirit and my Soul are connected to Heaven and to Earth and this knowing brings me to the awareness that I can add to the higher qualities of life because I am connected to the whole. My being is far-reaching and immeasurable. I contribute to existence simply by knowing. All of the guideposts are connected for me today to see my way to a profound new future. My vision is clear and I can clearly set my sights on this new course. Golden opportunities come with this new vision and I trust in my guidance to bring me to this new level of manifesting power. I check in with my inner lights, each day, by meditating and asking for all seven of the energy centers in my body to come into alignment with the outer symbols of guidance. I do this by becoming still and breathing until I feel the stillness. Then, I place my hand on each center in my body, one center at a time, to be activated by light. Next, I ask out loud for each center in my body to let me know what its energetic contribution to the new direction is and how best to use the energy to move forward on my new course of action. I write down each statement and connect each statement to the guiding star in the sky. I am now linked up physically and spiritually and ready to navigate my total self towards my new evolutionary direction.

Aquarius Homework

Aquarians manifest a storehouse of information through innovative telecommunications, technology, social networking and media, and global communication. They are typically found in the fields of psychology, science fiction authoring or film-making, speech writing, and aerospace engineering.

Consider these three Aquarian gifts:

- Opportunity – Become a creative influence
- Enlightenment – When you become aware that you are light
- Brotherhood – Separation doesn't exist anymore

Where do you see these occurring in your life?

Without Acknowledgment Progress Cannot Occur

Acknowledgement creates space for victory and gratitude, which automatically brings you to a level of completion so a new cycle of opportunity can occur in your life. When you celebrate your wins and acknowledge your victories with gratitude, you update your cells so that your ability to move forward is not hindered by a cellular holographic pattern that is stuck in the past. Cellular lag creates resistance and makes moving forward most difficult. The key is to stay continuously updated by acknowledging yourself for what you did do at the end of each day, rather than heading off to sleep thinking about what you did not do. By acknowledging what you did not do, you play into your karmic storage bank and keep your progress at bay. When you acknowledge yourself and your manifestations you are complete, and more cycles of opportunity become available to you in each new day. Be prepared for miracles!

Victory List

When a creation result is acknowledged it seals the deal. This makes room for more magnificence to expand into your life and increases your abundance factor adding to your ability to receive. As each aspect of your manifesting list arrives in your life, spend time allowing, acknowledging, and accepting it with the true gusto of gratitude! Keep your victory list active here.

Gratitude List

This fulfills the relationship between the giver and the receiver, which completes the cycle with the Universe so that a new beginning can be established.

February 8th
6:40 AM

New Moon in Aquarius

How to Use the Moon Book With Your Chart

Fill in the blanks on the Cosmic Check-In page. Then look up the degree of the Moon on the chart below. Take note of the "I" statement on the outside of the wheel where the Moon is located. Now, locate the same degree on your own chart and make a note of the house and corresponding "I" statement. Go back to the Cosmic Check-In page and circle the two statements from the charts and read what you wrote. This will give you an idea about what to expect from this moon phase on a personal level.

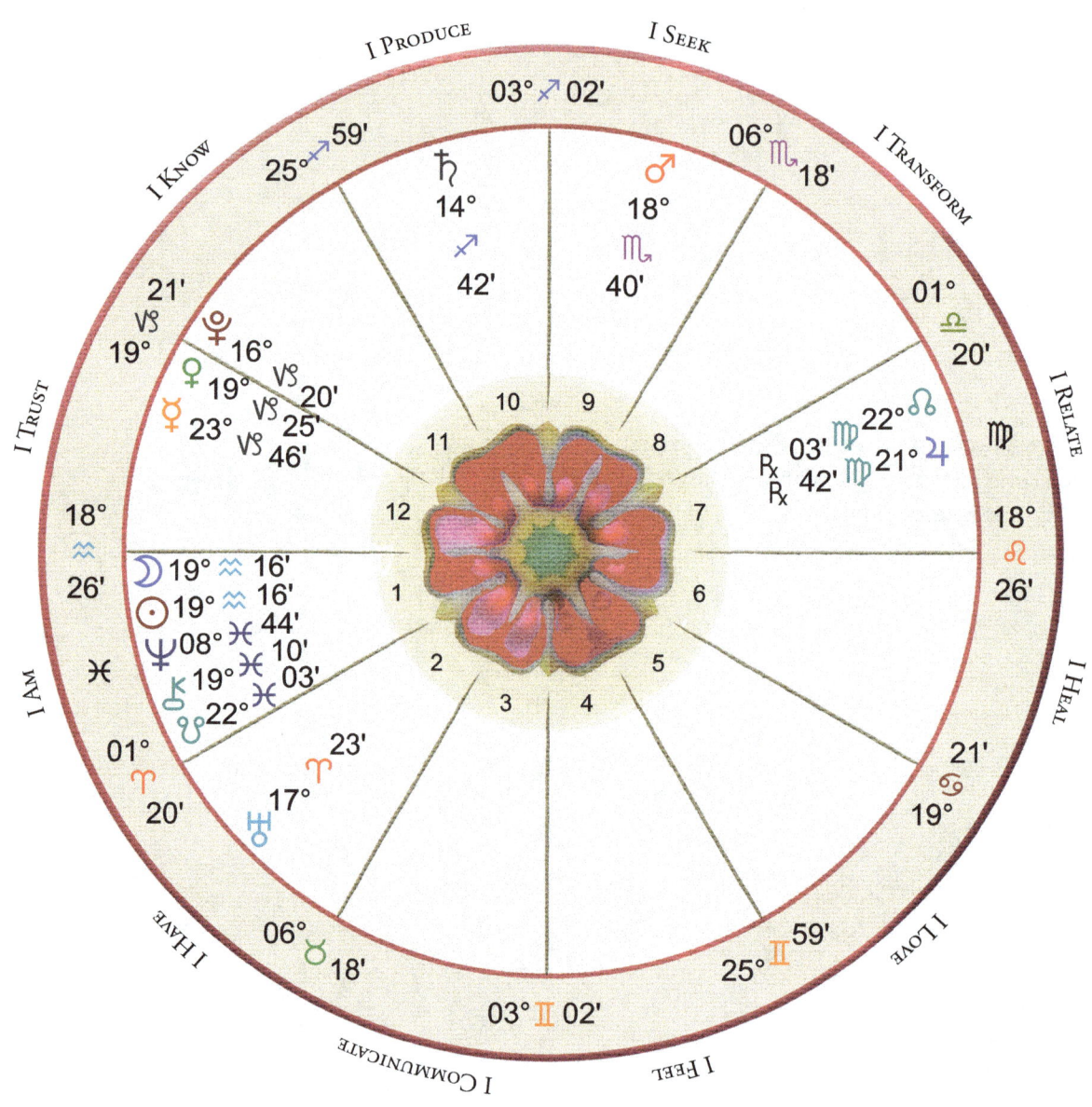

♈ Aries	♋ Cancer	♐ Sagittarius	☽ Moon	♄ Saturn	☊ North Node	V/C Void-of-Course
♉ Taurus	♌ Leo	♑ Capricorn	☿ Mercury	♅ Uranus	☋ South Node	▲ Super-Sensitivity
♊ Gemini	♍ Virgo	♒ Aquarius	♀ Venus	♆ Neptune	➡ Enters	▼ Low-Vitality
	♎ Libra	♓ Pisces	♂ Mars	♇ Pluto	℞ Retrograde	
	♏ Scorpio		☉ Sun	⚷ Chiron	SD Stationary Direct	

36

Cosmic Check-In

Take a moment to write a brief phrase for each "I" statement.
This activates all areas of your life for this creative cycle.

♒ I Know

♓ I Trust

♈ I Am

♉ I Have

♊ I Communicate

♋ I Feel

♌ I Love

♍ I Heal

♎ I Relate

♏ I Transform

♐ I Seek

♑ I Produce

February 22nd
3:24 AM

Full Moon in Virgo

Degree Choice Points
3° Virgo 34'

Light   Clever Responses

Shadow   Anxiety

Wisdom   You are not governed by concrete rules or traditions.

Statement   I Heal
- **Body**   Intestines
- **Mind**   Critical
- **Spirit**   Divinity in the Details

Element
Earth – Family lineage and DNA healing, knowing nutrition and abundance, healing power from the plant kingdom, body awareness, connection to small animals.

Fourth House Moon
7° Leo 47'

Fourth House Umbrella Theme
I Feel/I Love – The way your early environmental training was, how that set your foundation for living, and why you chose your mother.

Light   Political Idealism

Shadow   Propaganda

Wisdom   Manifest a goal free of doubt or fear.

The Sun is Opposite the Moon

Full moons are always in opposition to the Sun. This creates a feeling of tension between where you want to shine and how your feelings are flowing on a sensory level about the Sun's directive. The two forces seem like they are working against each other, yet they are on the same team displaying different techniques to obtain the same mission. The Virgo/Pisces polarity creates tension between doing your work and finding your path.

Virgo Goddess

Astraea is the virgin Goddess of Purity, who fled the Earth upon seeing weaponry, warfare, and the rise of patriarchy that destroyed the earth goddess culture during the Iron Age. She ascended to the heavens to become the constellation Virgo, to watch over the Earth until she will one day return issuing in a new Utopian age. Often depicted as a star maiden, she has wings and a shining halo or crown of stars, and carries a flaming torch or thunderbolt.

Ask Astraea to help you as you sort through the details to bring love and light into a fresh new perspective, free from the restrictions of the past. "Because it's always been done that way," is no longer a viable excuse. Sharing what you love, with the intention for the highest and best for all, enlists Astraea's blessings.

Build Your Altar

Colors   Green, blue, earth tones

Numerology   9 – Spirit springs from your heart

Tarot Card   The Hermit – Knowing your purpose and sharing it with the world

Gemstones   Emerald, sapphire

Plant remedy   Sage – The ability to hold and store light

Fragrance   Lavender – Management and storage of energy

Clearing the Slate

Remember a time when you experienced the following trigger points.
Write down what happened and perform Ho'oponopono, the Hawaiian forgiveness ritual.

Judgment

- I'm Sorry
- Please Forgive Me
- Thank You
- I Love You

Habitual Actions

- I'm Sorry
- Please Forgive Me
- Thank You
- I Love You

Avoiding the "big picture" by being obsessed by details

- I'm Sorry
- Please Forgive Me
- Thank You
- I Love You

Being Stubborn

- I'm Sorry
- Please Forgive Me
- Thank You
- I Love You

Letting "being perfect" stop your action

- I'm Sorry
- Please Forgive Me
- Thank You
- I Love You

February 22nd
3:24 AM

Full Moon in Virgo

Virgo Challenges and Victories

Say all of the statements in this section out loud. Then, underline the phrase that means the most to you. Use the phrase as your special affirmation for recalibrating throughout this phase of the moon.

Today I take time to go within to be silent. I imagine myself on a country road moving towards a beautiful mountain. I bask in the glory of the power of the mountain and know that it is calling me to the top. I find a pathway to the top and begin to climb. As I climb I become aware of a presence guiding me and empowering me to keep going, creating a sense of peacefulness within me.

I become aware of my own power in this silent journey to the top and revel in the serenity that nature and silence bring me. At last I am about to reach the summit and, just before I do, I feel the power drawing me to go within on a deeper level. I stop for a moment and look back at the path I have just climbed and know that my life's path is a remarkable gift. I connect to the center of the Earth and feel an inner glow.

The top of the mountain calls to me and, as I reach the top, a voice says to me, "Take in the view and look in all directions." As I turn 360-degrees, I sense a light igniting me in every direction. Then the voice says, "Look up!" Now, my awareness shifts and I see that I have become an illuminating light glowing in all six directions. Next I hear, "Sit in your silence and take in the vastness of who you are. Who you are is immeasurable." I sit, feeling the glow of light within me, and become aware of a greater plan for my life. I allow myself to receive this plan. I accept this assignment and slowly walk down the mountain, knowing that I can be a shining light for myself and others. I know I must take my light out to the world and share what I know to be my truth. Today, I become a messenger for the light.

Virgo Homework

Become integrated so that the light of your personality becomes soul-infused. When you are soul-infused and are in service to your Higher Self, you radiate love and light through the power of the inner self through all activities, thoughts, and emotions and become more magnificent. Learn the art of detachment and let your Soul take control.

Recalibrating List

Say this statement out loud three times before writing your recalibrating list!

I am a free spiritual being and it is my desire to be free to think and to express myself fully.

I hereby fully and completely free my mind from all adhesions to outdated philosophies, habits, relationships, groups of people, man-made laws, moral codes, all rules, set ideas and set ways of thinking, traditions, organizations, duty-motivated activities, guilt, judgment, and being misunderstood!

Virgo Recalibrating Ideas

Now is the time to activate a game change in my life, and give up finding fault with myself, my addiction to perfection, my addiction to detail, over-indulging in image management, pain-producing thinking patterns, judgment of others, resistance to being healthy, and destructive behaviors.

February 22nd
3:24 AM

Full Moon in Virgo

How to Use the Moon Book With Your Chart

Fill in the blanks on the Cosmic Check-In page. Then look up the degree of the Moon on the chart below. Take note of the "I" statement on the outside of the wheel where the Moon is located. Now, locate the same degree on your own chart and make a note of the house and corresponding "I" statement. Go back to the Cosmic Check-In page and circle the two statements from the charts and read what you wrote. This will give you an idea about what to expect from this moon phase on a personal level.

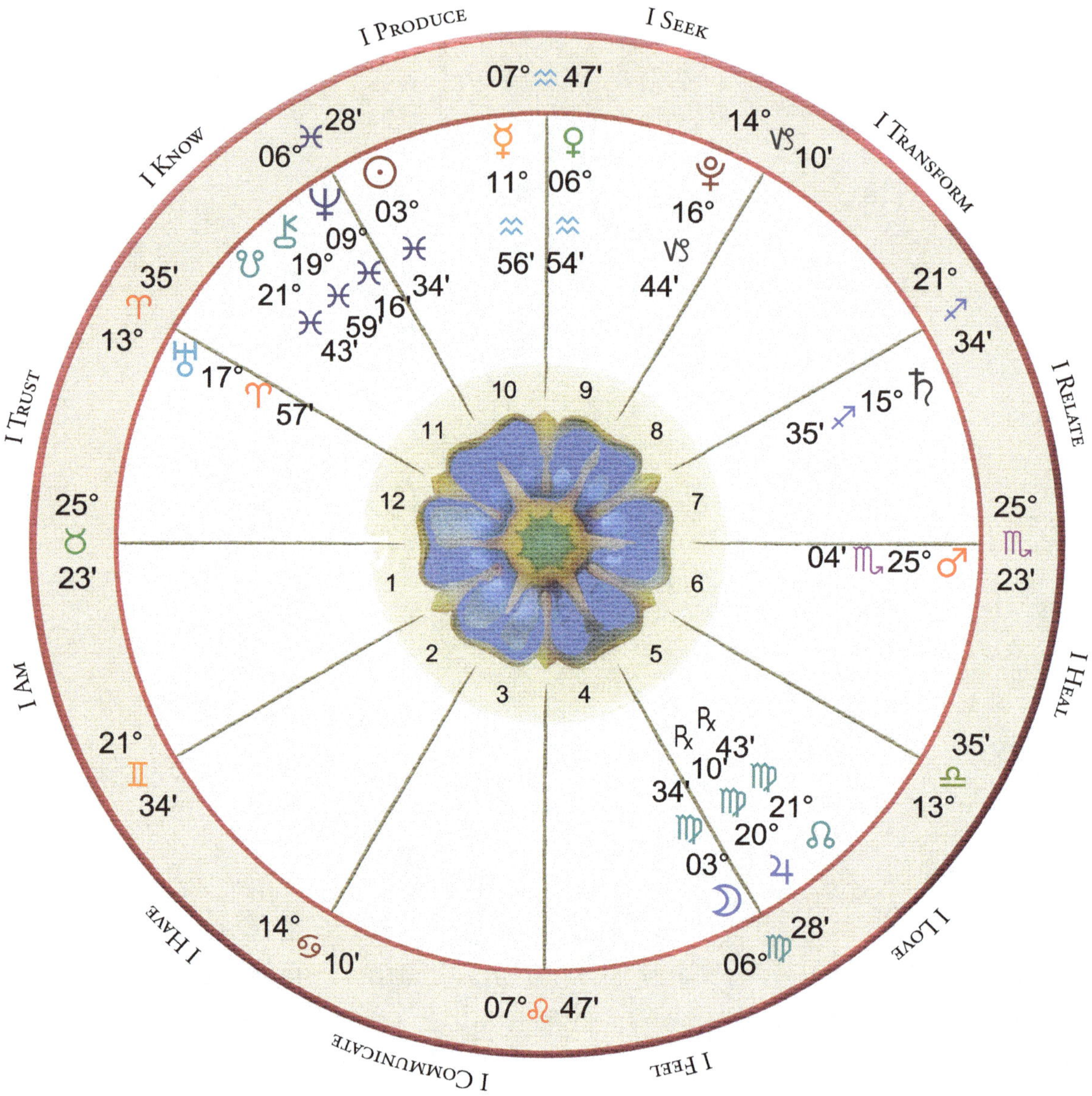

♈ Aries	♋ Cancer	♐ Sagittarius	☽ Moon	♄ Saturn	☊ North Node	V/C Void-of-Course
♉ Taurus	♌ Leo	♑ Capricorn	☿ Mercury	♅ Uranus	☋ South Node	▲ Super-Sensitivity
♊ Gemini	♍ Virgo	♒ Aquarius	♀ Venus	♆ Neptune	➡ Enters	• Low-Vitality
	♎ Libra	♓ Pisces	♂ Mars	♇ Pluto	℞ Retrograde	
	♏ Scorpio		☉ Sun	⚷ Chiron	S/D Stationary Direct	

44

Cosmic Check-In

Take a moment to write a brief phrase for each "I" statement.
This activates all areas of your life for this creative cycle.

♍ I Heal

♎ I Relate

♏ I Transform

♐ I Seek

♑ I Produce

♒ I Know

♓ I Trust

♈ I Am

♉ I Have

♊ I Communicate

♋ I Feel

♌ I Love

March Planetary Highlights

Jupiter is Retrograde in Virgo Until May 9

Where were you and who were you with in 2004? A review of that time period is coming up for recalibration. Start by asking yourself the questions, "What choices was I making about life then?" and, "How might I adjust those choices, especially as they relate to health and happiness?" Consciously set a new stage.

Saturn goes Retrograde in Sagittarius March 25 until August 15

Expect an adjustment in your career and a rewritten approach to your portion of production as it relates to your job activities.

March 5 – Mars Enters Sagittarius

Time for adventure, long trips, and study programs on ancient philosophies.

March 8 – Solar Eclipse

A deep connection can take place here, especially with a new spiritual community. The solar eclipse will break a 19-year pattern relating to old belief systems that are no longer juicy for you. Celebrate the release and advance. Your new Monopoly board awaits you!

March 8 – Neptune and Mercury are Coupled in Pisces Until March 18

It's not a good idea to make decisions or choices during these days, wait until the mist clears after the 18th.

March 8 – The New Moon in Pisces, Chiron, and the South Node are Connecting Throughout the Month

Old healing modalities and tools are being exchanged for more advanced applications. If you stay out of the way, you will receive a very bright, shiny toolbox and a teaching.

March 8 – Jupiter and the North Node are Dancing Together on the Ascendant

Expect an expansion of your self image by taking a very optimistic view of yourself, thus bringing about unlimited opportunities for a better future.

March 8 – Chiron Opposing Jupiter

This could have major benefits for healing humankind. Expect miracles and opportunities to make miracles happen. Pay attention and say YES!

March 19 – Sun Enters Aries – Spring Equinox

The Astrological New Year is here to awaken you from your Winter's sleep. Begin to participate in the Year of GENEROSITY! It is now time to plant your seeds.

March 21 – Mercury Enters Aries

It's time to express the new 2016 you.

March 23 – Lunar Eclipse

Set yourself free from any relationships that make you feel trapped or devoid of choice. The lunar eclipse will work on the inner plane of your awareness that has been contributing to this entrapment for the last 19 years.

March 23 – Karmic Awakening Pisces/Virgo

We may find ourselves feeling power coming from many sources and judging rather than adjusting so we can actually see our truth. Remember your ego wants to be right and your true nature simply wants to BE.

March 23 – Mars Conjunct Mid-Heaven Until the End of the Month

Expect a highly-competitive spirit to make itself known in whatever arena you fully intend to win. Public image becomes very important. You may even get an "Employee of the Month" award.

Super-Sensitivity – March 2-3, 29-30

Lots of new vibrations are entering the atmosphere right now. Slow down and let the dust settle. Rushing creates accidents and an overactive mind.

Low-Vitality – March 14-15

The Earth is depleted right now. Take extra care of yourself. Pushing leads to exhaustion.

SUNDAY	MONDAY	TUESDAY	WEDNESDAY	THURSDAY	FRIDAY	SATURDAY
		1 ♃℞ 7. Judging interferes with living.	**2** ♃℞▲ ☽ V/C 6:54pm 8. Know that you can manifest.	**3** ♃℞▲ ☽→♑ 2:01am 9. Walk with love in your feet.	**4** ♃℞ 10. Live in the now.	**5** ♃℞ ♀→♓ 2:25am ♂→♐ 6:30pm ☽ V/C 8:05am ☽→♒ 8:22am 2. Look at both sides of every issue.
6 ♃℞ 3. Your creativity knows no limits.	**7** ♃℞ ☽ V/C 2:46am ☽→♓ 11:08am 4. Be silent, be still, know yourself.	**8** ♃℞ ☽ V/C 5:54pm ● 18°♓56′ 5:56pm Solar Eclipse 5:58pm 5. Ride the wave of acceptance.	**9** ♃℞ ☽→♈ 11:39am 6. Beauty is polarity in motion.	**10** ♃℞ 7. Risk determines faith.	**11** ♃℞ ☽ V/C 10:23am ☽→♉ 11:43am 8. There is always more to be had.	**12** ♃℞ ♀→♓ 2:25am 9. A true humanitarian comes from love.
13 ♃℞ PDT ☽ V/C 1:46am ☽→♊ 2:03pm 10. Living in the past stunts learning.	**14** ♃℞▼ 2. Be gentle as you decide.	**15** ♃℞▼ ☽ V/C 10:02am ☽→♋ 5:56pm 4. To be secure, know all the parts.	**16** ♃℞ 5. Variety makes life interesting.	**17** ♃℞ St. Patrick's Day ☽ V/C 9:08pm 6. Let joy be your barometer for life.	**18** ♃℞ ☽→♌ 12:54am 7. Look beneath the surface and know.	**19** ♃℞ Spring Equinox ☉→♈ 9:31pm ☽ V/C 1:42pm 8. A team player respects everyone.
20 ♃℞ ☽→♍ 10:39am 9. Accept your importance in life.	**21** ♃℞ ☿→♈ 5:20pm ☽ V/C 8:54pm 10. A happy future stems from joy now.	**22** ♃℞ ☽→♎ 10:23pm 2. Harmony creates balance.	**23** ♃℞ ○ 3°♎17′ 5:02am Lunar Eclipse 4:48am 3. Choose happiness. It is an option.	**24** ♃℞ ☽ V/C 1:54pm 4. Is your workspace in order?	**25** ♃♄℞ ♄℞ ♐ 3:02am ☽→♏ 11:08am 5. A healthy body is an exercised body.	**26** ♃♄℞ 6. Create comfort in your home.
27 ♃♄℞ Easter ☽ V/C 12:25am ☽→♐ 11:46pm 7. Good students make good teachers.	**28** ♃♄℞ 8. Celebrate the success of another.	**29** ♃♄℞▲ ☽ V/C 6:54pm 9. Pray aloud from your heart.	**30** ♃♄℞▲ ☽→♑ 10:44am 10. See your future in a bright light.	**31** ♃♄℞ 2. Harmony breeds generosity.		

♈ Aries	♎ Libra	☉ Sun	♄ Saturn	☊ North Node	▲ Super Sensitivity	6. Love
♉ Taurus	♏ Scorpio	☽ Moon	♅ Uranus	☋ South Node	▼ Low Vitality	7. Learning
♊ Gemini	♐ Sagittarius	☿ Mercury	♆ Neptune	➡ Enters	2. Balance	8. Money
♋ Cancer	♑ Capricorn	♀ Venus	♇ Pluto	℞ Retrograde	3. Fun	9. Spirituality
♌ Leo	♒ Aquarius	♂ Mars	⚷ Chiron	SD Stationary Direct	4. Structure	10. Visionary
♍ Virgo	♓ Pisces	♃ Jupiter		V/C Void-of-Course	5. Action	11. Completion

Solar Eclipse
March 8th
5:56 PM

New Moon in Pisces

Degree Choice Points
  18° Pisces 56'

Light   Teacher/Student

Shadow   Patronizing

Wisdom   Your answers are in the lyrics of a song, the junk mail, or a friend's gift.

Statement   I Trust
  Body   Feet
  Mind   Super-sensitive
  Spirit   Mystical

Element
  Water – Grace, rhythm, cycles of awareness, Divine Feminine.

Sixth House Moon
  22° Aquarius 48'

Sixth House Umbrella Theme
  I Heal/I Know – The way you manage your body and appearance.

Light   Performance

Shadow   Attention-seeking

Wisdom   Personal power gains momentum by maintaining balance.

When the Sun is in Pisces

This is a time when you come in contact with your most Divine essence. It is a time to meditate and connect to your higher purpose. Let your intuition guide you to a program of service. Let your Soul take control and connect to a space beyond your ego. In order to do this, you must become free of your habits, hang ups, and fantasies. Compassion frees you from the slavery of self-interest and the lure of your personality's blind urges, emotional traps, and mental crystallizations. When the Soul takes control, you unite your personality with Divine essence and radiate the light needed to find your true pathway.

Pisces Goddess

This new moon, Canola, the Irish mistress of the harp, tugs at your heartstrings. In myth, Canola took a walk after quarrelling with her lover one night, and fell asleep outdoors to hypnotic music. The next morning she awoke to find that it was the sound of the wind passing through the sinews of a whale carcass; from this she invented the harp.

Trust the messages that come to you through song. Take a break to breathe, chant, and sing to your heart's content, knowing that the sound will carry your will and intention, with beauty, harmony, and balance, into the world, healing yourself and others. Bring the spring plants to life with your voice!

Build Your Altar

Colors Turquoise, blue, green, aqua

Numerology 5 – Ride the wave of acceptance

Tarot Card The Moon – The inner journey, reflection, illumination

Gemstones Amethyst, opal, jade, turquoise

Plant Remedy Passion flower – The ability to live in the here and now

Fragrance Lotus – Connecting to the Divine without arrogance

Manifesting List

This or something better than this comes to me in an easy and pleasurable way, for the good of all concerned. Thank you, Universe!

Pisces Manifesting Ideas

Now is the time to focus on manifesting connection with the Divine, creativity, healing powers, psychic abilities, sensitivity, compassion, and service.

Solar Eclipse
March 8th
5:56 PM

New Moon in Pisces

Pisces Challenges and Victories

Say all of the statements in this section out loud. Then, underline the phrase that means the most to you. Use the phrase as your special affirmation for manifesting throughout this phase of the moon.

I see my path clearly now. I know I must walk by myself on this journey into the deepest part of my Soul. It is time to clear the way and look beneath the surface to discover the parts of myself that I have placed in the unconscious world to be worked on at a later date. That later date is now. I am aware that the postponement of my inner reality can no longer be delayed.

Evolution is pulling me and it has become greater than my distractions, my fear, my denial, and my refusal to face what I have hidden from myself and others. I am aware of outside influences that pull me away from facing my inner realms. I know, without a doubt, that I am only as sick as the secrets I keep from myself and others. I see clearly how these distractions, illusions, and secrets need to be recognized so I can find the separated parts of myself that have been left in the dark, obscured from the light. I know that it is time to bring myself into wholeness and bring my shadow side to the light of my awareness.

I begin by closing my eyes and experiencing darkness. I imagine walking on a lonely road, in the dark, by myself. I pay particular attention to the sensations in my body and allow for the body to guide me to the places of dullness, numbness, fear, and anxiety. I simply allow for the intelligence of the body to coordinate the feeling with an image, person, or an event. I stay still and know, from the depth of my being, that recognition is all that is required of me right now. When recognition occurs, the light of awareness is ignited and the conscious world will take care of the rest. I know that the road to enlightenment requires me to first take the road into the dark side of my Soul.

Pisces Homework

Pisces manifest by using their psychic powers for counseling, therapy, hypnosis, the ministry, and creating spiritual schools or healing centers. They are also successful in visionary arts, acting, music, medical and pharmaceutical fields, and oceanography.

Take time to go within to discover where new pathways are open for advancement. Blessings pour forth to those who move toward these pathways in the spirit of service. Be open to these pathways and consider the ones that benefit our planet with new ideas, creative expression, and expanded views that lead people to higher levels of service.

Without Acknowledgment Progress Cannot Occur

Acknowledgement creates space for victory and gratitude, which automatically brings you to a level of completion so a new cycle of opportunity can occur in your life. When you celebrate your wins and acknowledge your victories with gratitude, you update your cells so that your ability to move forward is not hindered by a cellular holographic pattern that is stuck in the past. Cellular lag creates resistance and makes moving forward most difficult. The key is to stay continuously updated by acknowledging yourself for what you did do at the end of each day, rather than heading off to sleep thinking about what you did not do. By acknowledging what you did not do, you play into your karmic storage bank and keep your progress at bay. When you acknowledge yourself and your manifestations you are complete, and more cycles of opportunity become available to you in each new day. Be prepared for miracles!

Victory List

When a creation result is acknowledged it seals the deal. This makes room for more magnificence to expand into your life and increases your abundance factor adding to your ability to receive. As each aspect of your manifesting list arrives in your life, spend time allowing, acknowledging, and accepting it with the true gusto of gratitude! Keep your victory list active here.

Gratitude List

This fulfills the relationship between the giver and the receiver, which completes the cycle with the Universe so that a new beginning can be established.

Solar Eclipse
March 8th
5:56 PM

New Moon in Pisces

How to Use the Moon Book With Your Chart

Fill in the blanks on the Cosmic Check-In page. Then look up the degree of the Moon on the chart below. Take note of the "I" statement on the outside of the wheel where the Moon is located. Now, locate the same degree on your own chart and make a note of the house and corresponding "I" statement. Go back to the Cosmic Check-In page and circle the two statements from the charts and read what you wrote. This will give you an idea about what to expect from this moon phase on a personal level.

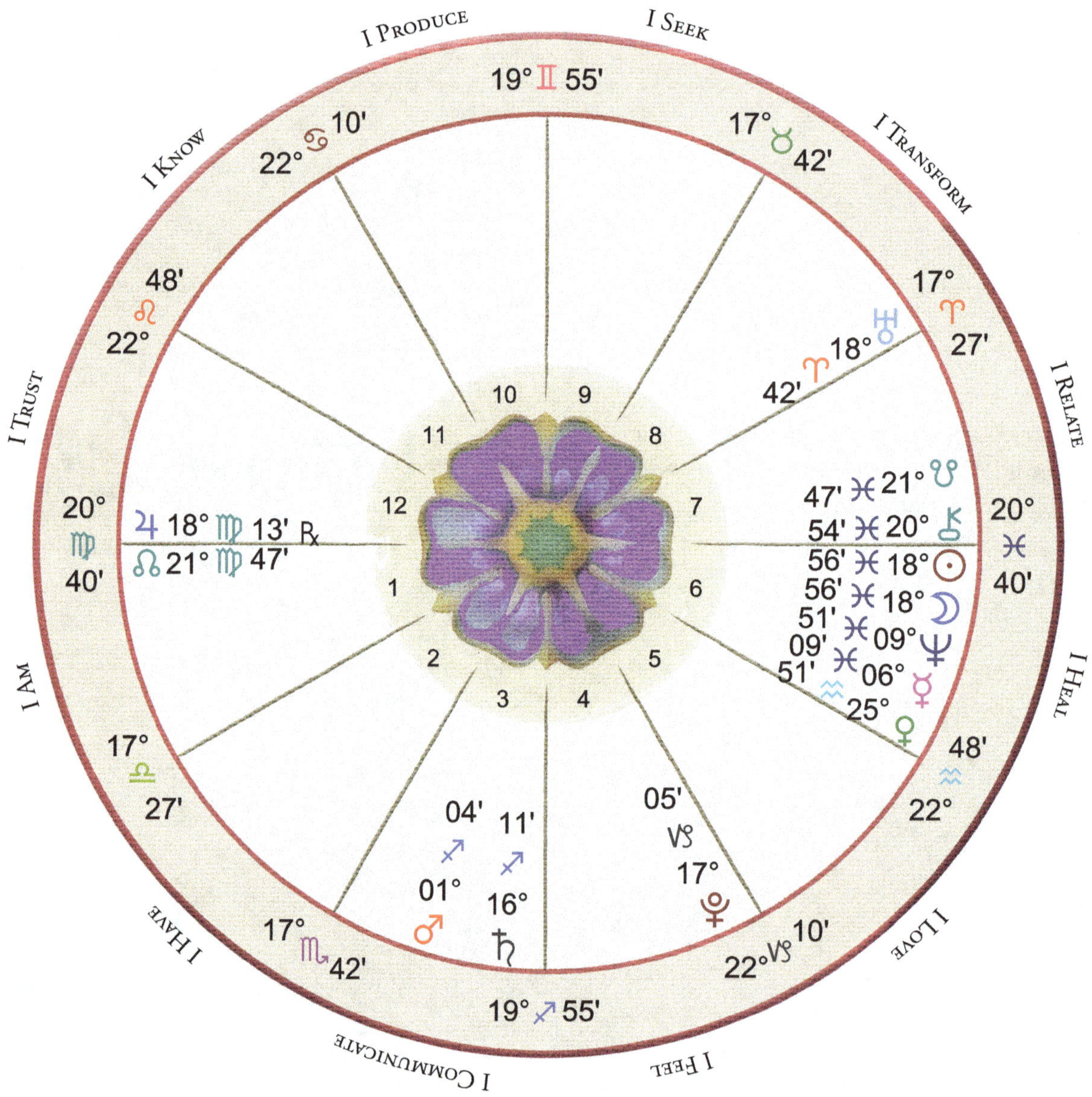

♈ Aries	♋ Cancer	♐ Sagittarius	☽ Moon	♄ Saturn	☊ North Node	V/C Void-of-Course
♉ Taurus	♌ Leo	♑ Capricorn	☿ Mercury	♅ Uranus	☋ South Node	▲ Super-Sensitivity
♊ Gemini	♍ Virgo	♒ Aquarius	♀ Venus	♆ Neptune	➡ Enters	▼ Low-Vitality
	♎ Libra	♓ Pisces	♂ Mars	♇ Pluto	℞ Retrograde	
	♏ Scorpio	☉ Sun	♃ Jupiter	⚷ Chiron	S/D Stationary Direct	

Cosmic Check-In

Take a moment to write a brief phrase for each "I" statement.
This activates all areas of your life for this creative cycle.

♓ I Trust

♈ I Am

♉ I Have

♊ I Communicate

♋ I Feel

♌ I Love

♍ I Heal

♎ I Relate

♏ I Transform

♐ I Seek

♑ I Produce

♒ I Know

Lunar Eclipse
March 23rd
5:02 AM

Full Moon in Libra

Degree Choice Points
3° Libra 17'

Light   Collective Focus

Shadow   Laborious Efforts

Wisdom   Use a Lemurian crystal to bend your mind, body, or the rules!!!

Statement   I Relate
  Body   Kidneys
  Mind   Social
  Spirit   Peace

Element
  Air – Need for new insights, active dreaming, freedom from attachments, forgiveness.

Seventh House Moon
23° Leo 24'

Seventh House Umbrella Theme
  I Relate/I Love – One-on-one relationships, defines your people attraction, and how you work in relationships with the people you attract.

Light   Spirit/Body Union

Shadow   Physical Neglect

Wisdom   Expand your perception of reality in the face of opposition.

Karmic Awakening

Virgo/Pisces – Conflicting issues relate to boundaries

The conflict here is getting lost in vastness due to lack of boundaries or restriction due to over-analyzing details.

Karmic stress will appear in the area of relating to yourself or others. The challenge happens when you receive an infusion of light, in the form of a spirit body union, and go flying off to "wonderland" while neglecting the physical. Watch out for temper tantrums that interfere with your inner peace due to living for another, thus forgetting yourself.

The Sun is Opposite the Moon

Full moons are always in opposition to the Sun. This creates a feeling of tension between where you want to shine and how your feelings are flowing on a sensory level about the Sun's directive. The two forces seem like they are working against each other, yet they are on the same team displaying different techniques to obtain the same mission. The Libra/Aries polarity creates tension between the idea of "We" versus "Me."

Libra Goddess

Ostara, Goddess of the Spring Equinox, walks into your life creating a carpet of fragrant flowers in her wake with each step upon the Earth. Freed from the ice and snow of Winter, she bathes in the moonlight and breathes out warmer breezes to turn up the temperatures. This moon is the harbinger, a rebirth of the Earth to fresh growth and abundance.

What is blooming new in your life? What do your seeds need to shed and break through to bask in the bright Spring sunlight? Take Ostara's blessing of jasmine or rose fragrance into the bath or shower and allow the warm water to wash away the old.

Build Your Altar

Colors Pink, green

Numerology 3 – Choose happiness – it is an option

Tarot Card Justice – The ability to stay in the center of polarity

Gemstones Rose quartz, jade

Plant remedy Olive trees – Stamina

Fragrance Eucalyptus – Clarity of breath

Clearing the Slate

Remember a time when you experienced the following trigger points.
Write down what happened and perform Ho'oponopono, the Hawaiian forgiveness ritual.

Guilt

- I'm Sorry
- Please Forgive Me
- Thank You
- I Love You

Need to Justify

- I'm Sorry
- Please Forgive Me
- Thank You
- I Love You

Feeling Wrong

- I'm Sorry
- Please Forgive Me
- Thank You
- I Love You

Defending

- I'm Sorry
- Please Forgive Me
- Thank You
- I Love You

Avoiding the moment due to spending time strategizing

- I'm Sorry
- Please Forgive Me
- Thank You
- I Love You

Lunar Eclipse
March 23rd
5:02 AM

Full Moon in Libra

Libra Challenges and Victories

Say all of the statements in this section out loud. Then, underline the phrase that means the most to you. Use the phrase as your special affirmation for recalibrating throughout this phase of the moon.

I am awakened to the reality of the Law of Cause and Effect. I take time out today to see what is coming back to me. I know my actions, my words, and my thoughts have life and manifest in a pattern that returns to me. Today, I am in a place where I can clearly see the results of my words, my actions, and my thoughts. I am aware that it is time for a review and, in so doing, I am given the opportunity to balance, integrate and redistribute these results in a more productive way. When I truly know and experience the Law of Cause and Effect (what I send out comes back to me), I can take responsibility for my actions, words, and thoughts, and set myself free of blame. When blame is gone from my thought pattern (self-inflicted or circumstantial), I am able to benefit from my review rather than wasting energy justifying or defending my position. I now accept the idea that I am free to reconcile with whatever I have labeled as an injustice in my life. I take the time to re-route my thinking towards making life a beneficial experience. Today, I accept that in changing my language I can change my life. Today, I prepare to take actions toward beneficial experiences. Today, I release the need to be right and accept the right to be. Today, I stop judging life and start living life.

Libra Homework

Let the fresh air blow away mental stagnation related to times when you let others' interests supersede your own. Drink an excess amount of water to alert your kidneys that the recalibration process has commenced. It's time to deepen your intention to be one with the light, promoting restoration on Earth.

Recalibrating List

Say this statement out loud three times before writing your recalibrating list!

I am a free spiritual being and it is my desire to be free to think and to express myself fully.

I hereby fully and completely free my mind from all adhesions to outdated philosophies, habits, relationships, groups of people, man-made laws, moral codes, all rules, set ideas and set ways of thinking, traditions, organizations, duty-motivated activities, guilt, judgment, and being misunderstood!

Libra Recalibrating Ideas

Now is the time to activate a game change in my life, and give up situations that are not balanced, people-pleasing and the need to be liked, sorrow over past relationships, unsupportive relationships, the need to be right, false accusations, and being misunderstood.

Lunar Eclipse
March 23rd
5:02 AM

Full Moon in Libra

How to Use the Moon Book With Your Chart

Fill in the blanks on the Cosmic Check-In page. Then look up the degree of the Moon on the chart below. Take note of the "I" statement on the outside of the wheel where the Moon is located. Now, locate the same degree on your own chart and make a note of the house and corresponding "I" statement. Go back to the Cosmic Check-In page and circle the two statements from the charts and read what you wrote. This will give you an idea about what to expect from this moon phase on a personal level.

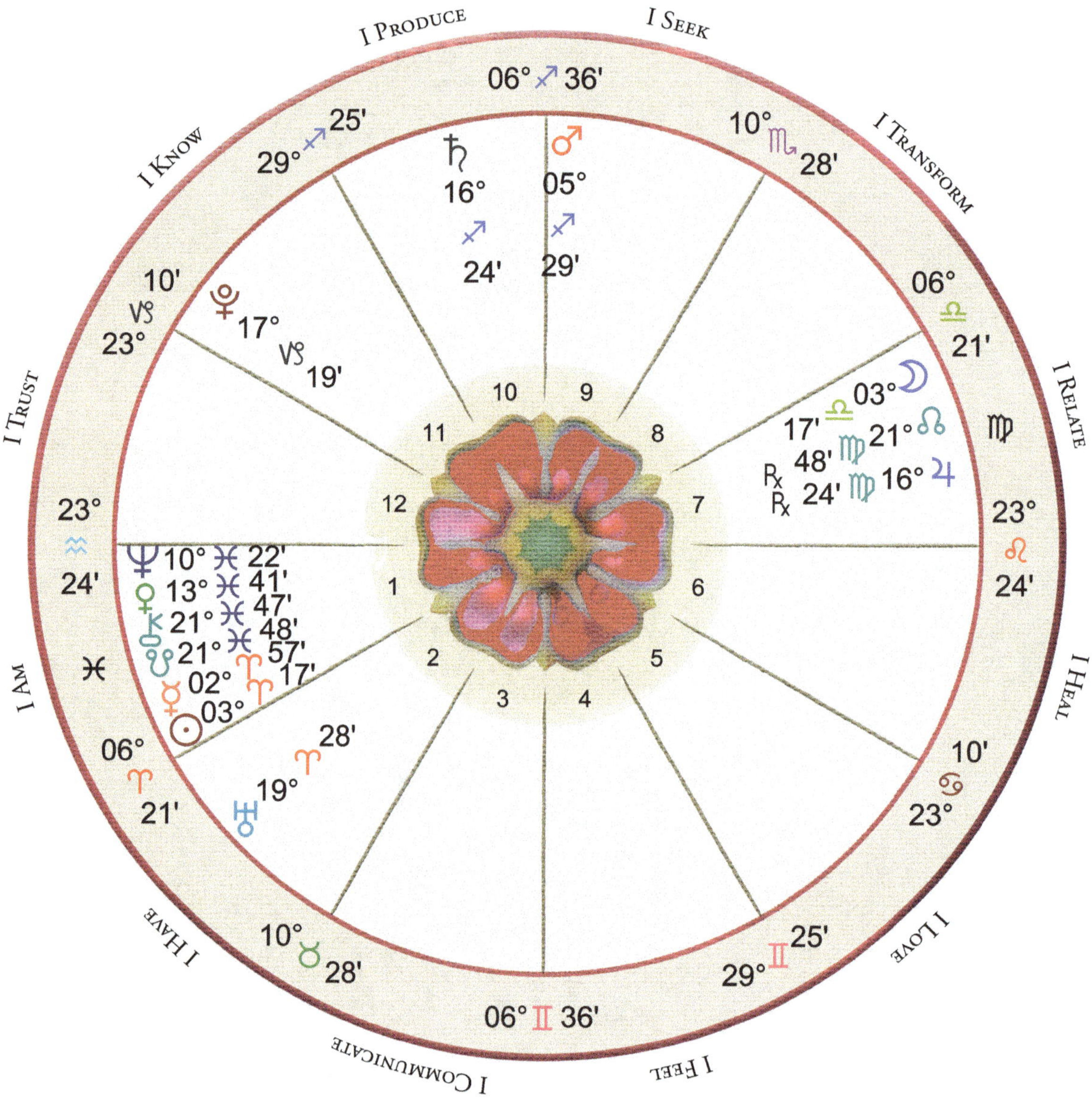

♈ Aries	♋ Cancer	♐ Sagittarius	☽ Moon	♄ Saturn	☊ North Node	V/C Void-of-Course
♉ Taurus	♌ Leo	♑ Capricorn	☿ Mercury	♅ Uranus	☋ South Node	▲ Super-Sensitivity
♊ Gemini	♍ Virgo	♒ Aquarius	♀ Venus	♆ Neptune	➡ Enters	♦ Low-Vitality
	♎ Libra	♓ Pisces	♂ Mars	♇ Pluto	℞ Retrograde	
	♏ Scorpio		☉ Sun	⚷ Chiron	S/D Stationary Direct	

62

Cosmic Check-In

Take a moment to write a brief phrase for each "I" statement.
This activates all areas of your life for this creative cycle.

♎ I Relate

♏ I Transform

♐ I Seek

♑ I Produce

♒ I Know

♓ I Trust

♈ I Am

♉ I Have

♊ I Communicate

♋ I Feel

♌ I Love

♍ I Heal

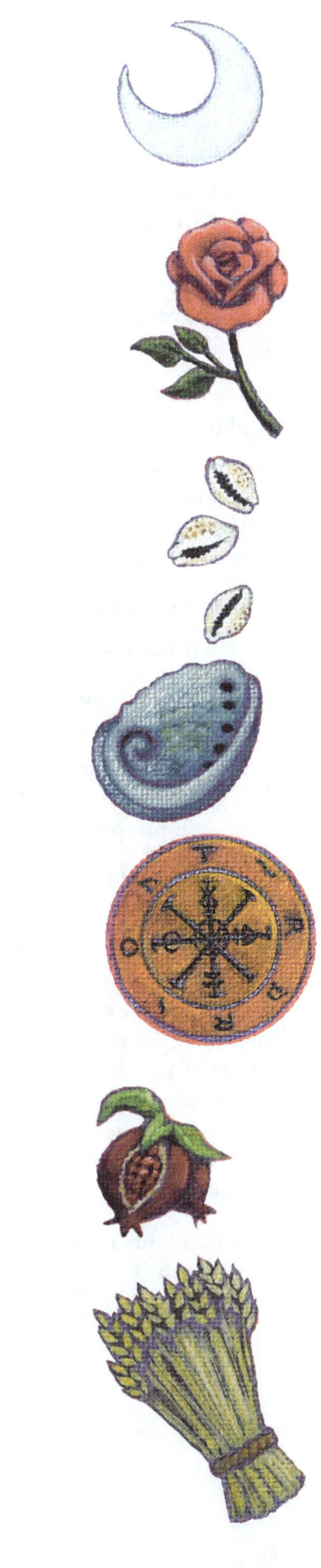

April Planetary Highlights

Jupiter is Retrograde in Virgo Until May 9

When Divinity is discovered in the details, life expands into a great adventure.

Saturn is Retrograde in Sagittarius Until August 13

As long as you accept your ability to inspire others, you will be fine.

Mars goes Retrograde on April 17 in Sagittarius Until June 29

The spirit of adventure could feel squelched and the broad strokes might be getting ignored during this time. Life could get confusing. Keep your intention focused and that might help lighten the load.

Pluto is Retrograde in Capricorn Until September 26

We now make choices based on freedom, not survival.

South Node and Chiron in Pisces Continue to be Coupled Throughout the Month

It's time to move away from self-healing and to stop trying to be your own doctor. Trust the fact that you have recalibrated your past pain and are now free to live a happier life.

North Node and Jupiter Stay Coupled for the Entire Month

Expect mutual generosity and goodwill during this time. Your attraction force will direct you to people and groups who share common philosophical and religious beliefs, influencing close bonds and lasting friendships. Jupiter may bring material wealth, good luck, support, and spiritual guidance to areas of influence according to your chart.

Mars Continues to Activate Mid-Heaven

This indicates an emerging influence that will present a deep need for personal recognition.

April 5 – Mercury Enters Taurus

It's time to communicate how you want your version of success to be.

April 5 – Venus Enters Aries

Impatience could get you in trouble where a new love interest is awakening. Rushing gives you immediate gratification, but you may miss a lasting concept. Remember, love is a process not a destination.

April 7 – The Sun, Moon, and Uranus are Tripled in Aries

Watch out! Tempers could be boiling over especially with your mother or female friends. This could come on suddenly and, out of the blue, you may notice yourself being quite cranky, impatient, or needing to dump out old, unnecessary stuff. Uranus has a long-term effect, so stay focused on flowing with feelings rather than exploding, otherwise you might regret it.

April 29 – Venus Enters Taurus

This coupling activates prosperity, beauty, art, and luxury. Shopping sprees are a must at this time, enjoy yourself! Throw a party and let yourself dance the dance of life!

April 21 – Venus and Uranus are Connecting in Aries

Expect an unusual love attraction to come into play. The energy is very spontaneous, so you might find yourself having a "stranger in paradise" experience.

Super-Sensitivity – April 25-26

The atmosphere could be delicate. It's global, so don't personalize it. Avoid chaos and go slow to avoid carelessness.

Low-Vitality – April 10-11

Now is the time to honor the Earth with prayers or working on the land in some way to assist in balancing. Exhaustion may be part of the pattern – if so, get rest.

Sunday	Monday	Tuesday	Wednesday	Thursday	Friday	Saturday
					1 ♃♄℞ ☽ V/C 9:38am ☽→♒ 6:36pm 3. Greet each day with a song.	**2** ♃♄℞ 4. Unify to raise the earthly vibration.
3 ♃♄℞ ☽ V/C 4:15pm ☽→♓ 10:45pm 5. Be willing to change often.	**4** ♃♄℞ 6. Full alignment in Self is well-being.	**5** ♃♄℞ ☿→♉ 4:10pm ♀→♈ 9:52am ☽ V/C 3:32am ☽→♈ 11:45pm 7. Use free choice in your experiences.	**6** ♃♄℞ 8. Generosity of spirit is abundance.	**7** ♃♄℞ ☽ V/C 7:56am ☽→♉ 11:10pm ● 18°♈04′ 4:25am 9. Everyone is spiritually connected.	**8** ♃♄℞ 10. Love is the promise for all.	**9** ♃♄℞ ☽ V/C 2:49am ☽→♊ 10:58pm 2. Allow the intuitive to become real.
10 ♃♄℞▼ 3. Strive to make a difference.	**11** ♃♄℞▼ ☽ V/C 11:56am 4. Send positive energy to the planet.	**12** ♃♄℞ ☽→♋ 1:06am 5. You can change anything.	**13** ♃♄℞ ☽ V/C 8:59pm 6. Embrace a friend with an open heart.	**14** ♃♄℞ ☽→♌ 6:52am 7. Reading expands your horizons.	**15** ♃♄℞ 8. Each human is a part of God.	**16** ♃♄℞ ☽ V/C 10:48am ☽→♍ 4:22pm 9. Know in your heart you are loved.
17 ♂♃♄℞ ♂ SR→8°♐54′ 5:15am 10. Forgiveness allows for closure.	**18** ♂♃♄♇℞ ♇ SR→17°♑29° 12:24am ☽ V/C 5:29am 2. When you are balanced, life works.	**19** ♂♃♄♇℞ ☽→♎ 4:23am ☉→♉ 8:31am 3. Creative opportunities are all around.	**20** ♂♃♄♇℞ ☽ V/C 11:13pm 4. Biology of creation exists within.	**21** ♂♃♄♇℞ ☽→♏ 5:17pm ○ 2°♏31′ 10:25pm 5. Choose to change your patterns.	**22** ♂♃♄♇℞ Passover Earth Day 6. At the core of your being is God.	**23** ♂♃♄♇℞ ☽ V/C 2:45pm 7. Wisdom is learning to act wisely.
24 ♂♃♄♇℞ ☽→♐ 5:46am 8. The only limit is the one you create.	**25** ♂♃♄♇℞▲ 9. Claim your Divinity.	**26** ♂♃♄♇℞▲ ☽ V/C 8:50am ☽→♑ 4:54pm 10. Live the dream you wish for now.	**27** ♂♃♄♇℞ 2. Look at both sides and then decide.	**28** ♂♃♄♇℞ ☿ SR→23°♉36′ 10:21am 3. Living creatively is living without fear.	**29** ☿♂♃♄♇℞ ♀→♉ 5:37pm ☽ V/C 12:07am ☽→♒ 1:46am 4. Respect is a firm foundation.	**30** ☿♂♃♄♇℞ ☽ V/C 7:55pm 5. Making changes enhances creativity.

♈ Aries	♎ Libra	☉ Sun	♄ Saturn	☊ North Node	▲ Super Sensitivity	6. Love
♉ Taurus	♏ Scorpio	☽ Moon	♅ Uranus	☋ South Node	▼ Low Vitality	7. Learning
♊ Gemini	♐ Sagittarius	☿ Mercury	♆ Neptune	➡ Enters	2. Balance	8. Money
♋ Cancer	♑ Capricorn	♀ Venus	♇ Pluto	℞ Retrograde	3. Fun	9. Spirituality
♌ Leo	♒ Aquarius	♂ Mars	⚷ Chiron	SD Stationary Direct	4. Structure	10. Visionary
♍ Virgo	♓ Pisces	♃ Jupiter		V/C Void-of-Course	5. Action	11. Completion

April 7th
4:25 AM

New Moon in Aries

Degree Choice Points
18° Aries 04'

Light	Imagination
Shadow	Vicariousness
Wisdom	Anything you can imagine is real somewhere.
Statement	I Am
Body	Head
Mind	Impulsive
Spirit	Initiation

Element
Fire – Championship energy, serving yourself first, Divine Masculine, all-consuming.

Second House Moon
13° Aries 40'

Second House Umbrella Theme
I Have/I Am – The way you make money and the way you spend your money.

Light	Revelation
Shadow	Sexual Manipulation
Wisdom	Your only role is to initiate in this situation.

Karmic Awakening

Leo/Aquarius – Restriction and tension occur when devotion is not available on an intimate level due to distractions happening in the outer world.

Karmic stress will appear when attention is going to the group rather than to your loved one. This can bring about an imbalance of choices between a mystical vision and obvious beneficial choices. If this gets out of hand, healing and restoration of trust will be required.

When the Sun is in Aries

Aries awakens the dreamer from Winter sleep and represents the raw energy of Spring, when the new shoots of life burst forth. Aries is the fundamental, straightforward approach to life. There is no challenge that is too great, no obstacle too daunting, and no rival too powerful for the Aries. Aries symbolizes initiation, leadership, strength, and potency. Competition and achievement are very important to Aries. Now is the time to be a pioneer and break all barriers to become the winner you are.

Aries Goddess

Pandora was created by Zeus, who was angry about Prometheus stealing the secret of fire. She was the first human woman, whose name means "the all-giving." The gods all conspired to each invest her with seductive gifts. Hesiod's story tells us that Pandora's curiosity led her to open a jar (not a box) that unleashed evils upon humanity. However, Pandora, also known as Anesidora, "she who sends up gifts" from the Earth, could instead be interpreted as opening the pithos (the vessel), an ancient symbol of the Divine Feminine, and generously gifting the world with fertility and creativity.

As you reinterpret your identity this moon, ask Pandora to help you get curious and creative about the "I" you present to the world and how that contributes to the "We."

Build Your Altar

Colors Red, black, white

Numerology 9 – Everyone is spiritually connected

Tarot Card Emperor – Success on all levels

Gemstones Diamond, red jasper, coral, obsidian

Plant Remedy Pomegranates, oak – Planting new life and rooting new life

Fragrance Ginger – The ability to ingest and digest life

Manifesting List

This or something better than this comes to me in an easy and pleasurable way, for the good of all concerned. Thank you, Universe!

Aries Manifesting Ideas

Now is the time to focus on manifesting personality power, leadership, strength, self-acceptance, winning, courage, personal appearance, and advancing to new frontiers.

April 7th
4:25 AM

New Moon in Aries

Aries Challenges and Victories

Say all of the statements in this section out loud. Then, underline the phrase that means the most to you. Use the phrase as your special affirmation for manifesting throughout this phase of the moon.

I am the author of my life. I accept that I am a winner and, in so doing, all doors are open to me. I hold the world in the palm of my hand and I know that there is not a mountain that I cannot climb. My ability to respond to life is in operation today and I direct my intention to bring me to the next level of self-determined achievement. The world and its systems are available for me to use as tools for my success and I use them with true excellence. I am organized and all systems are in place for me to make my mark on the world. I accept that my structured ground state and my dynamic energy are ready to make headway using pure determination, action, planning, and power. I will manage this plan and know that the sequence of events provided support me to make a breakthrough today.

I am willing to make my plan and take action on it. I gather my support team together today to focus on the appropriate action and encourage each person in their area of excellence and production. I am a great leader and my dynamic power is a good resource for others to determine their own success formula. I am aware that all parts of my team are important and place value on all areas of performance required to manifest in the world. I know how to place people in their best areas of expertise, so they can experience their own unique talent manifesting. Today, I honor my father for what he taught me by what he did, or didn't do, to encourage my ability to perform. I am the producer. I am the protector. I am the provider. I am the promoter. I am power. I am the author of my life.

Aries Homework

Aries manifest best through sales and promotions, and as a professional athlete, personal trainer or coach, martial arts expert, military professional, demolition expert, fireworks manufacturer, or wardrobe consultant.

Merge your light and dark forces so balance can occur. Then, give shape to your feelings through creative forms and learn to live in the duality of your Soul and watch your spirit soar! The embodiment of this duality connects you to the Unity, a requirement for these times.

Without Acknowledgment Progress Cannot Occur

Acknowledgement creates space for victory and gratitude, which automatically brings you to a level of completion so a new cycle of opportunity can occur in your life. When you celebrate your wins and acknowledge your victories with gratitude, you update your cells so that your ability to move forward is not hindered by a cellular holographic pattern that is stuck in the past. Cellular lag creates resistance and makes moving forward most difficult. The key is to stay continuously updated by acknowledging yourself for what you did do at the end of each day, rather than heading off to sleep thinking about what you did not do. By acknowledging what you did not do, you play into your karmic storage bank and keep your progress at bay. When you acknowledge yourself and your manifestations you are complete, and more cycles of opportunity become available to you in each new day. Be prepared for miracles!

Victory List

When a creation result is acknowledged it seals the deal. This makes room for more magnificence to expand into your life and increases your abundance factor adding to your ability to receive. As each aspect of your manifesting list arrives in your life, spend time allowing, acknowledging, and accepting it with the true gusto of gratitude! Keep your victory list active here.

This fulfills the relationship between the giver and the receiver, which completes the cycle with the Universe so that a new beginning can be established.

Gratitude List

April 7th
4:25 AM

New Moon in Aries

How to Use the Moon Book With Your Chart

Fill in the blanks on the Cosmic Check-In page. Then look up the degree of the Moon on the chart below. Take note of the "I" statement on the outside of the wheel where the Moon is located. Now, locate the same degree on your own chart and make a note of the house and corresponding "I" statement. Go back to the Cosmic Check-In page and circle the two statements from the charts and read what you wrote. This will give you an idea about what to expect from this moon phase on a personal level.

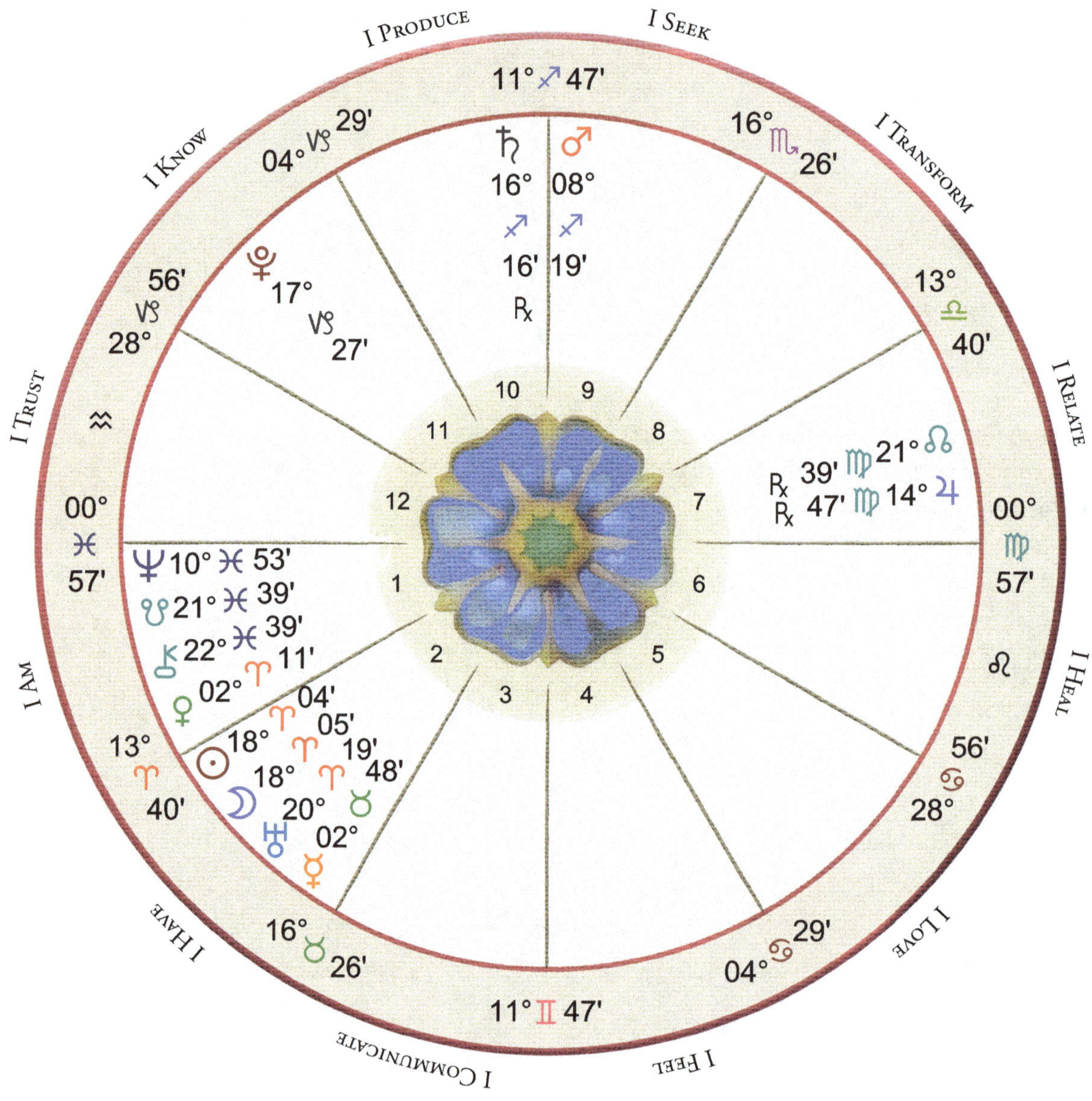

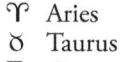

72

Cosmic Check-In

Take a moment to write a brief phrase for each "I" statement.
This activates all areas of your life for this creative cycle.

♈ I Am

♉ I Have

♊ I Communicate

♋ I Feel

♌ I Love

♍ I Heal

♎ I Relate

♏ I Transform

♐ I Seek

♑ I Produce

♒ I Know

♓ I Trust

April 21st
10:25 PM

Full Moon in Scorpio

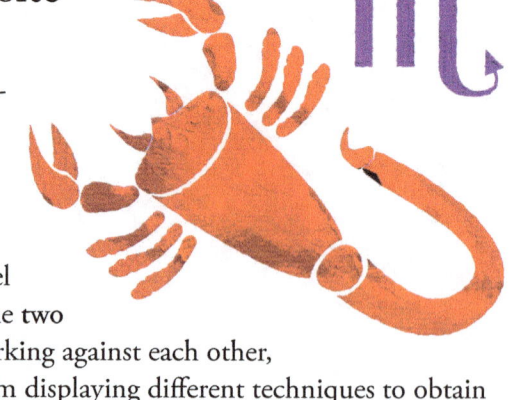

Degree Choice Points
2° Scorpio 31'

Light   Philosophic Thinking

Shadow   Bureaucracy

Wisdom   Yield to the changes in your life, the results are empowering.

Statement   I Transform
    Body   Sex Organs
    Mind   Intensity
    Spirit   Transformation

Element
Water – Seeks lowest ground to be contained, emotions that consume, the need for soul nourishment, sensitivity to others.

Eleventh House Moon
24° Libra 33'

Eleventh House Umbrella Theme
I Know/I Relate – Your approach to friends, social consciousness, teamwork, community service, and the future.

Light   Interdependence

Shadow   Irrelevance

Wisdom   Learn real MAGIC!

The Sun is Opposite the Moon

Full moons are always in opposition to the Sun. This creates a feeling of tension between where you want to shine and how your feelings are flowing on a sensory level about the Sun's directive. The two forces seem like they are working against each other, yet they are on the same team displaying different techniques to obtain the same mission. The Scorpio/Taurus polarity creates tension between sharing resources and living abundantly for yourself.

Scorpio Goddess

The concept of web thinking, in which all is intrinsically interconnected and related to the whole, comes to us through the creator myths of the Pueblo and Hopi people, as Grandmother Spider. She spun a sparkling dew-dropped web and threw it up into the night sky to create the stars.

Her interdependent web of light reminds us to promote the power of community and band together to take action when important issues affect the whole. Grandmother Spider can help you appreciate your own and others' unique contributions and talents, and show you how to combine them to create a strong and sustainable web of action.

Build Your Altar

Colors   Indigo, deep purple, scarlet

Numerology   5 – Choose to change your patterns

Tarot Card   Death – The ability to make changes

Gemstones   Topaz, tanzanite, onyx, obsidian

Plant remedy   Manzanita – Prepares the body for transformation

Fragrance   Sandalwood – Awakens your sensuality

Clearing the Slate

Remember a time when you experienced the following trigger points.
Write down what happened and perform Ho'oponopono, the Hawaiian forgiveness ritual.

Secrets

- I'm Sorry
- Please Forgive Me
- Thank You
- I Love You

Sharing Money

- I'm Sorry
- Please Forgive Me
- Thank You
- I Love You

Sexual Indiscretions

- I'm Sorry
- Please Forgive Me
- Thank You
- I Love You

Control Dramas

- I'm Sorry
- Please Forgive Me
- Thank You
- I Love You

Revenge

- I'm Sorry
- Please Forgive Me
- Thank You
- I Love You

April 21st
10:25 PM

Full Moon in Scorpio

Scorpio Challenges and Victories

Say all of the statements in this section out loud. Then, underline the phrase that means the most to you. Use the phrase as your special affirmation for recalibrating throughout this phase of the moon.

I will not compromise myself today. I know that transformation occurs when I stand tall in my truth, even if everything around me needs to die. I see death as a new beginning and know that in death comes new aliveness. I am willing to embrace transformation and open to the idea that change is in my favor. I know that in letting go, I give new life to myself. I am willing to accept that life is ever-changing and in a constant state of renewal; one cannot occur without the other.

Releasing is easy when I offer myself something new. When I allow for the motion of change to stay alive, I let go with one hand and receive with the other hand. The ever-present flow and motion keeps me alive and connected to the revitalizing power of Nature. When the power of Nature becomes apparent to me, I become aware that Nature abhors a vacuum. Rejuvenation is mine when I embrace change.

Scorpio Homework

The Scorpio moon creates the urge within us to make life happen. Pay attention to these urges so you can prepare yourself for greater action, intention, and purpose.

Recalibrating List

Say this statement out loud three times before writing your recalibrating list!

I am a free spiritual being and it is my desire to be free to think and to express myself fully.

I am now free and ready to make choices beyond survival!

Scorpio Recalibrating Ideas

Now is the time to activate a game change in my life, and give up resentment, jealousy, revenge, vendettas, betrayals, blocks to transformation, destructive relationships, unhealthy joint financial situations, obstacles to having a healthy sex life, resistance to changing paradigms, and karma relating to all issues of power.

Full Moon in Scorpio

April 21st
10:25 PM

How to Use the Moon Book With Your Chart

Fill in the blanks on the Cosmic Check-In page. Then look up the degree of the Moon on the chart below. Take note of the "I" statement on the outside of the wheel where the Moon is located. Now, locate the same degree on your own chart and make a note of the house and corresponding "I" statement. Go back to the Cosmic Check-In page and circle the two statements from the charts and read what you wrote. This will give you an idea about what to expect from this moon phase on a personal level.

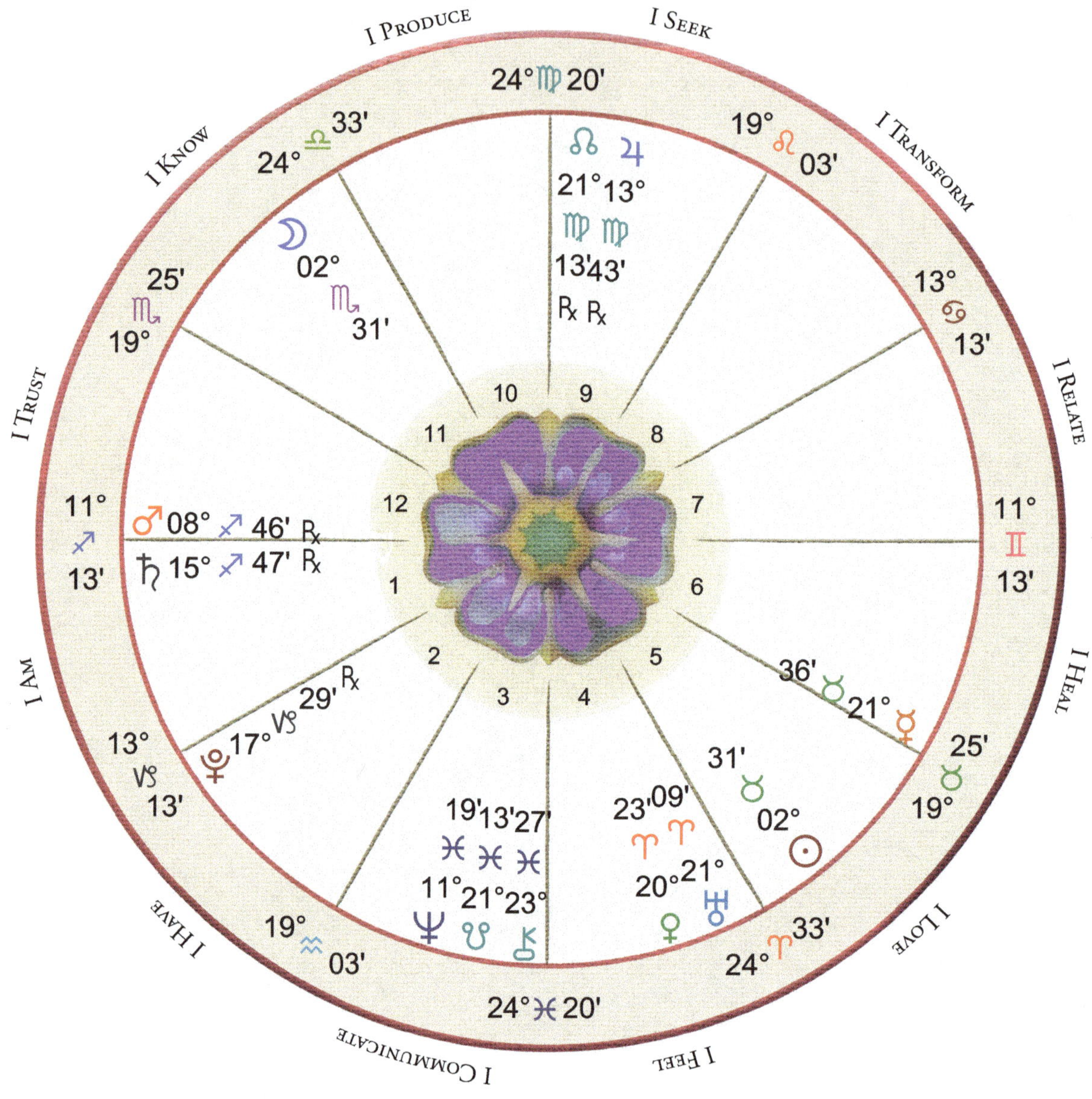

♈ Aries	♋ Cancer	♐ Sagittarius	☽ Moon	♄ Saturn	☊ North Node	V/C Void-of-Course
♉ Taurus	♌ Leo	♑ Capricorn	☿ Mercury	♅ Uranus	☋ South Node	▲ Super-Sensitivity
♊ Gemini	♍ Virgo	♒ Aquarius	♀ Venus	♆ Neptune	➡ Enters	• Low-Vitality
	♎ Libra	♓ Pisces	♂ Mars	♇ Pluto	℞ Retrograde	
	♏ Scorpio	☉ Sun	♃ Jupiter	⚷ Chiron	S/D Stationary Direct	

Cosmic Check-In

Take a moment to write a brief phrase for each "I" statement.
This activates all areas of your life for this creative cycle.

♏ I Transform

♐ I Seek

♑ I Produce

♒ I Know

♓ I Trust

♈ I Am

♉ I Have

♊ I Communicate

♋ I Feel

♌ I Love

♍ I Heal

♎ I Relate

May Planetary Highlights

Mercury is Retrograde in Taurus Until May 22

It's time to slow down and smell the roses.

Mars is Retrograde in Sagittarius Until June 29

Avoid travel if possible. If not, expect delays. You might feel stuck. If so, learn to work with options.

Jupiter is Retrograde in Virgo Until May 9

Avoid broad strokes – the answer is in the details.

Jupiter goes Direct in Virgo May 9

You will feel like the monkey is finally off of your back and your free will has returned. Go have some fun!

Pluto is Retrograde in Capricorn Until September 26

Create support systems for yourself personally and professionally.

Jupiter and the North Node are Conjunct All Month

Be willing to accept a vision of good fortune for your future.

Chiron and the South Node are Still Connected for the Month

Take a serious look at where holding on to the past keeps your body from working in the now.

May 20 – The Sun Enters Gemini

The power of your potential begins to speak to you. Take the reins and GO FOR IT!

May 21 – Full Moon Coupled with Mars in Sagittarius

Reflect on anger issues and make amends with them. Do what you can to avoid any new versions of anger. Learn to communicate when you feel the steam rising, rather than waiting for the flames to rise to the uncontrollable zone.

May 21 – Neptune Approaches the South Node

Expect a new assignment to come forward. It's what you have been waiting for.

May 24 – Venus Enters Gemini

It's time to flirt Big Time!

May 27 – Mars Retrograde Re-enters Scorpio

Yikes! Time to get it that control is an illusion and doesn't work.

Super-Sensitivity – May 22-23

There's double duty going on in the chaos department. Beware, be careful, and be well!

Low-Vitality – May 8-9

Don't stress if you are tired – simply go and take a nap.

Sunday	Monday	Tuesday	Wednesday	Thursday	Friday	Saturday
1 ☿♂♃♄♇℞ ☽→♓ 7:33am 6. Be yourself. Everyone else is taken.	**2** ☿♂♃♄♇℞ ☽ V/C 10:07pm 7. Sharing what you know helps others.	**3** ☿♂♃♄♇℞ ☽→♈ 10:04am 8. A good leader takes no prisoners.	**4** ☿♂♃♄♇℞ ☽ V/C 9:16pm 9. God is your essence.	**5** ☿♂♃♄♇℞ ☽→♉ 10:10am 10. Visualize the solution as here.	**6** ☿♂♃♄♇℞ ☽ V/C 7:10pm ● 16°♉41′ 12:31pm 2. Peace can heal hearts at the core.	**7** ☿♂♃♄♇℞ ☽→♊ 9:34am 3. Become a part of a creative team.
8 ☿♂♃♄♇℞ ▼ Mother's Day ☽ V/C 9:15pm 4. Perfection is being yourself.	**9** ☿♂♄♇℞ ▼ ♃SD-13°♍15′ 5:16am ☽→♋ 10:23am 5. Move beyond resistance.	**10** ☿♂♄♇℞ 6. Remove any clutter from your home.	**11** ☿♂♄♇℞ ☽ V/C 12:33am ☽→♌ 2:31pm 7. Teaching is the best way to learn.	**12** ☿♂♄♇℞ 8. Taking charge is not taking control.	**13** ☿♂♄♇℞ ☽ V/C 10:02am ☽→♍ 10:51pm 9. The spirit of love exists in the heart.	**14** ☿♂♄♇℞ 10. Release the baggage from the past.
15 ☿♂♄♇℞ 2. The truth is the truth regardless.	**16** ☿♂♄♇℞ ☽ V/C 2:20am ☽→♎ 10:32am 3. Use generosity as a circle of creation.	**17** ☿♂♄♇℞ 4. An organized approach is best.	**18** ☿♂♄♇℞ ☽ V/C 8:22am ☽→♏ 11:29pm 5. Remember, all of life is a transition.	**19** ☿♂♄♇℞ 6. Send someone you love a card.	**20** ☿♂♄♇℞ ☉→♊ 7:38am 7. Celebrate the wisdom of waiting.	**21** ☿♂♄♇℞ ☽ V/C 4:39am ☽→♐ 11:48am ○ 1°♐14′ 2:16pm 8. Everyone on the team counts.
22 ♂♄♇℞ ▲ ☿SD-14°♉20′ 6:21am 9. No one owns the essence of God.	**23** ♂♄♇℞ ▲ ☽ V/C 8:37am ☽→♑ 10:33pm 10. Choose to move beyond limits.	**24** ♂♄♇℞ ♀→♊ 2:46am 2. Be a good partner with the planet.	**25** ♂♄♇℞ ☽ V/C 6:11pm 3. What you create belongs to you.	**26** ♂♄♇℞ ☽→♒ 7:26am 4. Make sure your plan has options.	**27** ♂♄♇℞ ♂→♏ 6:52am 6. Loyalty and trust build relationships.	**28** ♂♄♇℞ ☽ V/C 1:18pm ☽→♓ 2:05pm 7. Know there is more to know.
29 ♂♄♇℞ 8. Money is intended to be used.	**30** ♂♄♇℞ Memorial Day ☽ V/C 4:10pm ☽→♈ 6:09pm 9. The love of Spirit is humble and pure.	**31** ♂♄♇℞ 10. Create a new beginning each day.				

♈ Aries	♎ Libra	☉ Sun	♄ Saturn	☊ North Node	▲ Super Sensitivity	6. Love
♉ Taurus	♏ Scorpio	☽ Moon	♅ Uranus	☋ South Node	▼ Low Vitality	7. Learning
♊ Gemini	♐ Sagittarius	☿ Mercury	♆ Neptune	➡ Enters	2. Balance	8. Money
♋ Cancer	♑ Capricorn	♀ Venus	♇ Pluto	℞ Retrograde	3. Fun	9. Spirituality
♌ Leo	♒ Aquarius	♂ Mars	⚷ Chiron	SD Stationary Direct	4. Structure	10. Visionary
♍ Virgo	♓ Pisces	♃ Jupiter		V/C Void-of-Course	5. Action	11. Completion

May 6th
12:31 PM

New Moon in Taurus

Degree Choice Points
  16° Taurus 41'

Light	Purpose
Shadow	Necessity Versus Desire
Wisdom	Accept that others' values are genuine.
Statement	I Have
Body	Neck
Mind	Collector
Spirit	Accumulation

Element
  Earth – Acquisition, increase and create abundance, practice generosity.

Tenth House Moon
  13° Taurus 08'

Tenth House Umbrella Theme
  I Produce/I Have – Your approach to status, career, honor, and prestige and why you chose your father.

Light	Live and Let Live
Shadow	Prying
Wisdom	Identify and release emotions that are not yours.

When the Sun is in Taurus

Taurus is the time when we see the true manifesting power, as the plants move to a higher aspiration of life and bloom. Once again, we become connected to the essence of beauty as a symbol of our divinity. Taurus is the connection between humanity and divinity. Taurus' job is to infuse matter with light through accumulating layers of substance. This is why they are such good shoppers and collectors. The more they accumulate, the more divinity they experience. This process brings about a sense of self-value which is directly commensurate to the amount of money they manifest. Personal resources are part of the pattern. Discover your value at this time.

Taurus Goddess

Today, Lakshmi, the Hindu Goddess of Abundance, walks into your life bearing gifts. She joyously showers you with success, wealth, well-being, luck, happiness, and fulfillment. Her blessings also include forgiveness and the generosity of spirit that allows you to reap the recognition for good work well done.

Working with feng shui, place a statue of Lakshmi in the left-hand corner of your room (looking in from the entrance) to honor her and to signal your receptivity. Are your hands and heart open and ready to receive? Make space for the new. Step confidently into the flow of abundance! Take Lakshmi's lead and shower everyone you meet with kindness and generosity!

Build Your Altar

Colors Green, pink, deep red, earth tones

Numerology 2 – Peace can heal hearts at the core

Tarot Card Hierophant – The ability to listen, inner-knowing

Gemstones Topaz, agate, smoky quartz, jade, rose quartz

Plant Remedy Angelica – Connecting Heaven and Earth

Fragrance Rose – Opening the heart

Manifesting List

This or something better than this comes to me in an easy and pleasurable way, for the good of all concerned. Thank you, Universe!

Taurus Manifesting Ideas
Now is the time to focus on manifesting success, money, property, luxury, beauty, personal value, and pleasure.

May 6th
12:31 PM

New Moon in Taurus

Taurus Challenges and Victories

Say all of the statements in this section out loud. Then, underline the phrase that means the most to you. Use the phrase as your special affirmation for manifesting throughout this phase of the moon.

Everything is possible for me today. My possibilities are endless. I have the power within me to make all of my dreams come true. I have the tools to make my talent a reality. I have the power to identify with my talent. Today, I focus my attention and intention on manifesting with my talent and, in so doing, I transform my ideas into reality. I recognize the part of me that is connected to the cosmic source of ideas and I express that source within me to manifest my creative power. I see my possibilities and act on them today. I am the creative power. I am all-knowing. I am an individual. There is no one else like me. I can manifest anything I desire. I intend it, I allow it, so be it.

Rules for Manifesting

Know what you want. Write it down. Say it out loud. Recognize that because you thought it, it can be so. Release your limiting beliefs. Override your limiting beliefs with power statements. Act as if you have already manifested your idea. Lastly, value yourself!

Taurus Homework

Taureans manifest best when buying, selling, and owning real estate, gardening and landscaping, selling and collecting art, manufacturing and selling fine furniture, singing or acting, and as a restaurateur, antique dealer, or interior designer.

The Taurus moon asks us to infuse light into form and, in so doing, the bridge between humanity and divinity is actualized and we can assume our stewardship in the physical world. When we release Spirit into matter, we become open to the idea that accumulation and actualization set us free to experience the abundance available to us here on Earth. Go shopping!

Without Acknowledgment Progress Cannot Occur

Acknowledgement creates space for victory and gratitude, which automatically brings you to a level of completion so a new cycle of opportunity can occur in your life. When you celebrate your wins and acknowledge your victories with gratitude, you update your cells so that your ability to move forward is not hindered by a cellular holographic pattern that is stuck in the past. Cellular lag creates resistance and makes moving forward most difficult. The key is to stay continuously updated by acknowledging yourself for what you did do at the end of each day, rather than heading off to sleep thinking about what you did not do. By acknowledging what you did not do, you play into your karmic storage bank and keep your progress at bay. When you acknowledge yourself and your manifestations you are complete, and more cycles of opportunity become available to you in each new day. Be prepared for miracles!

Victory List

When a creation result is acknowledged it seals the deal. This makes room for more magnificence to expand into your life and increases your abundance factor adding to your ability to receive. As each aspect of your manifesting list arrives in your life, spend time allowing, acknowledging, and accepting it with the true gusto of gratitude! Keep your victory list active here.

Gratitude List

This fulfills the relationship between the giver and the receiver, which completes the cycle with the Universe so that a new beginning can be established.

New Moon in Taurus

May 6th
12:31 PM

How to Use the Moon Book With Your Chart

Fill in the blanks on the Cosmic Check-In page. Then look up the degree of the Moon on the chart below. Take note of the "I" statement on the outside of the wheel where the Moon is located. Now, locate the same degree on your own chart and make a note of the house and corresponding "I" statement. Go back to the Cosmic Check-In page and circle the two statements from the charts and read what you wrote. This will give you an idea about what to expect from this moon phase on a personal level.

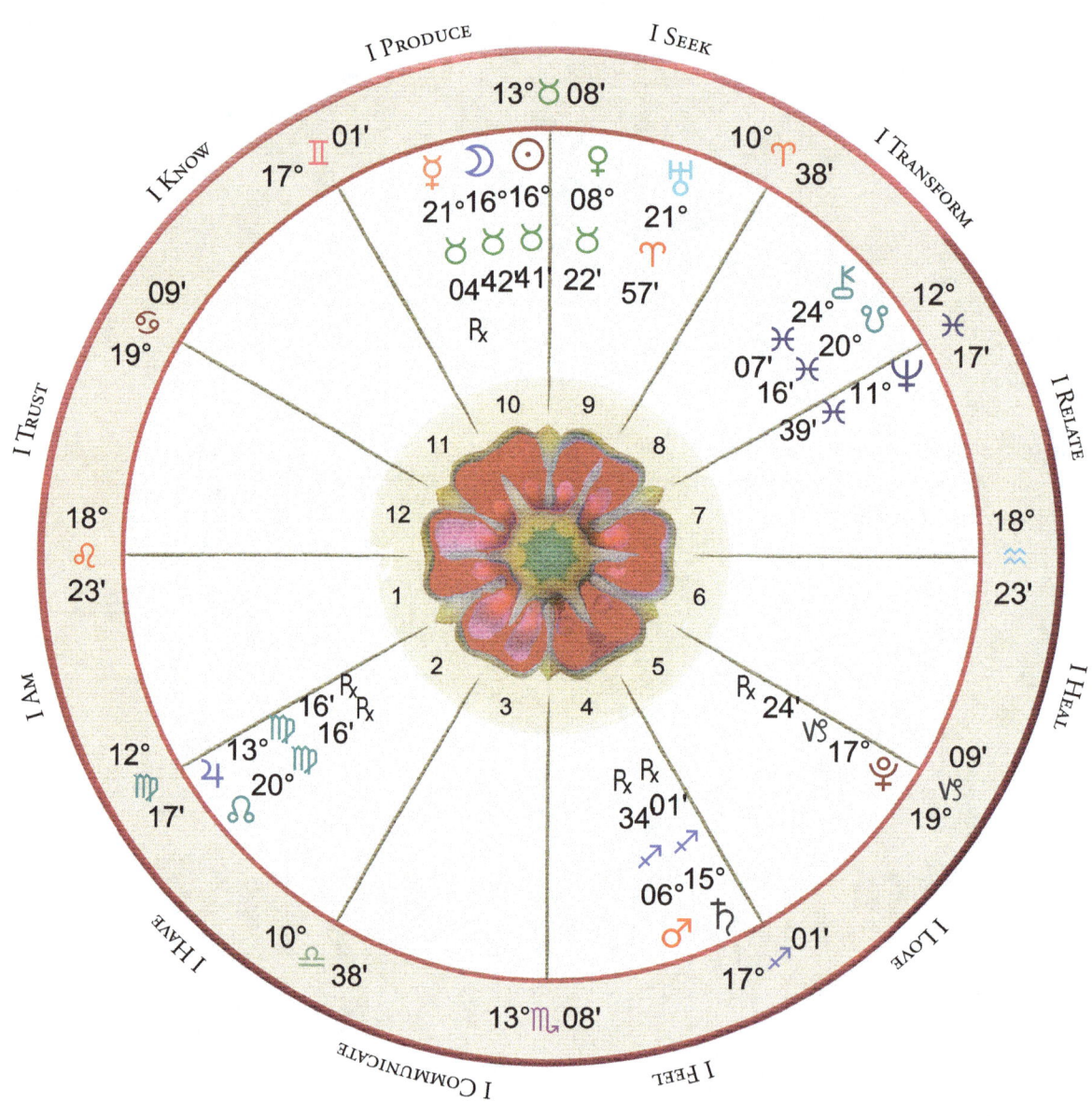

♈ Aries	♋ Cancer	♐ Sagittarius	☽ Moon	♄ Saturn	☊ North Node	V/C Void-of-Course
♉ Taurus	♌ Leo	♑ Capricorn	☿ Mercury	♅ Uranus	☋ South Node	▲ Super-Sensitivity
♊ Gemini	♍ Virgo	♒ Aquarius	♀ Venus	♆ Neptune	➡ Enters	▼ Low-Vitality
	♎ Libra	♓ Pisces	♂ Mars	♇ Pluto	℞ Retrograde	
	♏ Scorpio	☉ Sun	♃ Jupiter	⚷ Chiron	S/D Stationary Direct	

Cosmic Check-In

Take a moment to write a brief phrase for each "I" statement.
This activates all areas of your life for this creative cycle.

♉ I Have

♊ I Communicate

♋ I Feel

♌ I Love

♍ I Heal

♎ I Relate

♏ I Transform

♐ I Seek

♑ I Produce

♒ I Know

♓ I Trust

♈ I Am

May 21st
2:16 PM

Full Moon in Sagittarius

Degree Choice Points
1° Sagittarius 14'

Light   Ride the Waves

Shadow   Nervous Exhaustion

Wisdom   Receive messages from your dreams, meditations, and nature.

Statement   I Seek
     Body   Thighs
     Mind   Philosophical
     Spirit   Inspiration

Element
Fire – Ability to stand up for yourself, initiate projects, gives rise to the expression of the ego, enthusiasm and warmth, evolution.

Third House Moon
20° Scorpio 15'

Third House Umbrella Theme
I Communicate/I Transform – How you get the word out and the message behind the words.

Light   Conscientious Objection

Shadow   Anarchy

Wisdom   Be true to yourself with genuine self-expression.

The Sun is Opposite the Moon

Full moons are always in opposition to the Sun. This creates a feeling of tension between where you want to shine and how your feelings are flowing on a sensory level about the Sun's directive. The two forces seem like they are working against each other, yet they are on the same team displaying different techniques to obtain the same mission. The Sagittarius/Gemini polarity creates tension between the quest for higher knowledge and the need for academic accolades.

Sagittarius Goddess

Pythia was the title bestowed upon the priestess who channeled the Oracle of Delphi at the Temple of Apollo. The rambling prophecies she spoke were induced by breathing the vapors rising out of the chasm in the rocks, at a site formerly dedicated to the great Earth Goddess, Gaia.

Allow yourself quiet meditation time with your favorite divination tool (Tarot cards, pendulum, automatic writing) and give yourself over to messages you receive. Remember that Pythia calls forth her art through the magic of breathwork, which operates without hallucinogenic vapors! Seek the messages she delivers from the wisdom and stored history of the Earth. Find a rock to sit on and breathe!

Build Your Altar

Colors   Deep purple, turquoise, royal blue

Numerology   8 – Everyone on the team counts

Tarot Card   Temperance – Balancing the present with the past, updating yourself

Gemstone   Turquoise

Plant remedy   Madia – Seeing and hitting the target

Fragrance   Magnolia – Expanded beauty

Clearing the Slate

Remember a time when you experienced the following trigger points.
Write down what happened and perform Ho'oponopono, the Hawaiian forgiveness ritual.

Unfiltered Language

- I'm Sorry
- Please Forgive Me
- Thank You
- I Love You

Bluntness

- I'm Sorry
- Please Forgive Me
- Thank You
- I Love You

Exaggerating

- I'm Sorry
- Please Forgive Me
- Thank You
- I Love You

Excess

- I'm Sorry
- Please Forgive Me
- Thank You
- I Love You

Gambling or Risk-taking

- I'm Sorry
- Please Forgive Me
- Thank You
- I Love You

May 21st
2:16 PM

Full Moon in Sagittarius

Sagittarius Challenges and Victories

Say all of the statements in this section out loud. Then, underline the phrase that means the most to you. Use the phrase as your special affirmation for recalibrating throughout this phase of the moon.

Today, I blend my old self with my new self, my physical reality with my spiritual awareness, my positive thoughts with my negative thoughts, my past with my present, my feminine with my masculine, my rewards with my losses, my ups with my downs, and my higher self with my lower self. It is a day for me to refine and fine tune my life by looking at my extremes. I recognize what inspires me and what keeps me stuck. I find my center today by acknowledging my extremes. I am aware that balance comes to those who are able to locate the space in the center of these opposite energy fields. When I am in my center, my polarities are in motion. Healing cannot occur unless my polarities are moving and I know that healing is motion.

I am ready for a healing today and know that by visiting my opposites and determining their vast opposition to each other, I can find the paradoxes that I have chosen for myself and begin to heal. I am willing to experiment with this blending of opposites and become the alchemist of my own life. When I blend all aspects of myself, rather than separating them, I can truly become whole. Today is a day to integrate, rather than separate, in order to release the spark of light that stays prisoner when my polarities are in operation. When I find balance, motion occurs and the Law of Harmony takes over, putting paradoxical energies to rest, thus breaking the crystallization of polarity. The Law of Harmony is beauty in motion, promoting the flow of color, light, sound, and movement into form. Balance is a condition that keeps my spark in motion. I become the vertical line in the center of polarity today and carry the secret of balance. Balance cannot be my goal, motion is my goal today. When I am in motion, I can take action to evolve and to express all of myself freely.

Sagittarius Homework

Now is the time to use your physical body to release the feeling of being caged in by people or circumstances. Choose an activity that burns away confinement and allows you to feel the power of your passion.

The Sagittarius moon awakens us to know the spark of light that lives in our heart, thus elevating love in ourselves and in our world. This is when we come to realize what is in our highest and best good and we can begin to recalibrate all that is not lovable in our lives.

Recalibrating List

Say this statement out loud three times before writing your recalibrating list!

I am a free spiritual being and it is my desire to be free to think and to express myself fully.

I am now free and ready to make choices beyond survival!

Sagittarius Recalibrating Ideas

Now is the time to activate a game change in my life, and give up belief systems that no longer apply, attitudes that are not uplifting to me, addiction to excess and risk, the need to exaggerate based on low self-esteem, dishonesty, being too blunt, staying in the future and avoiding the NOW, overriding fear by being too optimistic, and preaching.

May 21st
2:16 PM

Full Moon in Sagittarius

How to Use the Moon Book With Your Chart

Fill in the blanks on the Cosmic Check-In page. Then look up the degree of the Moon on the chart below. Take note of the "I" statement on the outside of the wheel where the Moon is located. Now, locate the same degree on your own chart and make a note of the house and corresponding "I" statement. Go back to the Cosmic Check-In page and circle the two statements from the charts and read what you wrote. This will give you an idea about what to expect from this moon phase on a personal level.

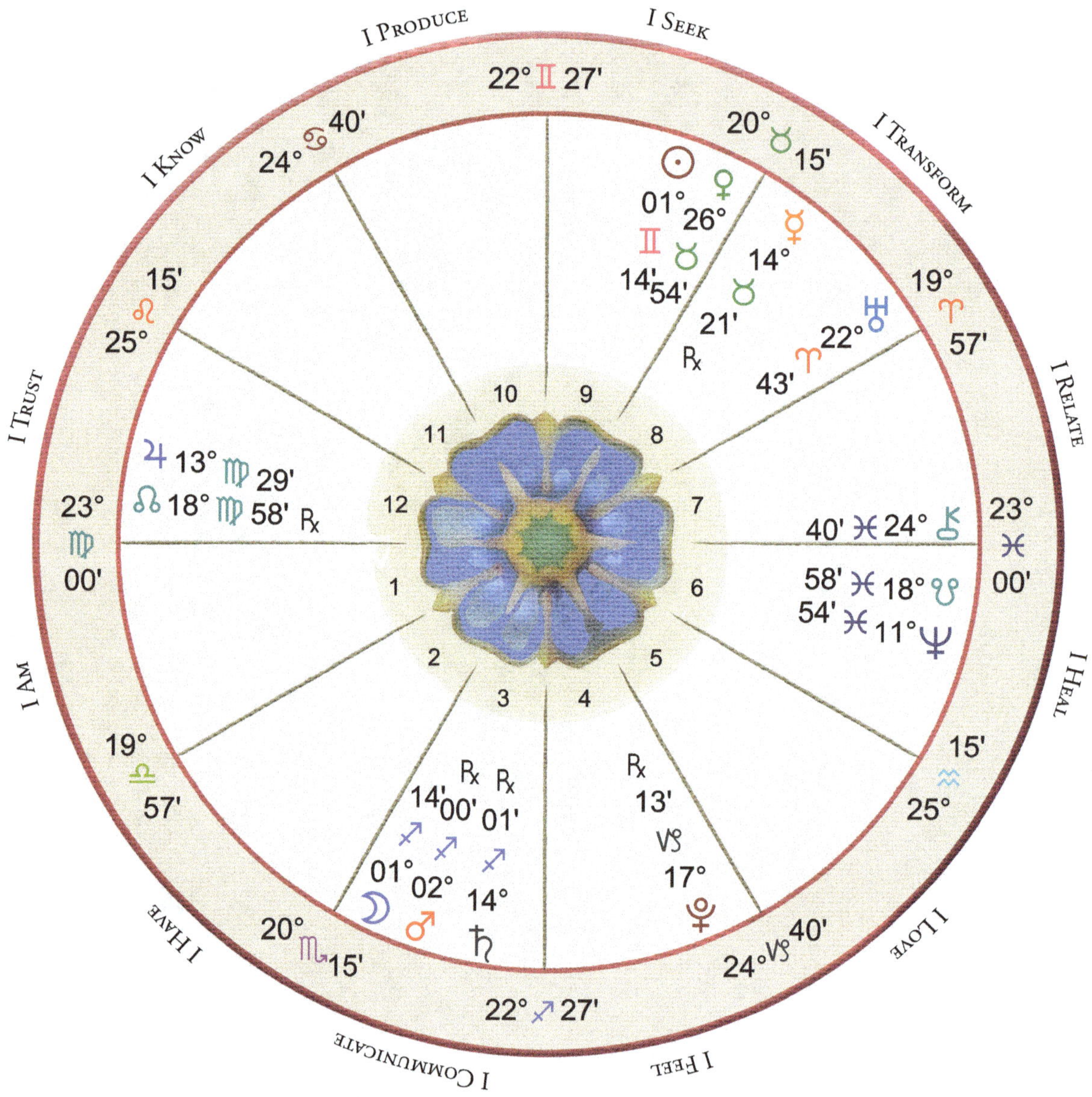

♈ Aries	♋ Cancer	♐ Sagittarius	☽ Moon	♄ Saturn	☊ North Node	V/C Void-of-Course
♉ Taurus	♌ Leo	♑ Capricorn	☿ Mercury	♅ Uranus	☋ South Node	▲ Super-Sensitivity
♊ Gemini	♍ Virgo	♒ Aquarius	♀ Venus	♆ Neptune	➡ Enters	▼ Low-Vitality
	♎ Libra	♓ Pisces	♂ Mars	♇ Pluto	℞ Retrograde	
	♏ Scorpio	☉ Sun	♃ Jupiter	⚷ Chiron	S/D Stationary Direct	

Cosmic Check-In

Take a moment to write a brief phrase for each "I" statement.
This activates all areas of your life for this creative cycle.

♐ I Seek

♑ I Produce

♒ I Know

♓ I Trust

♈ I Am

♉ I Have

♊ I Communicate

♋ I Feel

♌ I Love

♍ I Heal

♎ I Relate

♏ I Transform

June Planetary Highlights

Mars is Retrograde in Sagittarius Until June 29

Make sure that you know that the spirit of adventure is being revised, not forgotten. Hold on and breathe knowing full-well that it's time to rest and the 29th will be here soon enough.

Saturn is Retrograde in Sagittarius Until August 13

The suggestion box is full and now's the time to look and see what is being suggested. The Grand Teacher is waiting to see what you will do to adjust to a new way that is being presented. Remember Saturn is your friend and your teacher. Your reaction to the suggestions is more important than the actualization of the idea. Give flexibility a chance and all will be well.

Pluto is Retrograde in Capricorn Until September 26

Going deeper is part of this pattern, especially this month. Building strength from within is the key to the transformation being established. Forming, holding, and transforming are the appropriate actions here. Be willing to make choices based on love, not on survival.

Neptune goes Retrograde in Pisces on June 13

Pay attention to what is being promoted and promised to the masses, it will demonstrate to you how you might be being manipulated toward a "greater good" that is not so good. Keep your glasses on and see with awareness, rather than promise.

Mars goes Direct in Scorpio on June 29

Expect a burst of freedom on all levels, especially sexual. Before taking off like a rocket ship, ask yourself, "What did I learn from my perceived lock down?" Then, move forward!

June 12 – Mercury Enters Gemini

Expect conversation to be very active and interesting. Something new is being spoken about and will excite new potential if you listen!

June 17 – Venus Enters Cancer

A new level of fun and creativity will come into your home. Expect to spend some money on parties or interior design.

June 20 – The Sun Enters Cancer – Summer Solstice

Your garden of life is becoming full. Now is the time to weed out what no longer needs to be there and fertilize what needs to be enhanced.

June 29 – Mercury Enters Cancer

Remember to speak with a compassionate heart so that the homefront can move into a structure of being more based in love.

Neptune and the South Node Conjunct in Pisces the Entire Month

There is a sense here that something has been forgotten or left behind, especially in the area of healing or belief systems. See what the waters stir up and then it's up to you to see if it requires updating or releasing.

Jupiter and the North Node Continue Dancing in Virgo All Month

The future is being shown to us on a multi-dimensional level. Jupiter is giving us the big picture, wanting us to be inspired on a new level, and Virgo is forcing us to distill the process down to make it happen. This is a formula for successful living, however, it could be frustrating for those who can't establish validity in both areas of influence.

Low-Vitality – June 4-5

The atmosphere is filled with extra mental activity which can create a bit of chaos. It is best to be in your heart-center to avoid the swarm of unassigned thinking.

Super-Sensitivity – June 19-20

Stay centered, nurtured, and rested and all will be well.

Sunday	Monday	Tuesday	Wednesday	Thursday	Friday	Saturday
			1 ♂♄♇℞ ☽ V/C 8:42am ☽→♉ 7:46pm 2. Make no adjustments out of fear.	**2** ♂♄♇℞ 3. You can create anything you wish.	**3** ♂♄♇℞ ☽ V/C 4:02pm ☽→♊ 8:01pm 4. Create a structure that works for you.	**4** ♂♄♇℞ ▼ ● 14°♊53' 8:01pm 5. The only constant is change.
5 ♂♄♇℞ ▼ ☽ V/C 9:47am ☽→♋ 8:41pm 6. Make your home a place of joy.	**6** ♂♄♇℞ 7. Mental activity will raise your spirit.	**7** ♂♄♇℞ ☽ V/C 5:17pm ☽→♌ 11:47pm 8. See yourself manifesting your dreams.	**8** ♂♄♇℞ 9. Your heart holds deep compassion.	**9** ♂♄♇℞ 10. Find joy in creating each day anew.	**10** ♂♄♇℞ ☽ V/C 12:13am ☽→♍ 6:45am 2. Balance is not stagnant-it's active.	**11** ♂♄♇℞ 3. A playful attitude makes life easier.
12 ♂♄♇℞ ☿→♊ 4:24pm ☽ V/C 7:46am ☽→♎ 5:33pm 4. For more success be a team player.	**13** ♂♄♆♇℞ ♆℞-12°♓02' 1: 44pm 5. Discover a new approach and use it.	**14** ♂♄♆♇℞ Flag Day ☽ V/C 11:59pm 6. Take care of yourself first.	**15** ♂♄♆♇℞ ☽→♏ 6:18am 7. The light you show is always there.	**16** ♂♄♆♇℞ 8. See in everyone the Eternal Soul.	**17** ♂♄♆♇℞ ♀→♋ 12:40pm ☽ V/C 6:52am ☽→♐ 6:33pm 9. Balancing differences create peace.	**18** ♂♄♆♇℞ 10. Innovate and raise your vibration.
19 ♂♄♆♇℞ ▲ Father's Day 2. Once a decision is made, take action.	**20** ♂♄♆♇℞ ▲ Summer Solstice ☉→♋ 3:35pm ☽ V/C 4:02am ☽→♑ 4:54am ○ 29°♐33' 4:03am 3. Belief is adopting a known structure.	**21** ♂♄♆♇℞ 4. Strive for unity in all that you do.	**22** ♂♄♆♇℞ ☽ V/C 1:57am ☽→♒ 1:08pm 5. Follow the direction that feels best.	**23** ♂♄♆♇℞ 6. Live Love Everyday.	**24** ♂♄♆♇℞ ☽ V/C 8:47am ☽→♓ 7:30pm 7. Don't think, use thought.	**25** ♂♄♆♇℞ 8. Share your abundance.
26 ♂♄♆♇℞ ☽ V/C 12:54pm 9. An open heart is impassionate.	**27** ♂♄♆♇℞ ☽→♈ 12:07am 10. Your potential was set before birth.	**28** ♂♄♆♇℞ 2. Gather opinions and then decide.	**29** ♂♄♆♇℞ ♂SD 23°♏03' 4:39 pm ☽ V/C 12:45am ☽→♉ 3:03am ☿→♋ 4:25pm 3. Create opportunities for others.	**30** ♄♆♇℞ ☽ V/C 5:18pm 4. Teamwork sees everyone as equal.		

♈ Aries
♉ Taurus
♊ Gemini
♋ Cancer
♌ Leo
♍ Virgo

♎ Libra
♏ Scorpio
♐ Sagittarius
♑ Capricorn
♒ Aquarius
♓ Pisces

☉ Sun
☽ Moon
☿ Mercury
♀ Venus
♂ Mars
♃ Jupiter

♄ Saturn
♅ Uranus
♆ Neptune
♇ Pluto
⚷ Chiron

☊ North Node
☋ South Node
➜ Enters
℞ Retrograde
SD Stationary Direct
V/C Void-of-Course

▲ Super Sensitivity
▼ Low Vitality
2. Balance
3. Fun
4. Structure
5. Action

6. Love
7. Learning
8. Money
9. Spirituality
10. Visionary
11. Completion

June 4th
8:01 PM

New Moon in Gemini

Degree Choice Points
14° Gemini 53'

Light — Like-mindedness

Shadow — Seduction

Wisdom — Draw on feminine energy now to balance your creative power.

Statement — I Communicate
- **Body** — Lungs and Hands
- **Mind** — Intellect
- **Spirit** — Intelligence

Element
Air – Freedom from attachment, curiosity, flexibility, active-dreaming bridge between the mundane and spiritual worlds.

Sixth House Moon
25° Taurus 47'

Sixth House Umbrella Theme
I Heal/I Have – The way you manage your body and appearance.

Light — Storyteller/Bard/Poet

Shadow — Bottom Feeder

Wisdom — Organize your ideas to understand how they can be applied in the world.

Karmic Awakening

Virgo/Pisces – Conflicting issues relate to boundaries

The conflict here is getting lost in the vastness due to lack of boundaries or restriction due to over-analyzing details.

Karmic stress will happen when chatter out-weighs inspiration, the marketplace becomes more important than your spiritual rituals, or when academia becomes more important than higher knowledge.

When the Sun is in Gemini

This is a time when the ability to communicate is at the top of the priority list. Allow your thoughts to lead you to a formula for success so you can put your thoughts into action. Then, find the appropriate soapbox to stand on so your message can be heard. Right now is the time to make your message clear, enlightening, witty, and thought-provoking. Your bright mind is at its high throne and waiting for an audience. Try blogging, do a show on YouTube, join Toastmasters, write that screenplay, film yourself doing a travel show, start a discussion group, or write a newsletter for your neighborhood. Most of all, put your bright mind to work!

Gemini Goddess

Some of Zeus's favorite consorts were the nymphs who lived on Mount Kithairon. One in particular, Echo, incurred Zeus' wife Hera's wrath. As punishment for trying to protect Zeus, Hera cursed Echo with only being able to speak the last few words spoken to her. In love with Narcissus, Echo was unable to speak her own truth, and watched as Narcissus fell in love with himself, abetted by the words he spoke that Echo was forced to repeat back to him. After he died, Echo physically wasted away, leaving only the sound of her voice.

During this Gemini full moon, attend to your communications! Be curious about what ripples your speech and writing may generate. What reverberates and repeats? Is it your truth?

Build Your Altar

Colors Bright yellow, orange, multi-colors

Numerology 5 – The only constant is change

Tarot Card Lovers – Connecting to wholeness

Gemstones Yellow diamond, citrine

Plant Remedy Morning Glory – Thinking with your heart not your head

Fragrance Iris – The ability to focus the mind

Manifesting List

This or something better than this comes to me in an easy and pleasurable way, for the good of all concerned. Thank you, Universe!

Gemini Manifesting Ideas

Now is the time to focus on manifesting communications, a promotion, technology, ideas, non-judgmental communication, thinking outside of duality, a quiet mind, charisma and charm, and flirting.

June 4th
8:01 PM

New Moon in Gemini

Gemini Challenges and Victories

Say all of the statements in this section out loud. Then, underline the phrase that means the most to you. Use the phrase as your special affirmation for manifesting throughout this phase of the moon.

I am dark. I am light. I am day. I am night. The extremes in life exist within me, completing themselves in reality. The "I" that is "we" lives within me. I am one in the same. I am both.

I know that flow comes from accepting my opposite natures. Today, I accept my opposites and get into the flow. I am aware today of how my judgments separate me from people, events, experiences, and, most of all, from myself. Today, I am going to see where I have separated all of the parts of myself and begin to integrate into wholeness through acceptance and understanding. I begin by breathing. I breathe in wholeness and breathe out separation. I understand that breath is life and that life includes all facets of my experience to gain awareness. I know that I am Heaven. I know that I am Earth. I know that I am masculine. I know that I am feminine. Today, I become unified. Today, I integrate into wholeness. I breathe into all of these aspects of myself, knowing that in my totality I am connected to Oneness. The "I" that is "we" lives within me. I am one in the same. I am both.

Gemini Homework

Geminis manifest best through broadcasting and journalism, as a speech coach, comedian, political satirist, gossip columnist, negotiator, media specialist, manicurist, salesperson, teacher, or travel consultant.

Expect to awaken your will on seven levels…

- The will to direct – through the power of your original intention.
- The will to love – stimulating goodwill among humankind through cooperation.
- The will to act – by laying foundations for a happier world.
- The will to cooperate – the desire and demand for right relationships.
- The will to know – to think correctly and creatively so that every man/woman can find their outstanding characteristics.
- The will to persist – to be one with your light and represent the ideal standard for living.
- The will to organize – to carry forward direct inspiration through groups of goodwill.

Without Acknowledgment Progress Cannot Occur

Acknowledgement creates space for victory and gratitude, which automatically brings you to a level of completion so a new cycle of opportunity can occur in your life. When you celebrate your wins and acknowledge your victories with gratitude, you update your cells so that your ability to move forward is not hindered by a cellular holographic pattern that is stuck in the past. Cellular lag creates resistance and makes moving forward most difficult. The key is to stay continuously updated by acknowledging yourself for what you did do at the end of each day, rather than heading off to sleep thinking about what you did not do. By acknowledging what you did not do, you play into your karmic storage bank and keep your progress at bay. When you acknowledge yourself and your manifestations you are complete, and more cycles of opportunity become available to you in each new day. Be prepared for miracles!

Victory List

When a creation result is acknowledged it seals the deal. This makes room for more magnificence to expand into your life and increases your abundance factor adding to your ability to receive. As each aspect of your manifesting list arrives in your life, spend time allowing, acknowledging, and accepting it with the true gusto of gratitude! Keep your victory list active here.

Gratitude List

This fulfills the relationship between the giver and the receiver, which completes the cycle with the Universe so that a new beginning can be established.

June 4th
8:01 PM

New Moon in Gemini

How to Use the Moon Book With Your Chart

Fill in the blanks on the Cosmic Check-In page. Then look up the degree of the Moon on the chart below. Take note of the "I" statement on the outside of the wheel where the Moon is located. Now, locate the same degree on your own chart and make a note of the house and corresponding "I" statement. Go back to the Cosmic Check-In page and circle the two statements from the charts and read what you wrote. This will give you an idea about what to expect from this moon phase on a personal level.

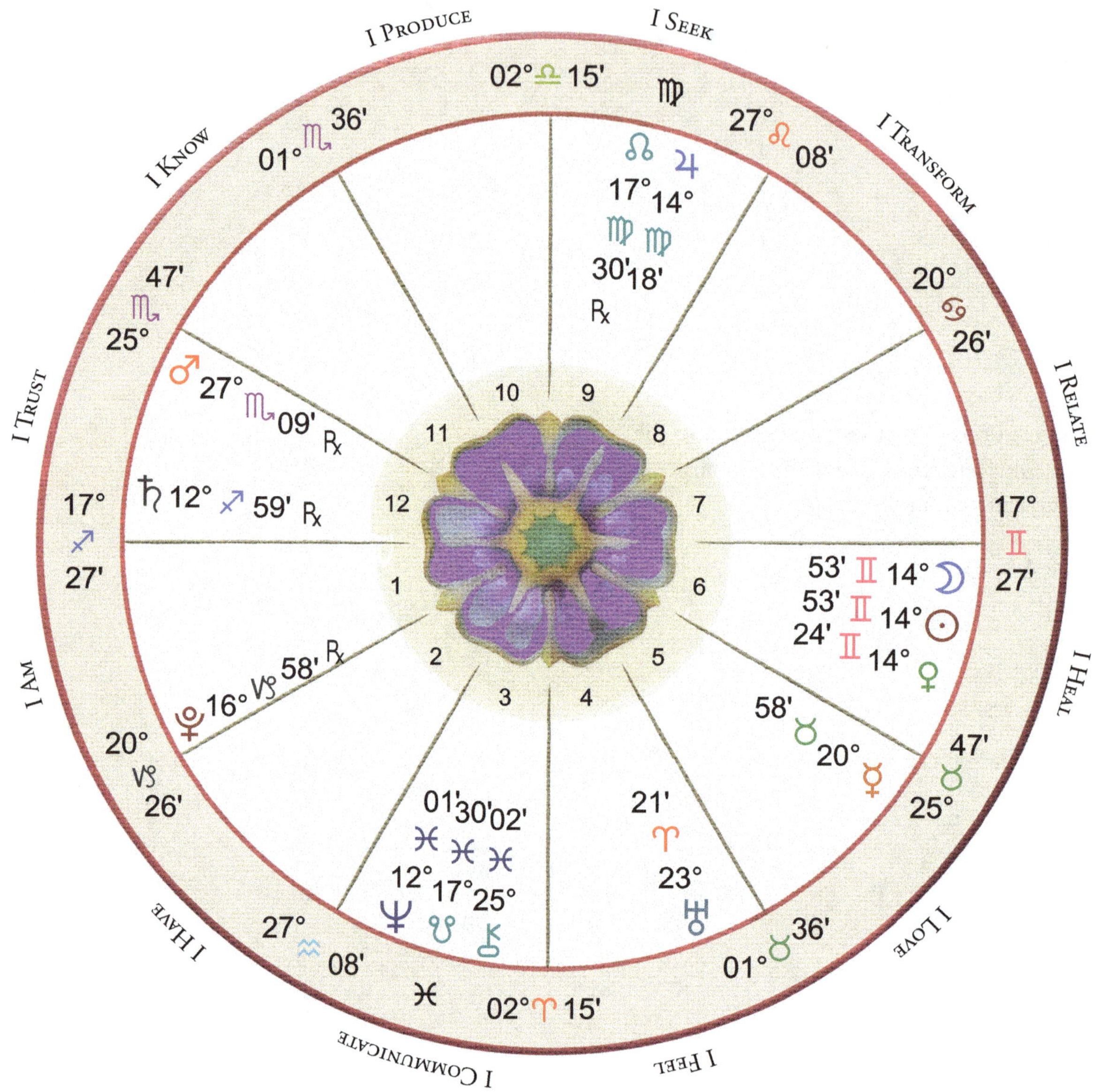

♈ Aries	♋ Cancer	♐ Sagittarius	☽ Moon	♄ Saturn	☊ North Node	V/C Void-of-Course
♉ Taurus	♌ Leo	♑ Capricorn	☿ Mercury	♅ Uranus	☋ South Node	▲ Super-Sensitivity
♊ Gemini	♍ Virgo	♒ Aquarius	♀ Venus	♆ Neptune	➡ Enters	• Low-Vitality
	♎ Libra	♓ Pisces	♂ Mars	♇ Pluto	℞ Retrograde	
	♏ Scorpio	☉ Sun	♃ Jupiter	⚷ Chiron	S/D Stationary Direct	

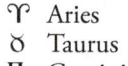

Cosmic Check-In

Take a moment to write a brief phrase for each "I" statement.
This activates all areas of your life for this creative cycle.

♊ I Communicate

♋ I Feel

♌ I Love

♍ I Heal

♎ I Relate

♏ I Transform

♐ I Seek

♑ I Produce

♒ I Know

♓ I Trust

♈ I Am

♉ I Have

June 20th
4:03 AM

Full Moon in Sagittarius

Degree Choice Points
29° Sagittarius 33'

Light   Mystical Adventurer

Shadow   Lust for Power

Wisdom   Reveal the available alternatives to others.

Statement   I Seek
     Body   Thighs
     Mind   Philosophical
     Spirit   Inspiration

Element
Fire – Ability to stand up for yourself, initiate projects, gives rise to the expression of the ego, enthusiasm and warmth, evolution.

Eighth House Moon
28° Sagittarius 35'

Eighth House Umbrella Theme
I Transform/I Seek – How you share money and other resources, what you keep hidden regarding sex, death, real estate, and regeneration.

Light   Self-worth

Shadow   Bored with Details

Wisdom   Restore your self-worth with a rose quartz healing.

Karmic Awakening

Taurus/Scorpio – my money or our money

Karmic stress will appear when the need for money comes up and the source is not defined. On the light side, from the point of view of interdependence, debts will be paid with ease and grace. If not, cheating could be a part of it and a healing would be required to reinstate trust.

The Sun is Opposite the Moon

Full moons are always in opposition to the Sun. This creates a feeling of tension between where you want to shine and how your feelings are flowing on a sensory level about the Sun's directive. The two forces seem like they are working against each other, yet they are on the same team displaying different techniques to obtain the same mission. The Sagittarius/Gemini polarity creates tension between the quest for higher knowledge and the need for academic accolades.

Sagittarius Goddess

Atalanta, whose name means "unswaying," is a feminist non-conformist who refuses to succumb to societal expectations. A virgin huntress, Atalanta adventured and quested with the Argonauts in search of the Golden Fleece. When her father finally said she must marry, she devised a foot race, challenging her suitors to beat her or be killed. Many men died in the attempt, but Hippomenes asked the Goddess Aphrodite for help. She gave him three golden apples that he rolled in front of Atalanta, to distract her. He won the race and Atalanta's hand, but only through Aphrodite's intervention.

This moon conjures Atalanta's spirit to adventure beyond the confines of the rat race to create your unique, uncharted pathway to the future! Do not sway from your course!

Build Your Altar

Colors Deep purple, turquoise, royal blue

Numerology 3 – Belief is adopting a known structure

Tarot Card Temperance – Balancing the present with the past, updating yourself

Gemstone Turquoise

Plant remedy Madia – Seeing and hitting the target

Fragrance Magnolia – Expanded beauty

Clearing the Slate

Remember a time when you experienced the following trigger points.
Write down what happened and perform Ho'oponopono, the Hawaiian forgiveness ritual.

Unfiltered Language

- I'm Sorry
- Please Forgive Me
- Thank You
- I Love You

Bluntness

- I'm Sorry
- Please Forgive Me
- Thank You
- I Love You

Exaggerating

- I'm Sorry
- Please Forgive Me
- Thank You
- I Love You

Excess

- I'm Sorry
- Please Forgive Me
- Thank You
- I Love You

Gambling or Risk-taking

- I'm Sorry
- Please Forgive Me
- Thank You
- I Love You

June 20th
4:03 AM

Full Moon in Sagittarius

Sagittarius Challenges and Victories

Say all of the statements in this section out loud. Then, underline the phrase that means the most to you. Use the phrase as your special affirmation for recalibrating throughout this phase of the moon.

Today, I blend my old self with my new self, my physical reality with my spiritual awareness, my positive thoughts with my negative thoughts, my past with my present, my feminine with my masculine, my rewards with my losses, my ups with my downs, and my higher self with my lower self. It is a day for me to refine and fine tune my life by looking at my extremes. I recognize what inspires me and what keeps me stuck. I find my center today by acknowledging my extremes. I am aware that balance comes to those who are able to locate the space in the center of these opposite energy fields. When I am in my center, my polarities are in motion. Healing cannot occur unless my polarities are moving and I know that healing is motion.

I am ready for a healing today and know that by visiting my opposites and determining their vast opposition to each other, I can find the paradoxes that I have chosen for myself and begin to heal. I am willing to experiment with this blending of opposites and become the alchemist of my own life. When I blend all aspects of myself, rather than separating them, I can truly become whole. Today is a day to integrate, rather than separate, in order to release the spark of light that stays prisoner when my polarities are in operation. When I find balance, motion occurs and the Law of Harmony takes over, putting paradoxical energies to rest, thus breaking the crystallization of polarity. The Law of Harmony is beauty in motion, promoting the flow of color, light, sound, and movement into form. Balance is a condition that keeps my spark in motion. I become the vertical line in the center of polarity today and carry the secret of balance. Balance cannot be my goal, motion is my goal today. When I am in motion, I can take action to evolve and to express all of myself freely.

Sagittarius Homework

Now is the time to use your physical body to release the feeling of being caged in by people or circumstances. Choose an activity that burns away confinement and allows you to feel the power of your passion.

The Sagittarius moon awakens us to know the spark of light that lives in our heart, thus elevating love in ourselves and in our world. This is when we come to realize what is in our highest and best good and we can begin to recalibrate all that is not lovable in our lives.

Recalibrating List

Say this statement out loud three times before writing your recalibrating list!

I am a free spiritual being and it is my desire to be free to think and to express myself fully.

I am now free and ready to make choices beyond survival!

Sagittarius Recalibrating Ideas

Now is the time to activate a game change in my life, and give up belief systems that no longer apply, attitudes that are not uplifting to me, addiction to excess and risk, the need to exaggerate based on low self-esteem, dishonesty, being too blunt, staying in the future and avoiding the NOW, overriding fear by being too optimistic, and preaching.

Full Moon in Sagittarius

June 20th
4:03 AM

How to Use the Moon Book With Your Chart

Fill in the blanks on the Cosmic Check-In page. Then look up the degree of the Moon on the chart below. Take note of the "I" statement on the outside of the wheel where the Moon is located. Now, locate the same degree on your own chart and make a note of the house and corresponding "I" statement. Go back to the Cosmic Check-In page and circle the two statements from the charts and read what you wrote. This will give you an idea about what to expect from this moon phase on a personal level.

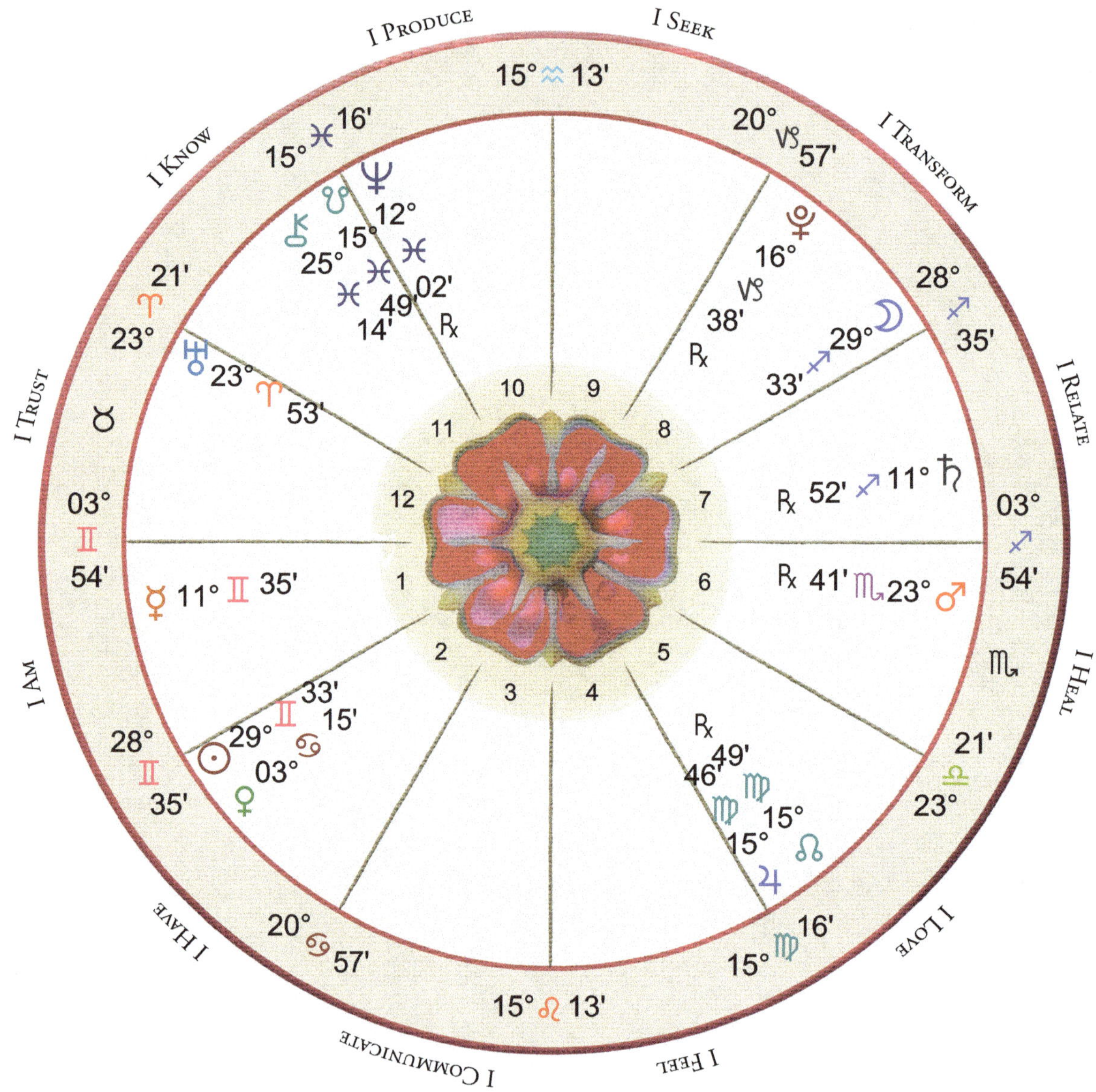

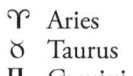

♈ Aries	♋ Cancer	♐ Sagittarius	☽ Moon	♄ Saturn	☊ North Node	V/C Void-of-Course
♉ Taurus	♌ Leo	♑ Capricorn	☿ Mercury	♅ Uranus	☋ South Node	▲ Super-Sensitivity
♊ Gemini	♍ Virgo	♒ Aquarius	♀ Venus	♆ Neptune	➡ Enters	• Low-Vitality
♎ Libra	♓ Pisces	♂ Mars	♇ Pluto	℞ Retrograde		
♏ Scorpio	☉ Sun	♃ Jupiter	⚷ Chiron	S/D Stationary Direct		

116

Cosmic Check-In

Take a moment to write a brief phrase for each "I" statement.
This activates all areas of your life for this creative cycle.

♐ I Seek

♑ I Produce

♒ I Know

♓ I Trust

♈ I Am

♉ I Have

♊ I Communicate

♋ I Feel

♌ I Love

♍ I Heal

♎ I Relate

♏ I Transform

July Planetary Highlights

Saturn is Retrograde in Sagittarius Until August 13

If you feel any burden on your shoulders, now is the time to face it and deal with it. Call upon your available support systems to get this done.

Neptune is Retrograde in Pisces Until November 19

Join a meditation group. Now is a time to connect with the collective spiritual unity.

Pluto is Retrograde in Capricorn Until September 26

We must remember, especially right now as the Sun reaches its zenith, that we've been in a holding and forming pattern. As Leo emerges, so do we. As our new light transforms into our new potential, we know how we are to shine for the year. We must see the power of holding patterns right now.

Uranus goes Retrograde in Aries July 29 and Continues into 2017

The recalibration of our future identity is still in operation. Uranus has been sitting on Aries for several years now asking for a clear version of your future self. This will still be in operation next year.

July 11 – Venus Enters Leo

YAY! It's party time!! Dance like no one's watching!

July 13 – Mercury Enters Leo

Speaking comes straight from the heart – Live Love Every Day!

July 22 – The Sun Enters Leo

It's time to shine! This year's private message about your 2016 potential is here. ACTIVATE IT NOW!

July 30 – Mercury Enters Virgo

Research is required now. Let the details speak to you, they have value!

Neptune Conjunct with the South Node All Month

The holding pattern for the past is still bleeding through. In order for it to heal, we must re-frame disappointment into victory.

Jupiter and the North Node are Weaving a Tapestry in Mid-heaven for This Month

The gifts of evolution and transformation will be made known to us through the benefits of Jupiter. They are all over the Universe waiting to be assigned to you. Accept and evolve – YES!

Low-Vitality – July 2-3, 29-31

Stay within your own boundaries on these days and all will be well.

Super-Sensitivity – July 15-17

Resting is required – let it happen.

120

Sunday	Monday	Tuesday	Wednesday	Thursday	Friday	Saturday
					1 ♄♆♇℞ ☽→♊ 4:44am 5. Treat yourself to something different.	**2** ♄♆♇℞ ▼ ☽ V/C 8:42pm 6. By being yourself compassion blooms.
3 ♄♆♇℞ ▼ ☽→♋ 6:19am 7. Embrace life without any blame.	**4** ♄♆♇℞ Independence Day ☽ V/C11:29pm ● 12°♋54′ 4:02am 8. Successful leaders listen to others.	**5** ♄♆♇℞ ☽→♌ 9:27am 9. Divine love is part of your energy.	**6** ♄♆♇℞ 10. New beginnings happen every day.	**7** ♄♆♇℞ ☽ V/C 5:06am ☽→♍ 3:40pm 2. Polarity completes the package.	**8** ♄♆♇℞ 3. Embrace your magnificence.	**9** ♄♆♇℞ ☽ V/C 8:27pm 4. Assemble all the parts before starting.
10 ♄♆♇℞ ☽→♎ 1:32am 5. Uniqueness flourishes in acceptance.	**11** ♄♆♇℞ ♀→♌ 10:35pm 6. Receptivity gives relationships life.	**12** ♄♆♇℞ ☽ V/C 8:00am ☽→♏ 1:52pm 7. Your thoughts are magnets.	**13** ♄♆♇℞ ☿→♌ 5:48pm 8. Good leadership empowers all.	**14** ♄♆♇℞ ☽ V/C 3:21pm 9. The Universe willingly responds.	**15** ♄♆♇℞ ▲ ☽→♐ 2:14am 10. Embrace all that life has to give.	**16** ♄♆♇℞ ▲ 2. Opinions are just suggestions.
17 ♄♆♇℞ ▲ ☽ V/C 1:56am ☽→♑ 12:32pm 3. Stimulation is the key to joy.	**18** ♄♆♇℞ 4. When all the pieces fit, life is a joy.	**19** ♄♆♇℞ ☽ V/C 3:56pm ☽→♒ 8:10pm ○ 27°♑40′ 3:58pm 5. The best exercise is consistency.	**20** ♄♆♇℞ 6. In lovely settings, food tastes better.	**21** ♄♆♇℞ ☽ V/C 6:55pm 7. Stillness is an active state.	**22** ♄♆♇℞ ☉→♌ 2:31am ☽→♓ 1:35am 8. Win by celebrating others.	**23** ♄♆♇℞ 9. The power of love can protect you.
24 ♄♆♇℞ ☽ V/C 12:06am ☽→♈ 5:32am 10. Drop the past, enjoy the now.	**25** ♄♆♇℞ ☽ V/C 11:18pm 2. Diversity enhances individuality.	**26** ♄♆♇℞ ☽→♉ 8:37am 3. Let your creativity flow.	**27** ♄♆♇℞ 4. Clutter confuses consciousness.	**28** ♄♆♇℞ ☽ V/C 8:12am ☽→♊ 11:16am 5. A consensus can establish a direction.	**29** ♄♅♆♇℞ ▼ ♅℞-24°♈30′ 2:07pm 6. Allow each room to have personality.	**30** ♄♅♆♇℞ ▼ ♀→♍ 11:19am ☽ V/C 4:46am ☽→♋ 2:08pm 7. Writing activates awareness.
31 ♄♅♆♇℞ ▼ 8. Be courageous, be the leader.						

♈ Aries	♎ Libra	☉ Sun	♄ Saturn	☊ North Node	▲ Super Sensitivity	6. Love
♉ Taurus	♏ Scorpio	☽ Moon	♅ Uranus	☋ South Node	▼ Low Vitality	7. Learning
♊ Gemini	♐ Sagittarius	☿ Mercury	♆ Neptune	➡ Enters	2. Balance	8. Money
♋ Cancer	♑ Capricorn	♀ Venus	♇ Pluto	℞ Retrograde	3. Fun	9. Spirituality
♌ Leo	♒ Aquarius	♂ Mars	⚷ Chiron	SD Stationary Direct	4. Structure	10. Visionary
♍ Virgo	♓ Pisces	♃ Jupiter		V/C Void-of-Course	5. Action	11. Completion

July 4th
4:02 AM

New Moon in Cancer

Degree Choice Points
12° Cancer 54'

Light   Willpower

Shadow   Overbearing

Wisdom   Share your bounty in order to sustain your wholeness.

Statement   I Feel
   Body   Stomach
   Mind   Worry
   Spirit   Nurturing

Element
   Water – Feelings, rhythm, cycles, supporting alignment, grace, creativity, receptivity, Divine Feminine.

Second House Moon
10° Cancer 50'

Second House Umbrella Theme
   I Have/I Feel – The way you make money and the way you spend your money.

Light   Humorist

Shadow   Camouflage

Wisdom   Hold the light for another to help them find their way.

Karmic Awakening

Pisces/Virgo – Conflicting issues relate to boundaries

The conflict here is getting lost in the vastness due to lack of boundaries or restriction due to over-analyzing details.

Karmic stress occurs when there are cross purposes between family life and professional life. The possibility of an escape pattern exists here or scapegoating. If avoidance is happening, a whole load of ancient wisdom will be lost as well as a position of leadership. Bigger karma will happen here if one tends to pass the buck, rather than take responsibility.

When the Sun is in Cancer

It is now time to build our structure and foundation. Cancer holds the wisdom of the Great Cosmic Architect. Her statement is, "I build a lighted house and therein I dwell." The key is to use the materials of light, love, and wisdom to build your house and become the creator of form. Look within to see what lights your home and your body. Also check security systems, early environmental training, and mother/child relationships to see what materials you are using to build the structure for your life. Use this creating moon to build the structure you want.

Cancer Goddess

Hecate is a household goddess who assists people at times of transitions, such as childbirth and death. She is depicted as holding a torch to light the way when you reach major crossroads in life. Associated with the Underworld and the bridge into death and rebirth, Hecate is often shown with three heads and a loyal dog at her side. Her ability to see through the veil of illusion allowed her to assist Demeter in her search for Persephone, because Hecate could see into Hades. She rules over the earth, sea, and sky.

Are you, or someone in your household, feeling restless or aimless? Call upon Hecate's ability to clear the pathway through discernment, the wisdom that comes with age, and the knowledge of cycles.

Build Your Altar

Colors   Shades of gray, milky/creamy colors

Numerology   8 – Successful leaders listen to others

Tarot Card   Chariot – The ability to move forward, victory through action

Gemstones   Pearl, moonstone, ruby

Plant Remedy   Shooting Star – The ability to move straight ahead

Fragrance   Peppermint – The essence of the Great Mother

Manifesting List

This or something better than this comes to me in an easy and pleasurable way, for the good of all concerned. Thank you, Universe!

Cancer Manifesting Ideas

Now is the time to focus on manifesting being a good mother, new ways to be a mom, nurturing and self-love, the ability to see joy, a clutter-free home, your dream home, and inner and outer security.

July 4th
4:02 AM

New Moon in Cancer

Cancer Challenges and Victories

Say all of the statements in this section out loud. Then, underline the phrase that means the most to you. Use the phrase as your special affirmation for manifesting throughout this phase of the moon.

Today I take advantage of my ability to take action and position myself for success. I clearly know that the road to success is before me, and all I need to do is move forward. I am aware that when I take action and move forward, the Universe fills in the dots. Whether I move left, right, or straight ahead doesn't matter—what matters is movement. Today, I release the indecisiveness that keeps me stuck. Today, I let go of vacillation that exhausts my mind. Today, I take my foot off of the brakes and find the gas pedal. I allow movement to occur, even if I don't know where I am going. When I take action, I trust that guideposts will appear. I am aware that action leads me to my new direction. So, today I know and GO! I remember that Karma comes to the space of non-action, while success comes through action. Action brings me to my victory. Standing still leads to regret, resentment, and chaos. I am aware that action can be as simple as taking a walk on the beach, buying fresh flowers to add a new dimension to my home, or simply going to a new restaurant for lunch. I take action today to break up a crystallized pattern and, in so doing, my life begins to show me newfound awareness and light to guide me.

Cancer Homework

Cancers manifest best when catering, writing cookbooks, in marriage and family counseling, providing childcare, giving massage, or when engaged in genealogy, arts and crafts, architecture, and home-building.

During the Cancer new moon cycle, we are asked to create light into form and turn it into beauty on four levels. Physically, we must feel nurtured and protected. Emotionally, we must set safe boundaries for the expression of our feelings. Mentally, we must release self-pity and embrace rightful thinking. Spiritually, we must hold the space for the infusion of light to shine inside all bodies on Earth.

Without Acknowledgment Progress Cannot Occur

Acknowledgement creates space for victory and gratitude, which automatically brings you to a level of completion so a new cycle of opportunity can occur in your life. When you celebrate your wins and acknowledge your victories with gratitude, you update your cells so that your ability to move forward is not hindered by a cellular holographic pattern that is stuck in the past. Cellular lag creates resistance and makes moving forward most difficult. The key is to stay continuously updated by acknowledging yourself for what you did do at the end of each day, rather than heading off to sleep thinking about what you did not do. By acknowledging what you did not do, you play into your karmic storage bank and keep your progress at bay. When you acknowledge yourself and your manifestations you are complete, and more cycles of opportunity become available to you in each new day. Be prepared for miracles!

Victory List

When a creation result is acknowledged it seals the deal. This makes room for more magnificence to expand into your life and increases your abundance factor adding to your ability to receive. As each aspect of your manifesting list arrives in your life, spend time allowing, acknowledging, and accepting it with the true gusto of gratitude! Keep your victory list active here.

Gratitude List

This fulfills the relationship between the giver and the receiver, which completes the cycle with the Universe so that a new beginning can be established.

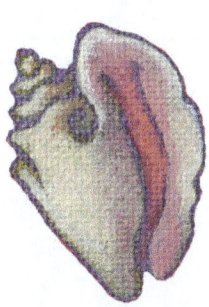

July 4th
4:02 AM

New Moon in Cancer

How to Use the Moon Book With Your Chart

Fill in the blanks on the Cosmic Check-In page. Then look up the degree of the Moon on the chart below. Take note of the "I" statement on the outside of the wheel where the Moon is located. Now, locate the same degree on your own chart and make a note of the house and corresponding "I" statement. Go back to the Cosmic Check-In page and circle the two statements from the charts and read what you wrote. This will give you an idea about what to expect from this moon phase on a personal level.

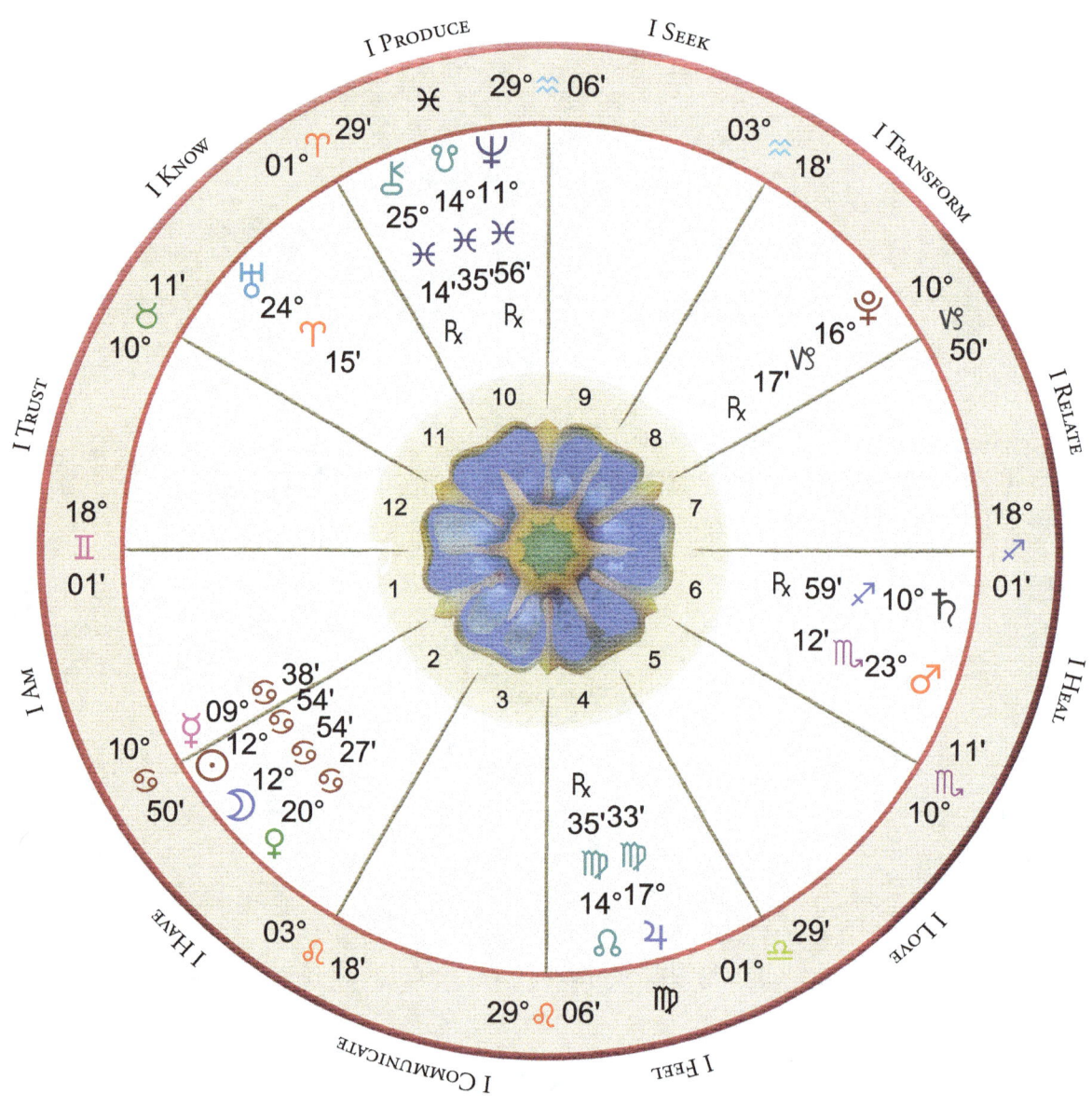

♈ Aries	♋ Cancer	♐ Sagittarius	☽ Moon	♄ Saturn	☊ North Node	V/C Void-of-Course
♉ Taurus	♌ Leo	♑ Capricorn	☿ Mercury	♅ Uranus	☋ South Node	▲ Super-Sensitivity
♊ Gemini	♍ Virgo	♒ Aquarius	♀ Venus	♆ Neptune	➡ Enters	• Low-Vitality
	♎ Libra	♓ Pisces	♂ Mars	♇ Pluto	℞ Retrograde	
	♏ Scorpio	☉ Sun	♃ Jupiter	⚷ Chiron	S/D Stationary Direct	

126

Cosmic Check-In

Take a moment to write a brief phrase for each "I" statement.
This activates all areas of your life for this creative cycle.

♋ I Feel

♌ I Love

♍ I Heal

♎ I Relate

♏ I Transform

♐ I Seek

♑ I Produce

♒ I Know

♓ I Trust

♈ I Am

♉ I Have

♊ I Communicate

July 19th
3:58 PM

Full Moon in Capricorn

The Sun is Opposite the Moon

Full moons are always in opposition to the Sun. This creates a feeling of tension between where you want to shine and how your feelings are flowing on a sensory level about the Sun's directive. The two forces seem like they are working against each other, yet they are on the same team displaying different techniques to obtain the same mission. The Capricorn/Cancer polarity creates tension between the quest for status and the need to feel secure.

Capricorn Goddess

The Goddess of hearth and home, Hestia, was once known as Chief of the Goddesses, and Hestia, the First and Last. Representing the central source, she embodies the virtues of a calm, stable, supportive, and well-centered mother and loving home-base. Hestia's symbols are the sacred flame and the circle. Choosing to stay home on Mount Olympus, she manages the estate and dependably provides a safe haven of unconditional love for all, even strangers. Connected by an umbilical cord at Delphi to the molten core of the Earth, Hestia's hearth flame will never be extinguished.

Allow your energy to tap into that root, running directly to the center of the Earth, and energize your ability to source and sustain your vision of your home, your community, and the Earth as sacred sanctuary.

Build Your Altar

Colors Forest green, earth tones

Numerology 5 – The best exercise is consistency

Tarot Card Devil – Confinement, attachment to form, look at the broader view

Gemstones Smoky quartz, topaz, garnet

Plant remedy Rosemary – Activates appropriate memory

Fragrance Frankincense – Assists the Soul's entry into the body

---

Degree Choice Points
27° Capricorn 50'

Light Community

Shadow Exclusivity

Wisdom Constructive emotional expression will fill the void created by expansion.

Statement I Produce
  Body Knees
  Mind Authority Issues
  Spirit Self-reliance

Element
Earth – Determination, endurance, stability, structure, overly-pragmatic, practical, stubborn.

Second House Moon
4° Capricorn 22'

Second House Umbrella Theme
I Have/I Produce – The way you make money and the way you spend your money.

Light Utilize

Shadow Exploit

Wisdom New experiences create fresh realities.

Clearing the Slate

Remember a time when you experienced the following trigger points.
Write down what happened and perform Ho'oponopono, the Hawaiian forgiveness ritual.

Responsibility

- I'm Sorry
- Please Forgive Me
- Thank You
- I Love You

Too much focus at work

- I'm Sorry
- Please Forgive Me
- Thank You
- I Love You

Too much focus on status and position

- I'm Sorry
- Please Forgive Me
- Thank You
- I Love You

Lacking Compassion

- I'm Sorry
- Please Forgive Me
- Thank You
- I Love You

Challenging Authority

- I'm Sorry
- Please Forgive Me
- Thank You
- I Love You

July 19th
3:58 PM

Full Moon in Capricorn

Capricorn Challenges and Victories

Say all of the statements in this section out loud. Then, underline the phrase that means the most to you. Use the phrase as your special affirmation for recalibrating throughout this phase of the moon.

I feel limited. I feel confined. I feel stuck. I feel there is no way out. Perhaps I am the target of someone's envy or jealousy, or perhaps I am jealous or I am envious. Maybe I am spending too much time in the outer world and putting too much value on material rewards, things, and possessions. Maybe I am trying to possess someone or limit their view or choice. I may feel there are no choices. Maybe I am living by someone else's rules and beliefs and forgot how to think for myself. I could also be overcome by fear and too terrorized to look at anything at all.

Today, I see and feel the limits of placing the source of love outside myself. I have tunnel vision and I seem to have forgotten to look at my options. I must ask myself today, "How many ways can I look at my life, my situation, or my perceived problems?" Today, I must expand my view to encompass 360-degrees instead of only 180-degrees. I begin by acknowledging to myself that today is the worst it is going to get. I know deep within me that if I allow myself to truly experience my bottom, the top will become visible to me. It is time to look at the brighter side. Begin by identifying the problem by writing it down on a piece of paper. Start with the phrase, "The problem is_____." Fill in the blank. Then, list as many solutions to the problem as you can. List at least three. Then, say these solutions out loud every day until the answer comes to you through a person, an idea, an event, or a choice.

Capricorn Homework

Put on a good pair of walking shoes and get ready to walk your blues away. It is time to get outside and feel the loving power of Mother Earth. The green of the trees refreshes your stagnant energy while you exhaust yourself to a point of vulnerability. Then, and only then, will you feel freedom. Give yourself permission to throw your watch away and learn to live in the moment.

The Capricorn moon is the reincarnation of Spirit emerging from the dark waters of our past emotions and releasing us from our fear of change and our fear of loss. Awaken your powerful and positive spiritual connection to be open to new possibilities. Ask yourself to release your emotional loyalty to the past. We are reminded of our need for material and emotional security at this time. In order to ensure this, we must learn to build a foundation for ourselves that is lit from within, made from the materials of love, goodwill, and intelligence.

Recalibrating List

Say this statement out loud three times before writing your recalibrating list!

I am a free spiritual being and it is my desire to be free to think and to express myself fully.

From this day forward I resolve to be true – first to myself and my highest self, and then to the highest self in me which is the Source of Love That I Am.

Capricorn Recalibrating Ideas

Now is the time to activate a game change in my life, and give up obstacles to success, authority issues, sorrow and sadness, fear that blocks me, arrogance, irritability, limitations of time, priorities that are no longer valid, control and domination, the need to do it all alone, and taking on excessive responsibility.

Full Moon in Capricorn

July 19th
3:58 PM

How to Use the Moon Book With Your Chart

Fill in the blanks on the Cosmic Check-In page. Then look up the degree of the Moon on the chart below. Take note of the "I" statement on the outside of the wheel where the Moon is located. Now, locate the same degree on your own chart and make a note of the house and corresponding "I" statement. Go back to the Cosmic Check-In page and circle the two statements from the charts and read what you wrote. This will give you an idea about what to expect from this moon phase on a personal level.

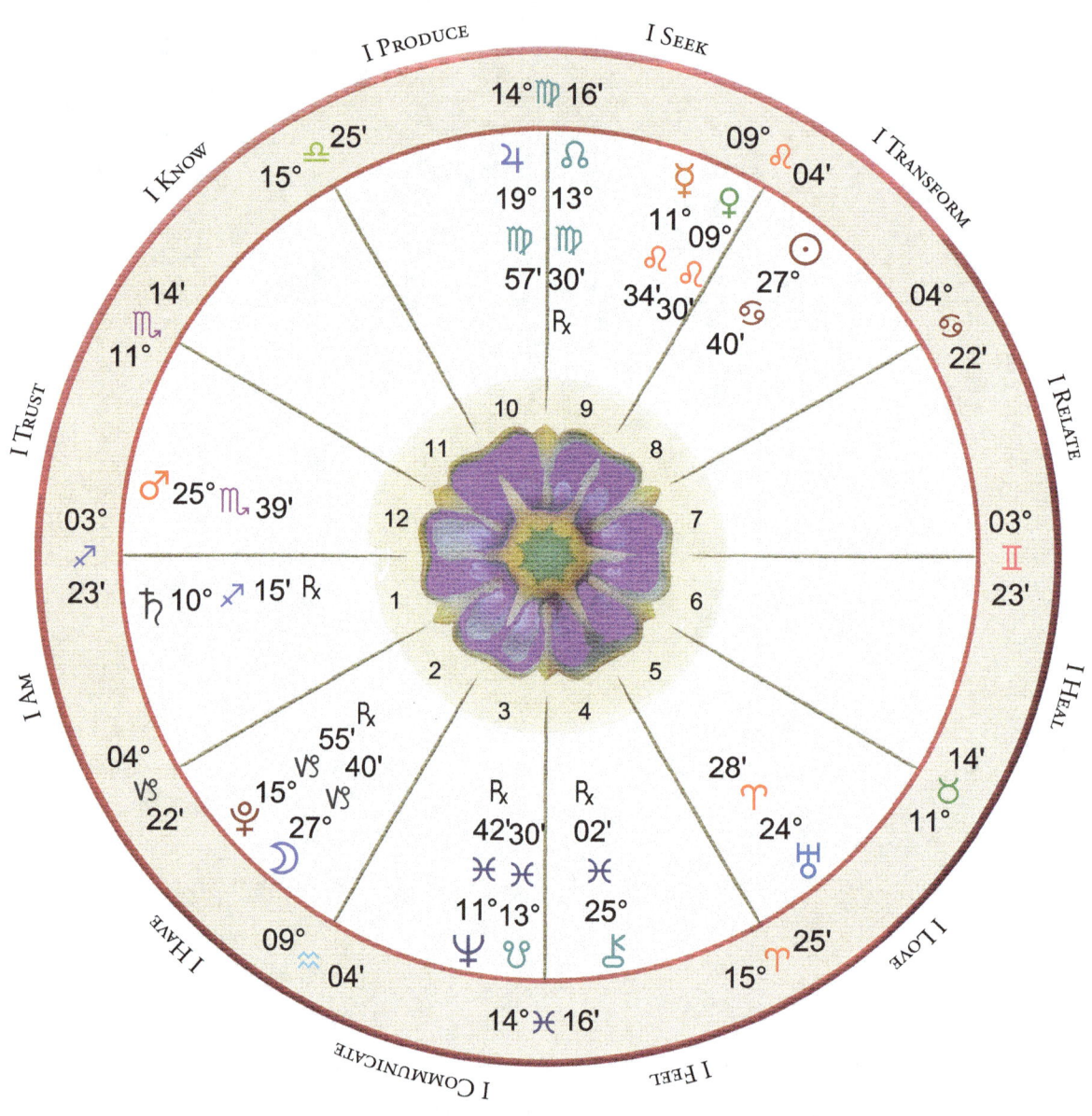

♈ Aries	♋ Cancer	♐ Sagittarius	☽ Moon	♄ Saturn	☊ North Node	V/C Void-of-Course
♉ Taurus	♌ Leo	♑ Capricorn	☿ Mercury	♅ Uranus	☋ South Node	▲ Super-Sensitivity
♊ Gemini	♍ Virgo	♒ Aquarius	♀ Venus	♆ Neptune	➔ Enters	▼ Low-Vitality
	♎ Libra	♓ Pisces	♂ Mars	♇ Pluto	℞ Retrograde	
	♏ Scorpio		☉ Sun	⚷ Chiron	S/D Stationary Direct	

134

Cosmic Check-In

Take a moment to write a brief phrase for each "I" statement.
This activates all areas of your life for this creative cycle.

♑ I Produce

♒ I Know

♓ I Trust

♈ I Am

♉ I Have

♊ I Communicate

♋ I Feel

♌ I Love

♍ I Heal

♎ I Relate

♏ I Transform

♐ I Seek

August Planetary Highlights

Saturn is Retrograde in Sagittarius Until August 13

Ask yourself these two questions: "Does my spiritual connection stay strong within me in the face of adversity?" "Does my spirituality get inspired when I discover something new?"

Neptune is Retrograde in Pisces Until November 19

Connect with your deeper form of devotion, and bring it into a group so that your spiritual connection can multiply.

Uranus is Retrograde Through the End of the Year

The renegade rebel is in charge here. See if you can make a choice to evolve with ease and grace, rather than rebellion. Be willing to share what you know in order to inspire those around you.

Mercury goes Retrograde in Virgo on August 30

This is a super time to put your mind to work doing research. The gleaning will be very rewarding and awaken parts of you that were sandwiched inside too many details.

Pluto is Retrograde in Capricorn Until September 26

Survival issues are up for review. If you are still stymied by them, now is the time to absolutely get over it. The first thing to do is to give something away. Capitalize on the generosity theme for the year. Donate to a cause that means something to you and your community. It is best if it is a thing, rather than a service, because when the "letting go" is over, an empty space will be defined. Face the perceived survival issue in the emptiness. Breathe through it.

August 2 – Mars Enters Sagittarius

Woohoo! Adventure, sports, travel, and pilgrimages will all come into your vision at this time – know that this could be the greatest time of your life! Allow yourself to receive it and go. Start by getting travel books and looking for travel adventure groups, and get involved. Special interest travel to learn about philosophy, culture, and ancient civilizations is calling you. Now is the time – Go! Go! Go!

August 5 – Venus Enters Virgo

The focus switches from beauty to hygiene, health, and workouts. Set the stage for your body to be revitalized. Remember to make it fun and you will be able to stick with it! Proper scheduling makes it work better for the Virgo element.

August 22 – The Sun Enters Virgo

This is an important time for feminine aspects to be brought to the surface, so that the new feminine formulas can be made available to women. Be willing to receive this download.

August 29 – Venus Enters Libra

Now's the time to manifest a relationship. Feel the true power of intimacy wrapping around you.

August 2 – Venus Conjunct with Mid-Heaven in Leo

This is a day to shine! Your potential will be lighting the way for your radiance to direct itself in the best possible way.

August 18 – Mercury Dances with Jupiter

This is a time when full expression from the heart of compassion and unconditional love can be spoken. It will be a test to speak from your heart and be exact with your words – no exaggerating allowed. Stay close to your truth when speaking.

August 18 – Mars and Saturn are Coupled in Sagittarius

Expect a feeling of confinement to occur – no escaping. It's best to do research and expand your mind by taking a class on a favorite subject.

Super-Sensitivity – August 12-13

No rushing – stay home and stay safe.

Low-Vitality – August 25-27

Resting is a must to help restore the Earth at this time.

SUNDAY	MONDAY	TUESDAY	WEDNESDAY	THURSDAY	FRIDAY	SATURDAY
	1 ♄♅♆♇℞ ☽ V/C 5:43pm ☽→♌ 6:11pm 9. We are never alone.	**2** ♄♅♆♇℞ ♂→♐ 10:50am ● 10°♌58' 1:46pm 10. A new level is transformative.	**3** ♄♅♆♇℞ ☽ V/C 9:12am 2. Finding the answer brings balance.	**4** ♄♅♆♇℞ ☽→♍ 12:33am 3. Experience is the source of creativity.	**5** ♄♅♆♇℞ ♀→♍ 8:28am ☽ V/C 8:20pm 4. Joy in the workplace is productive.	**6** ♄♅♆♇℞ ☽→♎ 9:56am 5. Choose to change.
7 ♄♅♆♇℞ 6. Friendship grows where trust exists.	**8** ♄♅♆♇℞ ☽ V/C 10:41am ☽→♏ 9:51pm 8. Failure is part of the road to success.	**9** ♄♅♆♇℞ 9. Those who create peace are blessed.	**10** ♄♅♆♇℞ ☽ V/C 10:21pm 10. Stay up-to-date with technology.	**11** ♄♅♆♇℞ ☽→♐ 10:23am 2. Choose what works best for you.	**12** ♄♅♆♇℞ ▲ 3. Once you know be willing to believe.	**13** ♅♆♇℞ ▲ ♄SD 9°♐46' 2:51am ☽ V/C 10:36am ☽→♑ 9:11pm 4. Grace under pressure is maturity.
14 ♅♆♇℞ 5. Make exercise a daily routine.	**15** ♅♆♇℞ ☽ V/C 7:44pm 6. Cheer others on to victory.	**16** ♅♆♇℞ ☽→♒ 4:52am 7. Disagreeing can lead to clarity.	**17** ♅♆♇℞ 8. When you are in charge, lead gently.	**18** ♅♆♇℞ ☽ V/C 2:26am ☽→♓ 9:34am ○ 25°♒52' 2:28am 9. Do community service today.	**19** ♅♆♇℞ 10. Plan your future and live in the now.	**20** ♅♆♇℞ ☽ V/C 5:20am ☽→♈ 12:18pm 2. Do the adaptability dance.
21 ♅♆♇℞ 3. The ability to laugh is healthy.	**22** ♅♆♇℞ ☉→♍ 9:40am ☽ V/C 4:47am ☽→♉ 2:19pm 4. Common sense is powerful.	**23** ♅♆♇℞ 5. Making progress requires interaction.	**24** ♅♆♇℞ ☽ V/C 12:37pm ☽→♊ 4:39pm 6. With heart connections we thrive.	**25** ♅♆♇℞ ▼ 7. You know best what's best for you.	**26** ♅♆♇℞ ▼ ☽ V/C 5:30pm ☽→♋ 8:06pm 8. Success is a dream manifested.	**27** ♅♆♇℞ ▼ 9. Be a generous humanitarian.
28 ♅♆♇℞ ☽ V/C 11:23pm 10. Vacations refresh the spirit.	**29** ♅♆♇℞ ♀→♎ 7:08pm ☽→♌ 1:11am 2. Partnership requires quality.	**30** ☿♅♆♇℞ ☿℞ 29°♍04' 6:05am ☽ V/C 9:19pm 3. Add joy in your life every day.	**31** ☿♅♆♇℞ ☽→♍ 8:22am 4. Investing wisely creates stability.			

♈ Aries
♉ Taurus
♊ Gemini
♋ Cancer
♌ Leo
♍ Virgo
♎ Libra
♏ Scorpio
♐ Sagittarius
♑ Capricorn
♒ Aquarius
♓ Pisces
☉ Sun
☽ Moon
☿ Mercury
♀ Venus
♂ Mars
♃ Jupiter
♄ Saturn
♅ Uranus
♆ Neptune
♇ Pluto
⚷ Chiron
☊ North Node
☋ South Node
→ Enters
℞ Retrograde
SD Stationary Direct
V/C Void-of-Course
▲ Super Sensitivity
▼ Low Vitality
2. Balance
3. Fun
4. Structure
5. Action
6. Love
7. Learning
8. Money
9. Spirituality
10. Visionary
11. Completion

August 2nd
1:46 PM

New Moon in Leo

Degree Choice Points
10° Leo 58'

Light   Playfulness

Shadow   Fending for Oneself

Wisdom   Dissolve the mental wall that causes separation.

Statement   I Love
- **Body**   Heart
- **Mind**   Self-confidence
- **Spirit**   Generosity

Element
Fire – Passion, enthusiasm, warmth, centered in personal identity.

Ninth House Moon
19° Cancer 35'

Ninth House Umbrella Theme
I Seek/I Feel – The way you approach spirituality, philosophy, journeys, higher knowledge, and aspiration.

Light   Sublime Romance

Shadow   Emotional Blackmail

Wisdom   Allow others the time they need to change.

When the Sun is in Leo

This is the time when you feel the power from the Sun, the heart of the Cosmos. Leo has a direct relationship with the Sun's heart. The Sun rules your identity. Now is the time to shine and stand tall in the center of your life. Allow yourself to feel the power of your individual conscious Self. When you align with the power of the Sun, you become radiant. This radiance gives you the power to transmit energy into life. Personal fulfillment becomes a reality when you align your will with love. Remember to live love every day!

Leo Goddess

Aphrodite sashays into the Summer party, full of moxie and ready to flirt! The Goddess of Beauty and Love is enlivening all aspects of your life with joyful play!

Get into your Feminine Light. Giggle, dance, and sing! What a great time for a girl's night out or karaoke on the beach beside a roaring bonfire! Work it! Swish your skirts and strut your stuff! Tap into Aphrodite's inner light for fun and frolic. Aphrodite reminds us that play is also our spiritual work. Bring some joy and fun into it!

Build Your Altar

Colors   Royal purple, royal blue, orange

Numerology   10 – A new level is transformative

Tarot Card   Sun – To stand tall in the center of life

Gemstones   Peridot, emerald, amber

Plant Remedy   Sunflower – Standing tall in the center of your garden

Fragrance   Jasmine – Remembering your Soul's original intention

Manifesting List

This or something better than this comes to me in an easy and pleasurable way, for the good of all concerned. Thank you, Universe!

Leo Manifesting Ideas

Now is the time to focus on manifesting new love or new ways of loving, new creative ways of expressing myself, bonding with those I love, quality time with those I love, knowledge of my Soul's intention, fun with my children, being a bright beaming light, and connecting to the hearts of humanity.

August 2nd
1:46 PM

New Moon in Leo

Leo Challenges and Victories

Say all of the statements in this section out loud. Then, underline the phrase that means the most to you. Use the phrase as your special affirmation for manifesting throughout this phase of the moon.

Today, I am at the center of bliss, happiness, abundance, and total celebration. It is my time to shine and feel the power of my true self blasting the Universe, the entire planet, and all of life with the light of my awareness. There is nothing that can stop me today, because I am free to be me. When I am free to be me, I can stand naked in the daylight and have nothing to hide. I truly know that all of life loves me and I love all of life. I feel the radiance and vibration of my being activating me with aliveness, vitality, and charisma. I know that I can make a difference because I celebrate life by infusing, sparking, and igniting matter with light. I am open and ready to embrace all that comes to me with joy. I say "YES!" to all opportunities today; knowing that today is my day. I am in the flow of abundance and I let abundance flow through me.

The child within me is open and ready to play full out; there is not a cloud in the sky today that can eclipse me or place a shadow on me and keep me from my true level of power. I am aware that the child state of being within me simply says yes to action and action is power. When I take action today, my possibilities are endless because they are generated from my true self and motivated by happiness, joy, and freedom. The child within me is able to play full out because I have birthed myself beyond my old perception of blocks. I know that in taking this true power, to be motivated by happiness, pathways on all levels and in all dimensions can open to the empowerment of joy. Empowerment is mine today because I am shining from within myself and I know my deepest self is connected to the source. Empowerment occurs when I live from the inside out. Today, I wave the banner of my being from within, feel the glow, and go.

Leo Homework

Leos manifest best through fashion and jewelry design, glamour, politics, super-modeling, movie stardom, child advocacy, fundraising, toy and game design, image consulting, authoring children's books, sales, and cardiology.

Leo gets you closer to your essential self, reminding you of your Soul's original intention. You become ready to receive the benefits of reflective light and radiating light at the same time, so that you can see your personality and your Soul connecting to love which constitutes a new level of fulfillment. Expect purification, transmutation, communication, and mastery to be part of your personal experience.

Without Acknowledgment Progress Cannot Occur

Acknowledgement creates space for victory and gratitude, which automatically brings you to a level of completion so a new cycle of opportunity can occur in your life. When you celebrate your wins and acknowledge your victories with gratitude, you update your cells so that your ability to move forward is not hindered by a cellular holographic pattern that is stuck in the past. Cellular lag creates resistance and makes moving forward most difficult. The key is to stay continuously updated by acknowledging yourself for what you did do at the end of each day, rather than heading off to sleep thinking about what you did not do. By acknowledging what you did not do, you play into your karmic storage bank and keep your progress at bay. When you acknowledge yourself and your manifestations you are complete, and more cycles of opportunity become available to you in each new day. Be prepared for miracles!

Victory List

When a creation result is acknowledged it seals the deal. This makes room for more magnificence to expand into your life and increases your abundance factor adding to your ability to receive. As each aspect of your manifesting list arrives in your life, spend time allowing, acknowledging, and accepting it with the true gusto of gratitude! Keep your victory list active here.

This fulfills the relationship between the giver and the receiver, which completes the cycle with the Universe so that a new beginning can be established.

Gratitude List

August 2nd
1:46 PM

New Moon in Leo

How to Use the Moon Book With Your Chart

Fill in the blanks on the Cosmic Check-In page. Then look up the degree of the Moon on the chart below. Take note of the "I" statement on the outside of the wheel where the Moon is located. Now, locate the same degree on your own chart and make a note of the house and corresponding "I" statement. Go back to the Cosmic Check-In page and circle the two statements from the charts and read what you wrote. This will give you an idea about what to expect from this moon phase on a personal level.

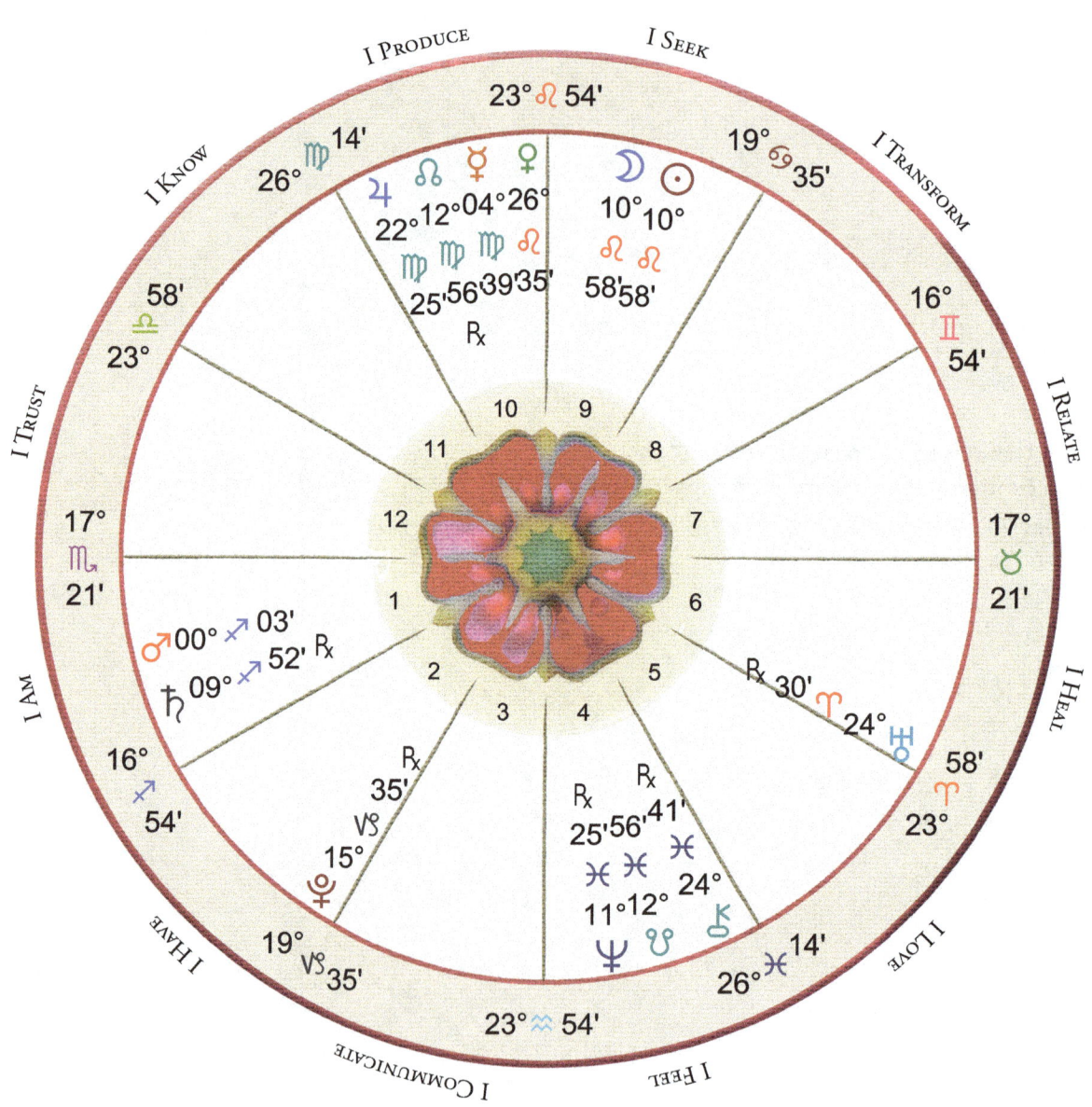

♈ Aries	♋ Cancer	♐ Sagittarius	☽ Moon	♄ Saturn	☊ North Node	V/C Void-of-Course
♉ Taurus	♌ Leo	♑ Capricorn	☿ Mercury	♅ Uranus	☋ South Node	▲ Super-Sensitivity
♊ Gemini	♍ Virgo	♒ Aquarius	♀ Venus	♆ Neptune	➔ Enters	• Low-Vitality
♎ Libra	♓ Pisces		♂ Mars	♇ Pluto	℞ Retrograde	
♏ Scorpio			☉ Sun	⚷ Chiron	S/D Stationary Direct	

144

Cosmic Check-In

Take a moment to write a brief phrase for each "I" statement.
This activates all areas of your life for this creative cycle.

♌ I Love

♍ I Heal

♎ I Relate

♏ I Transform

♐ I Seek

♑ I Produce

♒ I Know

♓ I Trust

♈ I Am

♉ I Have

♊ I Communicate

♋ I Feel

August 18th
2:28 AM

Full Moon in Aquarius

Degree Choice Points
25° Aquarius 52'

Light   Practical Goals

Shadow   Resisting Efficiency

Wisdom   Your desires are met by helping the Earth.

Statement   I Know
  Body   Ankles
  Mind   True Genius
  Spirit   Vision

Element
Air – Curiosity, learning, flexibility, and direct consciousness towards form.

Ninth House Moon
22° Capricorn 44'

Ninth House Umbrella Theme
I Seek/I Know – The way you approach spirituality, philosophy, journeys, higher knowledge, and aspiration.

Light   Performance

Shadow   Attention-seeking

Wisdom   Personal power gains momentum by maintaining balance.

Karmic Awakening

Taurus/Scorpio – My money or our money

Karma becomes activated when a question arises regarding money and who pays. The way the chart is set up is very simple, so if it is followed, karma won't happen. When spending, if the desired object is for one person in the relationship, that person must pay. If it is something that is desired for the couple it is paid for by shared resources.

The Sun is Opposite the Moon

Full moons are always in opposition to the Sun. This creates a feeling of tension between where you want to shine and how your feelings are flowing on a sensory level about the Sun's directive. The two forces seem like they are working against each other, yet they are on the same team displaying different techniques to obtain the same mission. The Aquarian/Leo polarity creates tension between the quest for group interaction and the recognition of self.

Aquarius Goddess

The Egyptian Goddess Maat ushers in a time of discovery about who you are at the core, as your most balanced and beneficent self, and about the work you came here to do in this lifetime. According to the Egyptian Book of the Dead, Maat is the goddess you visit upon your death. She places her single ostrich feather on the scale to be weighed against your heart. If you have lived a virtuous life, and reached your highest potential as a kind and decent human being, your heart will be as light as Maat's feather, and you would cross over. If not, you will be devoured by the Goddess Ammit and would be reborn into duality for another lifetime.

Let this moon show you your potential and re-orient yourself to your life's highest work and purpose. The Egyptian word for heart was "ib." Ask yourself, who will "I be" in this lifetime?

Build Your Altar

Colors Electric colors, neon, multi-colors, pearl white

Numerology 9 – Do community service today

Tarot Card Star – Being guided by a higher source

Gemstones Aquamarine, amethyst, opal

Plant remedy Queen of the Night Cactus – The ability to see in the dark

Fragrance Myrrh – Healing the nervous system

Clearing the Slate

Remember a time when you experienced the following trigger points.
Write down what happened and perform Ho'oponopono, the Hawaiian forgiveness ritual.

Stubborn

- I'm Sorry
- Please Forgive Me
- Thank You
- I Love You

Spiritual Elitism

- I'm Sorry
- Please Forgive Me
- Thank You
- I Love You

Frenzy and Chaos

- I'm Sorry
- Please Forgive Me
- Thank You
- I Love You

Living in the future

- I'm Sorry
- Please Forgive Me
- Thank You
- I Love You

Rebellion

- I'm Sorry
- Please Forgive Me
- Thank You
- I Love You

August 18th
2:28 AM

Full Moon in Aquarius

Aquarius Challenges and Victories

Say all of the statements in this section out loud. Then, underline the phrase that means the most to you. Use the phrase as your special affirmation for recalibrating throughout this phase of the moon.

Today my true potential can be realized. All I have to do is take a risk and know that my faith is in operation. My future is very bright and offers me a promise of things to come. Today is a day of destiny. I have chosen this day to determine a DESTINY PROMISE I MADE TO MYSELF BEFORE I CAME INTO THIS LIFE. All that is required of me is to move out of my comfort zone and take a risk. I am aware that faith cannot be determined without risk. I take the risk to move into the next space of creation in my life. I release fear and move into faith, knowing full well that my logic and reason are part of the fear that keeps me stuck.

I am reminded that the kingdom of heaven is open to the child. I find the child within me today to embrace what life has for me with open arms and a spirit of adventure. I know my true potential lives inside my magical child and she/he is willing to play and go for the gusto. I am here in this life to fulfill my promise to experience life to the fullest and to release the fear of judgment that has hounded me and kept me from playing full-out. I remember that when I experience, I gather a knowledge base within my Soul and keep my agreement with myself and the Universe. I connect to my super-consciousness and take on the bigger view of my life and all that it has to offer me when I risk reason and take a leap of faith. I know in the depth of my awareness that, if I jump off the diving board, there will be water in the pool. I am willing to risk reason for an experience. Everything I ever wanted is one step outside my comfort zone. I go for the GUSTO today! I release my fear today and turn it into faith. I trust in the promise of things to come. I know my potential is realized today, and that all I have to do is say "YES!" to life!

Aquarius Homework

The Aquarius moon reminds us of our connection to solar fire (the heart of the Sun) also known as the Heart of the Cosmos. During this time, we get our vitality recharged and our potent power comes into play motivating the masses to receive more energy to transmute into the new world. Voice all that you know to be true to the point of self-realization where your authentic purpose can be revealed to you. This is the moment where you have released all that has kept you from your true sense of freedom. Remember to replenish all the electrolytes in your system.

Recalibrating List

Say this statement out loud three times before writing your recalibrating list!

I am a free spiritual being and it is my desire to be free to think and to express myself fully.

Freedom is mine when I live my Truth!

Aquarius Recalibrating Ideas

Now is the time to activate a game change in my life, and give up resistance to authority figures, blocks to living in the moment, unnecessary rebellion, non-productive frenzy and fantasy, the need to be spontaneous, and people who aren't team players.

August 18th
2:28 AM

Full Moon in Aquarius

How to Use the Moon Book With Your Chart

Fill in the blanks on the Cosmic Check-In page. Then look up the degree of the Moon on the chart below. Take note of the "I" statement on the outside of the wheel where the Moon is located. Now, locate the same degree on your own chart and make a note of the house and corresponding "I" statement. Go back to the Cosmic Check-In page and circle the two statements from the charts and read what you wrote. This will give you an idea about what to expect from this moon phase on a personal level.

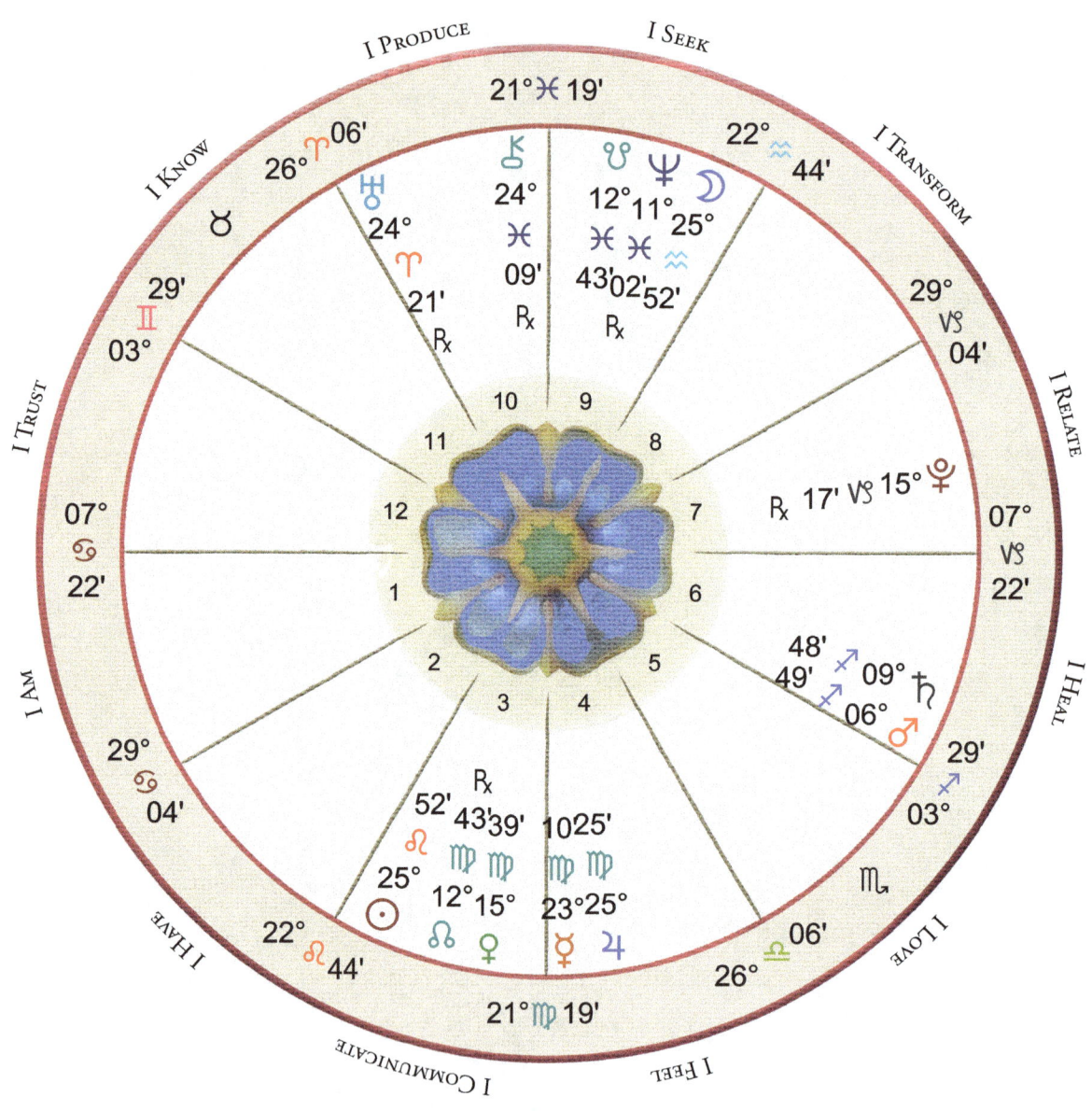

♈ Aries	♋ Cancer	♐ Sagittarius	☽ Moon	♄ Saturn	☊ North Node	V/C Void-of-Course
♉ Taurus	♌ Leo	♑ Capricorn	☿ Mercury	♅ Uranus	☋ South Node	▲ Super-Sensitivity
♊ Gemini	♍ Virgo	♒ Aquarius	♀ Venus	♆ Neptune	➡ Enters	• Low-Vitality
	♎ Libra	♓ Pisces	♂ Mars	♇ Pluto	℞ Retrograde	
	♏ Scorpio	☉ Sun	♃ Jupiter	⚷ Chiron	SD Stationary Direct	

152

Cosmic Check-In

Take a moment to write a brief phrase for each "I" statement.
This activates all areas of your life for this creative cycle.

♒ I Know

♓ I Trust

♈ I Am

♉ I Have

♊ I Communicate

♋ I Feel

♌ I Love

♍ I Heal

♎ I Relate

♏ I Transform

♐ I Seek

♑ I Produce

September Planetary Highlights

Mercury is Retrograde in Virgo Until September 21

Mercury is happy in Virgo, especially when it's retrograde, because of the intense interest in details. The best use of this process is to take on a research project. You will be in bliss!

Uranus is Retrograde in Aries Through the End of the Year

Uranus is doing a major clean-up of the old way of doing things. This must happen so that the new paradigms come into our consciousness with ease and grace. An innovative mindset is the key and Uranus won't stop until it happens.

Neptune is Retrograde in Pisces Until November 19

We are learning the expression of our spiritual process and how that applies in our lives right now. In the moment when you get a flash of insight, notice where you are and what kind of people you have attracted.

Pluto is Retrograde in Capricorn Until September 26

This is a time to watch out for slippery thoughts that lead you down the rabbit hole to places you may not want to go.

September 1 – Solar Eclipse in Virgo

You will be eclipsing 19 years of bad habits and poor health habits, plus healing your mind from poor judgements that keep you from working at your highest level.

September 1 – Mars and Saturn Conjunct

This is not a good time to travel. The idea of adventure is not an option right now. It's best to go within and make knowing yourself a real adventure.

September 1 – Virgo Cluster – The Sun, Moon, Jupiter, Mercury, and the North Node – Lasting for 10 days

This is an interesting cluster that brings future endeavors into the limelight of potential. Act on this now and your platform will get you to the right audience.

September 16 – Lunar Eclipse in Pisces

Release 19 years of false, outdated beliefs in order to set yourself free!

September 9 – Jupiter Enters Libra

This is a time when beauty, harmony, and good fortune bring on an attunement for all. There is a grace that becomes a requirement for all living environments. We all become aware of our outstanding characteristics. The concept for living is exceptional.

September 22 – The Sun Enters Libra – Fall Equinox

It's time to enter the harvest and celebrate the fruits of your labor. Remember your generosity has brought you much fruit – savor it in every way. Now that the light is diminishing, prepare to go within and let yourself be embraced.

September 27 – Mars Enters Capricorn

This is a major power process. Prepare yourself for the energy required to be the champion of your cause.

September 16 – Chiron and The Moon Conjunct in Pisces

With this coupling we could call this moon a healing moon. Let the healing waters of Pisces bring you to a place where suffering ends.

Super-Sensitivity – September 9-10

Know your boundaries and stay away from chaos.

Low-Vitality – September 21-22

Rest and nurture yourself today. Let the Earth get a nap too.

Sunday	Monday	Tuesday	Wednesday	Thursday	Friday	Saturday
				1 ☿♅♆♇℞ ● 9°♍21′ 2:04am Solar Eclipse 2:08am 5. Take another route for variety.	**2** ☿♅♆♇℞ ☽ V/C 3:12pm ☽→♎ 5:55pm 6. Add something new to your home.	**3** ☿♅♆♇℞ 7. Relax the mental process by exercise.
4 ☿♅♆♇℞ ☽ V/C 5:30pm 8. Be willing to share your wealth.	**5** ☿♅♆♇℞ Labor Day ☽→♏ 5:38am 9. For best results, pray out loud.	**6** ☿♅♆♇℞ 10. Keep abreast of what is current.	**7** ☿♅♆♇℞ ☽ V/C 5:42pm ☽→♐ 6:19pm 2. Look at both sides of an issue.	**8** ☿♅♆♇℞ 3. Enjoy watching children at play.	**9** ☿♅♆♇℞▲ ♃→♎ 4:19am ☽ V/C 5:50pm 4. Create a space that is inviting.	**10** ☿♅♆♇℞▲ ☽→♑ 5:54am 5. Having several choices is delightful.
11 ☿♅♆♇℞ 6. The best homes are peaceful.	**12** ☿♅♆♇℞ ☽ V/C 2:59am ☽→♒ 2:28pm 7. Wisdom comes from experience.	**13** ☿♅♆♇℞ 8. Intention equals manifesting.	**14** ☿♅♆♇℞ ☽ V/C 8:31am ☽→♓ 7:22pm 9. A prayer has unlimited potential.	**15** ☿♅♆♇℞ 10. See the world through new eyes.	**16** ☿♅♆♇℞ ☽ V/C 12:05pm ☽→♈ 9:22pm Lunar Eclipse 11:55am ○ 24°♓20′ 12:06pm 2. Decide to decide.	**17** ☿♅♆♇℞ 3. Find joy in the work you do.
18 ☿♅♆♇℞ ☽ V/C 1:10pm ☽→♉ 9:57pm 4. The most grounded path is logic.	**19** ☿♅♆♇℞ 5. Wait for the opportunity to act.	**20** ☿♅♆♇℞ ☽ V/C 8:32pm ☽→♊ 10:52pm 6. Kindness sets the tone for generosity.	**21** ♅♆♇℞▼ ☿ S/D - 14°♍49′ 10:32pm 7. Trusting intuition leads to action.	**22** ♅♆♇℞▼ Fall Equinox ☉→♎ 7:22am 8. Manifestation follows action.	**23** ♅♆♇℞ ☽ V/C 12:56am ☽→♋ 1:33am 9. Silence will show you what you know.	**24** ♅♆♇℞ ☽ V/C 6:41pm 10. A good formula has potential.
25 ♅♆♇℞ ☽→♌ 6:48am 2. Our conviction is based on experience.	**26** ♅♆℞ ♇ S/D - 14°♑55′ 8:00am 3. Sing along with the radio.	**27** ♅♆℞ ♂→♑ 1:08am ☽ V/C 1:52pm ☽→♍ 2:42pm 4. Restructure for success today.	**28** ♅♆℞ 5. Strive for clarity before taking action.	**29** ♅♆℞ ☽ V/C 3:04am 6. Good relationships thrive on love.	**30** ♅♆℞ ☽→♎ 12:52am ● 8°♎15′ 5:11pm 7. Accept limitation and transcend it.	

♈ Aries	♎ Libra	☉ Sun	♄ Saturn	☊ North Node	▲ Super Sensitivity	6. Love
♉ Taurus	♏ Scorpio	☽ Moon	♅ Uranus	☋ South Node	▼ Low Vitality	7. Learning
♊ Gemini	♐ Sagittarius	☿ Mercury	♆ Neptune	→ Enters	2. Balance	8. Money
♋ Cancer	♑ Capricorn	♀ Venus	♇ Pluto	℞ Retrograde	3. Fun	9. Spirituality
♌ Leo	♒ Aquarius	♂ Mars	⚷ Chiron	S/D Stationary Direct	4. Structure	10. Visionary
♍ Virgo	♓ Pisces	♃ Jupiter		V/C Void-of-Course	5. Action	11. Completion

Solar Eclipse
September 1st
2:04 AM

New Moon in Virgo

Degree Choice Points
9° Virgo 21'

Light   Intelligence

Shadow   Fragmentation

Wisdom   Obscurity maintains the integrity of your commitment.

Statement   I Heal
    Body   Intestines
    Mind   Critical
    Spirit   Divinity in the Details

Element
Earth – Family lineage and DNA healing, healing power from the plant kingdom, knowing nutrition, and abundance. Body awareness. Connection to small animals.

Third House Moon
0° Virgo 12'

Third House Umbrella Theme
I Communicate/I Heal – How you get the word out and the message behind the words.

Light   Dependable

Shadow   Labeling

Wisdom   Trust your future sight.

Karmic Awakening

Aries/Libra – karma lives between the "I am" and the "We are"

Karmic stress happens when confusion takes place around where energy needs to be focused. Is this for me or is it for me and my relationship? The best option is to avoid having to ever make this choice. Know the difference between personal and professional areas of your life.

When the Sun is in Virgo

Virgo is called the "Womb of Time" in which the seeds of great value are planted, shielded, nourished, and revealed. It is the labor of Virgo that brings the Christ Principle into manifestation within individuals and humanity. This unification occurs when we feel the power within us to serve. When we serve, we give birth to Divinity. Virgo time is when we all have a chance to raise the standard of excellence in our lives and on the Earth. The Virgo intelligence stores and maintains light in a precise manner. Attention to detail is Virgo's great gift to life.

Virgo Goddess

Mayan Goddess of medicine and midwifery, Ixchel, enters quietly in her jaguar form, to sit and observe. How are you being healed and how are you assisting the healing of others? Jaguar medicine is powerful for clearing attachments and cords that no longer serve you.

Call upon Ixchel to help you find precision and clarity through your words. Let her help you end negative self-talk. Enlist her to walk your boundaries and protect you fiercely, as though you were her little cub. Locate a stone or amulet you can carry in your pocket to remind you of her power, just like shaman and physicians of old would carry in their medicine bundles. When Ixchel has your back, you can roar!

Build Your Altar

Colors   Earth tones, blue, green

Numerology   5 – Take another route for variety

Tarot Card   The Hermit – Being a shining light for all of life

Gemstones   Emerald, malachite, sapphire

Plant Remedy   Sagebrush – The ability to hold and store light

Fragrance   Lavender – Management and storage of energy

Manifesting List

This or something better than this comes to me in an easy and pleasurable way, for the good of all concerned. Thank you, Universe!

Virgo Manifesting Ideas

Now is the time to focus on manifesting a high standard of excellence, a healthy lifestyle, self-acceptance, discernment without judgment, healing abilities, a contribution to nature, and a healthy body.

Solar Eclipse
September 1st
2:04 AM

New Moon in Virgo

Virgo Challenges and Victories

Say all of the statements in this section out loud. Then, underline the phrase that means the most to you. Use the phrase as your special affirmation for manifesting throughout this phase of the moon.

Today, I recognize what I love most about myself. I am the source of my love, my life, and my experience. I will set aside time today to nurture myself. I allow myself to receive these gifts and know in my heart that it is natural for me to love myself. I discover, deep within myself, the knowing that the love I give myself is commensurate to the love I am willing to receive from others. I am aware that what I expect from others cannot be truly expressed or experienced if I cannot give to myself first. I can never be disappointed when I know that love is a natural resource for me today.

Today, I honor the Earth by acknowledging what she has given me. I take time out to walk in the woods or on the beach, to feel the power of the creative pulse of the creative forces flowing through my body with the energy of being alive. I spend time in my garden and plant flowers to enhance the idea of beauty today. I honor my body today and get a massage. I spend quality time sharing joyful moments with those who love to connect from the heart and realize the blessings that come from living my life with love.

Virgo Homework

Virgos manifest best through working with herbology, folk medicine, environmental industries, organic farming, recycling, horticulture, acupuncture, healing arts, nutritional counseling, yoga instruction, and editing.

The Virgo moon cycle gives birth to Divinity in its own unique way, understanding the Soul's blueprint to be a temple of beauty. This creates what is known as the "crisis of perfection" within the minds of humankind during this time. We become aware of Spirit ascending and descending at the same time and must recognize that these contradicting energies are working within us in order to give birth to Divinity.

Without Acknowledgment Progress Cannot Occur

Acknowledgement creates space for victory and gratitude, which automatically brings you to a level of completion so a new cycle of opportunity can occur in your life. When you celebrate your wins and acknowledge your victories with gratitude, you update your cells so that your ability to move forward is not hindered by a cellular holographic pattern that is stuck in the past. Cellular lag creates resistance and makes moving forward most difficult. The key is to stay continuously updated by acknowledging yourself for what you did do at the end of each day, rather than heading off to sleep thinking about what you did not do. By acknowledging what you did not do, you play into your karmic storage bank and keep your progress at bay. When you acknowledge yourself and your manifestations you are complete, and more cycles of opportunity become available to you in each new day. Be prepared for miracles!

Victory List

When a creation result is acknowledged it seals the deal. This makes room for more magnificence to expand into your life and increases your abundance factor adding to your ability to receive. As each aspect of your manifesting list arrives in your life, spend time allowing, acknowledging, and accepting it with the true gusto of gratitude! Keep your victory list active here.

Gratitude List

This fulfills the relationship between the giver and the receiver, which completes the cycle with the Universe so that a new beginning can be established.

Solar Eclipse
September 1st
2:04 AM

New Moon in Virgo

How to Use the Moon Book With Your Chart

Fill in the blanks on the Cosmic Check-In page. Then look up the degree of the Moon on the chart below. Take note of the "I" statement on the outside of the wheel where the Moon is located. Now, locate the same degree on your own chart and make a note of the house and corresponding "I" statement. Go back to the Cosmic Check-In page and circle the two statements from the charts and read what you wrote. This will give you an idea about what to expect from this moon phase on a personal level.

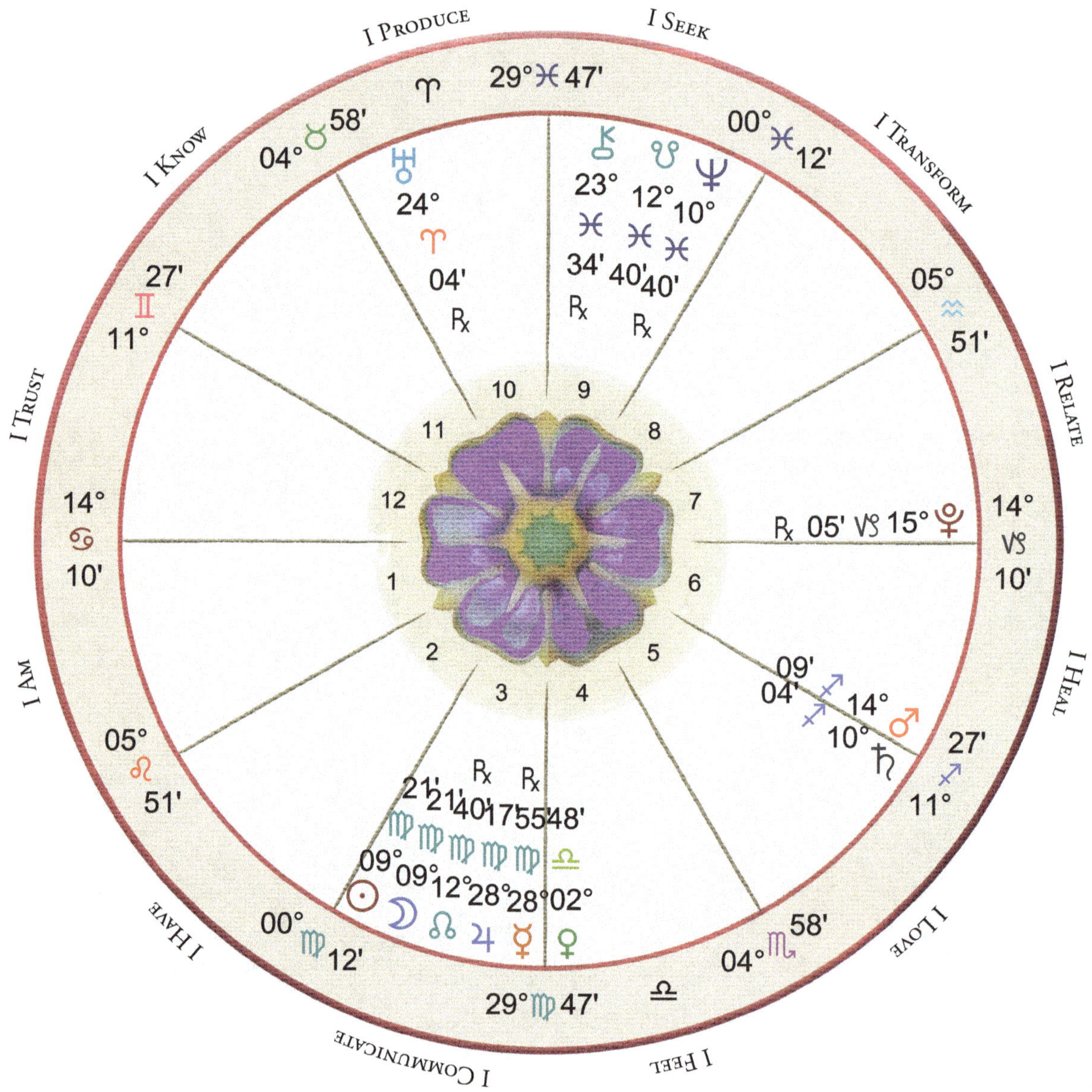

♈ Aries	♋ Cancer	♐ Sagittarius	☽ Moon	♄ Saturn	☊ North Node	V/C Void-of-Course
♉ Taurus	♌ Leo	♑ Capricorn	☿ Mercury	♅ Uranus	☋ South Node	▲ Super-Sensitivity
♊ Gemini	♍ Virgo	♒ Aquarius	♀ Venus	♆ Neptune	➡ Enters	• Low-Vitality
	♎ Libra	♓ Pisces	♂ Mars	♇ Pluto	℞ Retrograde	
	♏ Scorpio		☉ Sun	⚷ Chiron	S/D Stationary Direct	

Cosmic Check-In

Take a moment to write a brief phrase for each "I" statement.
This activates all areas of your life for this creative cycle.

♍ I Heal

♎ I Relate

♏ I Transform

♐ I Seek

♑ I Produce

♒ I Know

♓ I Trust

♈ I Am

♉ I Have

♊ I Communicate

♋ I Feel

♌ I Love

Lunar Eclipse
September 16th
12:06 PM

Full Moon in Pisces

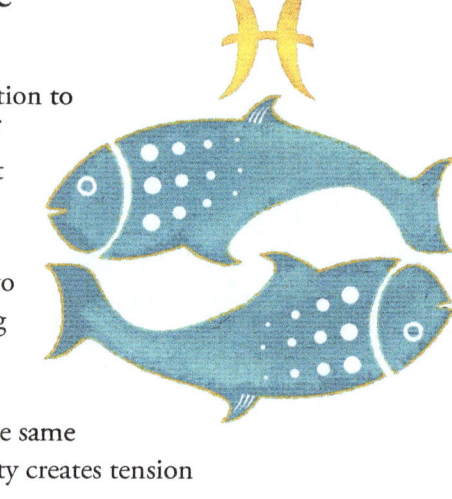

Degree Choice Points
  24° Pisces 20'

Light Authentic Talent

Shadow Directionless

Wisdom Focus on the present. DO IT!!!

Statement I Trust
  Body Feet
  Mind Super-sensitive
  Spirit Mystical

Element
  Water – Feeling, rhythm, living by cycles, flowing, escapism from reality.

Fourth House Moon
  14° Aquarius 16'

Fourth House Umbrella Theme
  I Feel/I Trust – The way your early environmental training was and how that set your foundation for living, and why you chose your mother.

Light Precision

Shadow Drudgery

Wisdom Nothing is out of order; there is no need for drama.

The Sun is Opposite the Moon

Full moons are always in opposition to the Sun. This creates a feeling of tension between where you want to shine and how your feelings are flowing on a sensory level about the Sun's directive. The two forces seem like they are working against each other, yet they are on the same team displaying different techniques to obtain the same mission. The Pisces/Virgo polarity creates tension between addiction and perfection.

Pisces Goddess

Lady Change'e, the Chinese Moon Goddess, is honored at the full moon closest to the Autumnal Equinox, with the sharing of moon cakes, whose round shape symbolizes completeness and togetherness. She ascended to the Moon after drinking the Elixir of Immortality. It had been gifted to her husband after he slew nine out of ten wayward sons of an emperor who had turned into suns and were scorching the Earth. If she and her husband had split the elixir, they would each be immortal, but her mistake in drinking it all (or her sacrifice, depending on the telling) means she will spend eternity on the Moon.

Depicted with a companion rabbit, a magical potion maker, Change'e is beneficent, and will grant your wishes, but remember she favors those who are careful what they wish for, and who take initiative towards working to make their own dreams a reality. Trust in the process of transformation, like the changing colors of the leaves, but also put both of your feet firmly on the path towards wholeness.

Build Your Altar

Colors Greens, blues, amethyst, aquamarine

Numerology 2 – Decide to decide

Tarot Card The Hanged Man – Learning to let go

Gemstones Opal, turquoise, amethyst

Plant remedy Passion flower – The ability to live in the here and now

Fragrance White lotus – Connecting to the Divine without arrogance

Clearing the Slate

Remember a time when you experienced the following trigger points.
Write down what happened and perform Ho'oponopono, the Hawaiian forgiveness ritual.

Unrealistic

- I'm Sorry
- Please Forgive Me
- Thank You
- I Love You

Escape Dramas

- I'm Sorry
- Please Forgive Me
- Thank You
- I Love You

Addictions

- I'm Sorry
- Please Forgive Me
- Thank You
- I Love You

Emotionally Unreliable

- I'm Sorry
- Please Forgive Me
- Thank You
- I Love You

Aimless

- I'm Sorry
- Please Forgive Me
- Thank You
- I Love You

Lunar Eclipse
September 16th
12:06 PM

Full Moon in Pisces

Pisces Challenges and Victories

Say all of the statements in this section out loud. Then, underline the phrase that means the most to you. Use the phrase as your special affirmation for recalibrating throughout this phase of the moon.

The best thing I can do for myself today is to get out of the way, so life can take its own course without the interference of my control drama. I take time out to let go and let things be. I have become too involved in the details and have lost sight of the vastness of the Universe, and the infinite possibilities that are available to me at all times and in every moment. I am aware that all I need is a different way of seeing what I have perceived as a problem, and that my view is limited by my needs, rather than by accepting things as they are. I trust that, when I get out of the way and give space to the power of NOW, all is in Divine Order and everything works out for the good of all concerned. This is the day when doing nothing gets me everything. I allow myself to experience the void. I empty myself of my rigidity, small-mindedness, racing thoughts, the need to be right, and to control outcomes. I know that non-action will present me with right action. I give the Universe a chance and trust the view to be larger than mine. When I accept myself as I am, I learn what I can become. I remove myself from all of the mind chatter and allow for silence to do its work. I am aware that a quiet mind brings me peace (the absence of conflict). In turning upside down, I see how right-side-up things really are. Acceptance brings me perspective. Acceptance sets me free. Acceptance brings me wholeness. Acceptance widens my mind.

Pisces Homework

Get a foot massage to bring your energy back to the ground. Feel the power of your path on the bottom of your feet. Now that you are back to your body, it is time to make a list of the ways your boundaries get breached. After the completion of your list, read it out loud and then throw it in the ocean.

Recalibrating List

Say this statement out loud three times before writing your recalibrating list!

I am a free spiritual being and it is my desire to be free to think and to express myself fully.

From this day forward I resolve to be true – first to myself and my highest self, and then to the highest self in me which is the Source of Love That I Am.

Pisces Recalibrating Ideas

Now is the time to activate a game change in my life, and give up addictions, illusions and fantasy, escape dramas, martyrdom, victimhood, and mental chaos.

Lunar Eclipse
September 16th
12:06 PM

Full Moon in Pisces

How to Use the Moon Book With Your Chart

Fill in the blanks on the Cosmic Check-In page. Then look up the degree of the Moon on the chart below. Take note of the "I" statement on the outside of the wheel where the Moon is located. Now, locate the same degree on your own chart and make a note of the house and corresponding "I" statement. Go back to the Cosmic Check-In page and circle the two statements from the charts and read what you wrote. This will give you an idea about what to expect from this moon phase on a personal level.

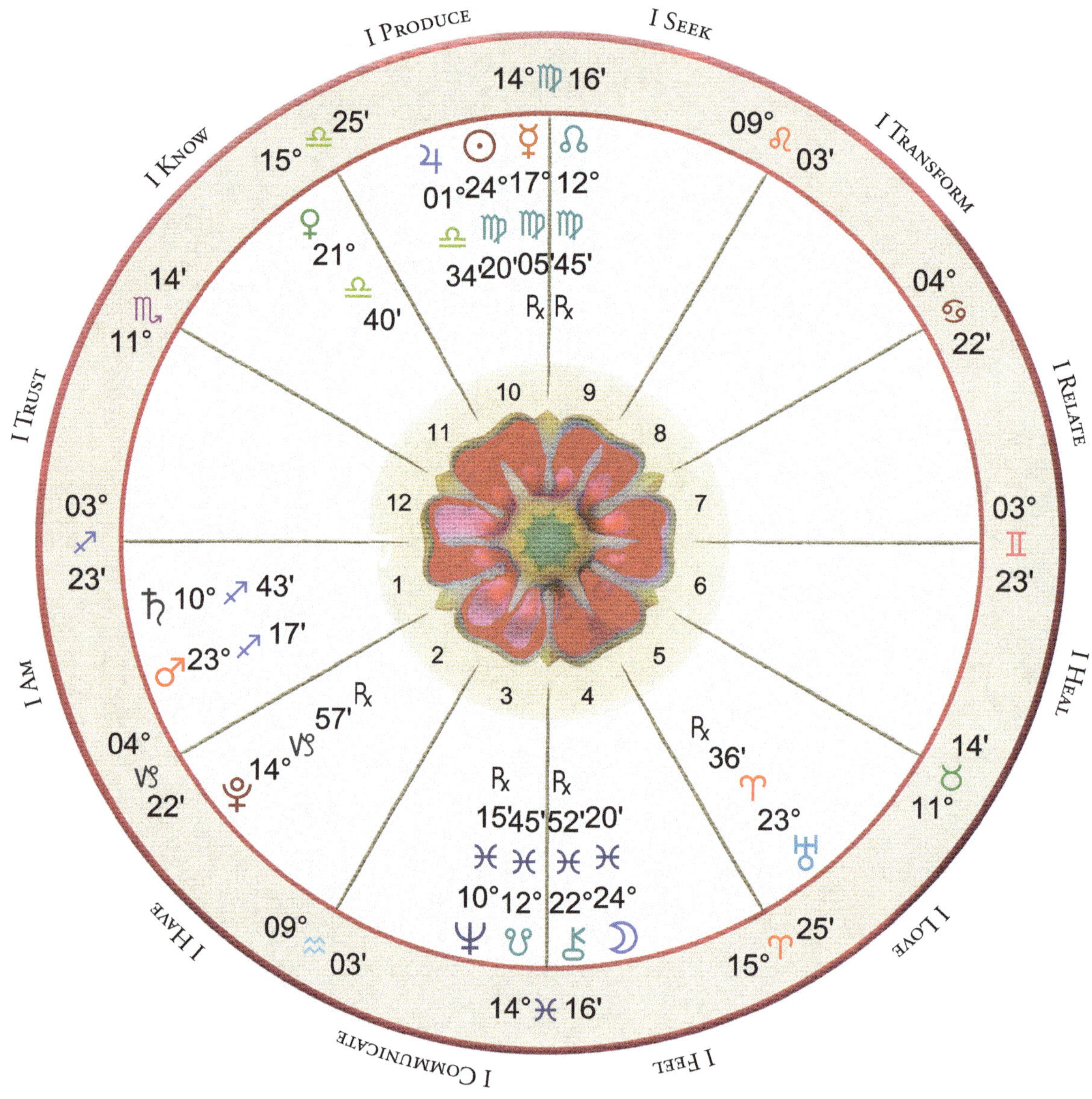

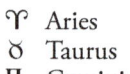

♈ Aries	♋ Cancer	♐ Sagittarius	☽ Moon	♄ Saturn	☊ North Node	V/C Void-of-Course
♉ Taurus	♌ Leo	♑ Capricorn	☿ Mercury	♅ Uranus	☋ South Node	▲ Super-Sensitivity
♊ Gemini	♍ Virgo	♒ Aquarius	♀ Venus	♆ Neptune	➔ Enters	▼ Low-Vitality
	♎ Libra	♓ Pisces	♂ Mars	♇ Pluto	℞ Retrograde	
	♏ Scorpio	☉ Sun	♃ Jupiter	⚷ Chiron	S/D Stationary Direct	

Cosmic Check-In

Take a moment to write a brief phrase for each "I" statement.
This activates all areas of your life for this creative cycle.

♓ I Trust

♈ I Am

♉ I Have

♊ I Communicate

♋ I Feel

♌ I Love

♍ I Heal

♎ I Relate

♏ I Transform

♐ I Seek

♑ I Produce

♒ I Know

September 30th
5:11 PM

New Moon in Libra

When the Sun is in Libra

Libra energy gives us the opportunity to bridge the gap between the higher and lower mind; abstract thinking versus concrete thinking. During Libra time, the light and dark forces are in balance and you are given a chance to experience harmony. Harmony occurs when you keep your polarities in motion and put paradox to rest, thus breaking the crystallization of polarity.

Now is the time to weigh your values through the light of your Soul. Libra asks you to look at what is increasing and decreasing in your life. Start with friendship, courage, sincerity, and understanding, and keep going until your scale is in motion.

Libra Goddess

The Black Madonna, is a goddess archetype found all over the world, in her many associations as Isis, Mary Magdalene, Sara, Kali, or Virgin of Guadalupe. She offers up compassion and understanding for the human condition. Black is all colors, completely absorbed, and in her blackness she encompasses all and gives solace and miracles to any seeking comfort. Often depicted with a child in arms, a halo or ring of stars around her head, and a moon at her feet, the Black Madonna is the protectress of those who are marginalized. She is connected seamlessly to Heaven and Earth, as a fully incarnated woman and mother who has known deep sorrow, passion, joy, and love.

Grant her real life experience equal weight with the images of virginal perfection offered up as ideal, and she will help you have compassion for yourself and others experiencing the struggle of living and relating.

Build Your Altar

Colors Pink, green

Numerology 7 – Accept limitation and transcend it

Tarot Card Justice – The Law of Cause and Effect

Gemstones Jade, rose quartz

Plant Remedy Olive trees – Stamina

Fragrance Eucalyptus – Clarity of breath

Degree Choice Points
8° Libra 14'

Light Symmetry

Shadow Severity

Wisdom Use alternative forms of communication to develop confidence.

Statement I Relate
  Body Kidneys
  Mind Social
  Spirit Peace

Element
Air – Promotes curiosity, insights, perspectives, bridges the mundane to the Divine.

Seventh House Moon
8° Virgo 47'

Seventh House Umbrella Theme
I Relate/I Heal – One-on-one relationships, defines your people attraction, and how you work in relationships with the people you attract.

Light Mind Expansion

Shadow Agitation

Wisdom Envision a diversity of beings and realms.

Manifesting List

This or something better than this comes to me in an easy and pleasurable way, for the good of all concerned. Thank you, Universe!

Libra Manifesting Ideas

Now is the time to focus on manifesting relationships, wholeness, being loving, lovable, and loved, living life as an art form, balance and equality, integrity, accuracy, diplomacy, and peace.

September 30th
5:11 PM

New Moon in Libra

Libra Challenges and Victories

Say all of the statements in this section out loud. Then, underline the phrase that means the most to you. Use the phrase as your special affirmation for manifesting throughout this phase of the moon.

I feel the call of the higher worlds awakening me to a new vibration. This call is to move beyond judgment and move to a place of acceptance, understanding, unconditional confidence, and love. I am at a place in my life where I can embrace the world of acceptance and wholeness, because I have birthed myself anew, beyond the imprisonment and crystallization of polarity and righteousness. My black and white worlds of right and wrong have integrated and blended into gray, the color of wisdom, where true knowledge exists. Knowledge simply is, and the need for proof does not exist where wisdom lives.

The only requirement is experience. I know that everything that comes before me is a direct reflection of my own experience and, in embracing this concept, I can now receive the gift of infinite awareness. I am in a place of awareness that came before and goes beyond where good and evil exist. I have within me, the presence of unconditional confidence to go where true love lives. I no longer need to prove myself.

I am now simply being myself. I release the need to be right and accept the right to BE. I no longer need to be forgiven, because I am neither wrong nor right. I no longer need to define myself. Acceptance has no reason for defense. I no longer need to be guilty; duty motivation is no longer a reality. I know that where there is judgment, there is separation. I know understanding unifies. I accept the call of the higher worlds and express myself freely and fully without fear of judgment. I accept myself as I am, so I can learn what I can become.

Libra Homework

Libras manifest best through the legal industry, beauty industry, diplomatic service, match-making, urban development, mediation, feng shui, spa ownership, clutter-busting and space clearing, romance writing, wedding consulting, fashion design, and as librarians.

It is time to weigh and measure the values of relationship, friendship, courage, sensitivity, sincerity, and understanding. Look at what is increasing and what is decreasing in these areas.

Without Acknowledgment Progress Cannot Occur

Acknowledgement creates space for victory and gratitude, which automatically brings you to a level of completion so a new cycle of opportunity can occur in your life. When you celebrate your wins and acknowledge your victories with gratitude, you update your cells so that your ability to move forward is not hindered by a cellular holographic pattern that is stuck in the past. Cellular lag creates resistance and makes moving forward most difficult. The key is to stay continuously updated by acknowledging yourself for what you did do at the end of each day, rather than heading off to sleep thinking about what you did not do. By acknowledging what you did not do, you play into your karmic storage bank and keep your progress at bay. When you acknowledge yourself and your manifestations you are complete, and more cycles of opportunity become available to you in each new day. Be prepared for miracles!

Victory List

When a creation result is acknowledged it seals the deal. This makes room for more magnificence to expand into your life and increases your abundance factor adding to your ability to receive. As each aspect of your manifesting list arrives in your life, spend time allowing, acknowledging, and accepting it with the true gusto of gratitude! Keep your victory list active here.

Gratitude List

This fulfills the relationship between the giver and the receiver, which completes the cycle with the Universe so that a new beginning can be established.

September 30th
5:11 PM

New Moon in Libra

How to Use the Moon Book With Your Chart

Fill in the blanks on the Cosmic Check-In page. Then look up the degree of the Moon on the chart below. Take note of the "I" statement on the outside of the wheel where the Moon is located. Now, locate the same degree on your own chart and make a note of the house and corresponding "I" statement. Go back to the Cosmic Check-In page and circle the two statements from the charts and read what you wrote. This will give you an idea about what to expect from this moon phase on a personal level.

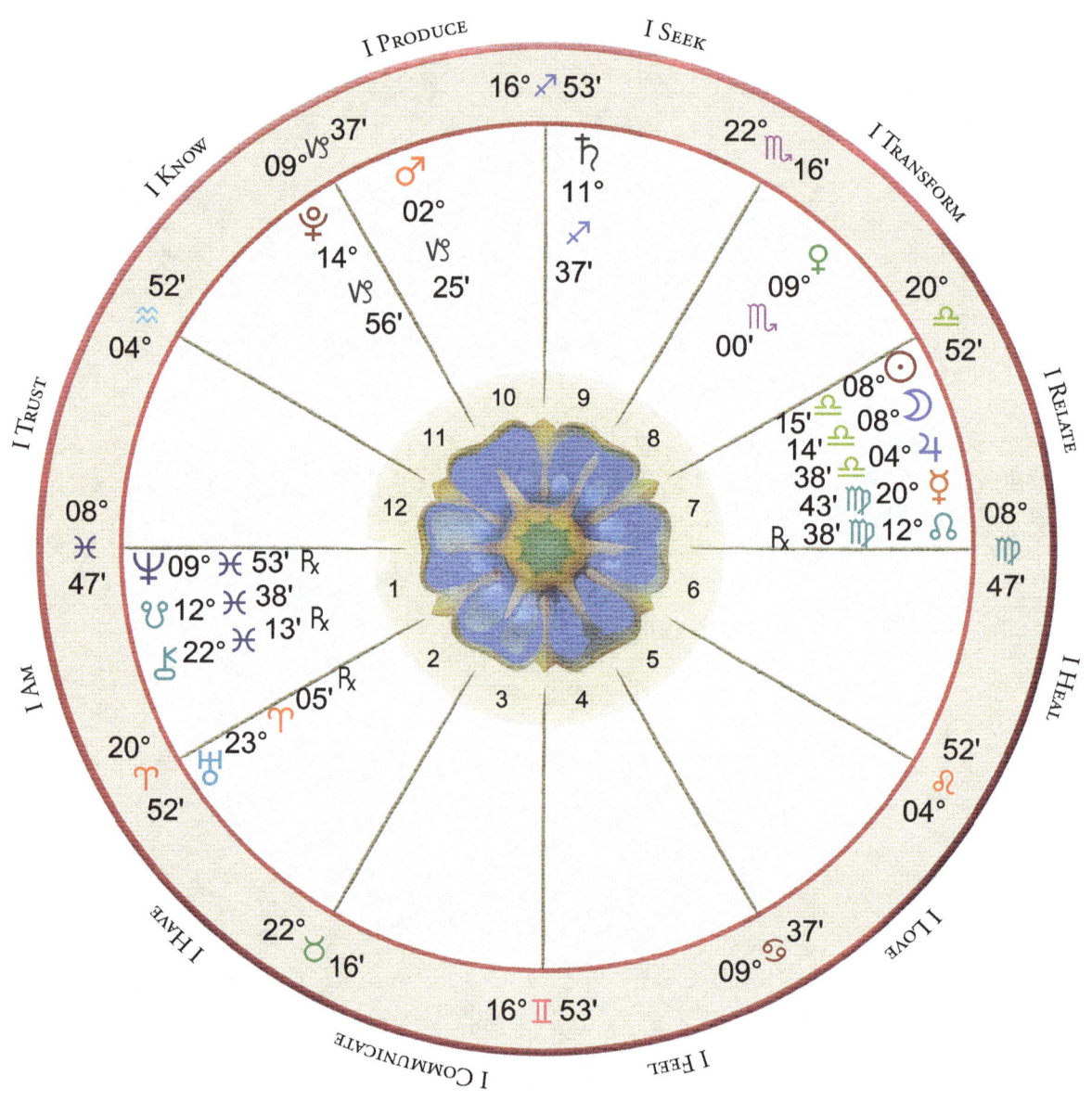

♈ Aries	♋ Cancer	♐ Sagittarius	☽ Moon	♄ Saturn	☊ North Node	V/C Void-of-Course
♉ Taurus	♌ Leo	♑ Capricorn	☿ Mercury	♅ Uranus	☋ South Node	▲ Super-Sensitivity
♊ Gemini	♍ Virgo	♒ Aquarius	♀ Venus	♆ Neptune	➔ Enters	• Low-Vitality
	♎ Libra	♓ Pisces	♂ Mars	♇ Pluto	℞ Retrograde	
	♏ Scorpio		☉ Sun	⚷ Chiron	S/D Stationary Direct	

Cosmic Check-In

Take a moment to write a brief phrase for each "I" statement.
This activates all areas of your life for this creative cycle.

♎ I Relate

♏ I Transform

♐ I Seek

♑ I Produce

♒ I Know

♓ I Trust

♈ I Am

♉ I Have

♊ I Communicate

♋ I Feel

♌ I Love

♍ I Heal

October Planetary Highlights

Uranus is Retrograde in Aries Until the End of the Year

This is an important time to get clear on all that is new about you.

Neptune is Retrograde in Pisces Until November 19

By now you have made a clear connection with your unified field of influence and are gathering up steam by presenting a spiritual platform that is very inspiring.

October 7 – Mercury Enters Libra

Expect conversations to be very uplifting. You will know the perfect wording to get your message out.

October 18 – Venus Enters Sagittarius

Celebrate a great feeling of adventure. Your social life will be quite active and may include travel.

October 22 – The Sun Enters Scorpio

It's time to keep your focus intact. Set the stage for healing on a very deep level.

October 24 – Mercury Enters Scorpio

Expect a deep sense of self to come to the surface to set yourself free. Research is in order and will come to you with ease and grace right now.

October 16 – Moon Conjunct with Uranus in Aries

Yikes! This could be quite an explosive time, especially in the woman's world. Break through old stereotypes and family paradigms will transform. Be willing to accept the change and things will run smoothly – resistance could be hell!

October 16 – The Sun Opposes Uranus

More Yikes!! Dormant potential comes alive and is activated. If acceptance happens, you and many others will be rewarded. Follow the light – it knows where to go.

October 16 – Mars and Pluto Conjunct in Capricorn

Expect to revise your financial arena. New paradigms will arise. Follow the action and know that we have been waiting for this.

October 30 – Venus and Saturn Conjunct in Sagittarius

It's time to get acquainted with being practical again. This is a very short transit, so it won't be that bad.

Super-Sensitivity – October 6-7

Avoid chaos!!

Low-Vitality – October 19-20

Get rest.

Sunday	Monday	Tuesday	Wednesday	Thursday	Friday	Saturday
						1 ♅♆℞ ☽ V/C 10:42pm 8. Love what you do, do what you love.
2 ♅♆℞ Rosh Hashana ☽→♏ 12:42pm 9. Forgiveness starts with self.	3 ♅♆℞ 10. With reflection, the past is clearer.	4 ♅♆℞ ☽ V/C 6:04pm 2. Temper action with balance.	5 ♅♆℞ ☽→♐ 1:26am 3. The peacemaker respects all life.	6 ♅♆℞▲ ☽ V/C 11:25pm 4. A team player diminishes ego.	7 ♅♆℞▲ ☿→♎ 12:57am ☽→♑ 1:39pm 5. Growth exists within friction.	8 ♅♆℞ 6. Flowers are always an appropriate gift.
9 ♅♆℞ ☽ V/C 9:50am ☽→♒ 11:32pm 7. Judge not and pray for everyone.	10 ♅♆℞ Columbus Day 8. Your desire is achievable.	11 ♅♆℞ Yom Kippur ☽ V/C 4:48pm 9. You are part of the light creation.	12 ♅♆℞ ☽→♓ 5:42am 10. Our future starts today.	13 ♅♆℞ 2. Make your decision from the heart.	14 ♅♆℞ ☽ V/C 12:13am ☽→♈ 8:08am 3. Live, love, and laugh joyfully.	15 ♅♆℞ ☽ V/C 9:23pm ○ 23°♈14° 9:24pm 4. Generosity is practical in nature.
16 ♅♆℞ ☽→♉ 8:04am 5. Change is the evolution of life.	17 ♅♆℞ ☽ V/C 7:46am 6. Surprise someone with a dinner party.	18 ♅♆℞ ♀→♐ 12:02am ☽→♊ 7:29am 7. Exploratory research can be fun.	19 ♅♆℞▼ 8. Celebrate someone's success.	20 ♅♆℞▼ ☽ V/C 4:16am ☽→♋ 8:28am 10. One door closes and another opens.	21 ♅♆℞ 2. Balance and order create harmony.	22 ♅♆℞ ☉→♏ 4:47pm ☽ V/C 12:13pm ☽→♌ 12:33pm 3. Combating fear adds value to life.
23 ♅♆℞ 4. Standing firm promotes growth.	24 ♅♆℞ ☿→♏ 1:47pm ☽ V/C 5:20am ☽→♍ 8:16pm 5. Welcome change as a blessing.	25 ♅♆℞ 6. Beauty exists in the polarity.	26 ♅♆℞ ☽ V/C11:32am 7. An error can be a new beginning	27 ♅♆℞ ☽→♎ 6:50am 8. Generosity speaks to abundance in life.	28 ♅♆℞ 9. Prayer makes all the difference.	29 ♅♆℞ ☽ V/C 3:09am ☽→♏ 7:00pm 10. If it's finished, let it go.
30 ♅♆℞ ● 7°♏44′ 10:39am 11. The possibilities are endless.	31 ♅♆℞ Halloween ☽ V/C 7:43pm 3. The first creation is a new birth.					

♈ Aries	♎ Libra	☉ Sun	♄ Saturn	☊ North Node	▲ Super Sensitivity	6. Love
♉ Taurus	♏ Scorpio	☽ Moon	♅ Uranus	☋ South Node	▼ Low Vitality	7. Learning
♊ Gemini	♐ Sagittarius	☿ Mercury	♆ Neptune	➡ Enters	2. Balance	8. Money
♋ Cancer	♑ Capricorn	♀ Venus	♇ Pluto	℞ Retrograde	3. Fun	9. Spirituality
♌ Leo	♒ Aquarius	♂ Mars	⚷ Chiron	SD Stationary Direct	4. Structure	10. Visionary
♍ Virgo	♓ Pisces	♃ Jupiter		V/C Void-of-Course	5. Action	11. Completion

October 15th
9:24 PM

Full Moon in Aries

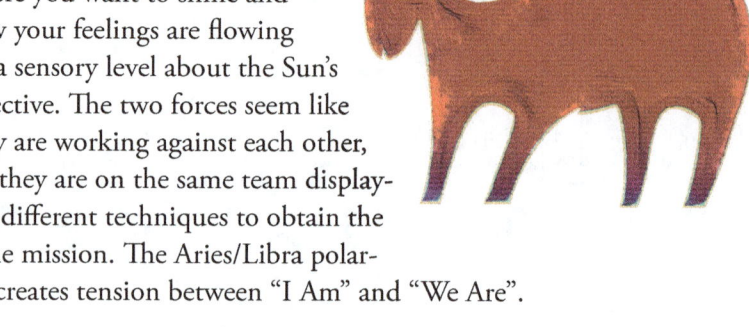

Degree Choice Points
23° Aries 14'

Light Abundant Opportunities

Shadow Pettiness

Wisdom You've been heard, there's no need to repeat yourself.

Statement I Am
  Body Head and Face
  Mind Ego
  Spirit Awakening

Element
  Fire – Inspiration, action, initiation, passion, enthusiasm, the Divine Masculine – "It's my way or the highway!"

Eleventh House Moon
  4° Aries 46'

Eleventh House Umbrella Theme
  I know/I am - Your approach to friends, social consciousness, teamwork, community service, and the future.

Light Self-transcendence

Shadow Obliviousness

Wisdom Learn through osmosis from extra-planetary intelligence.

The Sun is Opposite the Moon

Full moons are always in opposition to the Sun. This creates a feeling of tension between where you want to shine and how your feelings are flowing on a sensory level about the Sun's directive. The two forces seem like they are working against each other, yet they are on the same team displaying different techniques to obtain the same mission. The Aries/Libra polarity creates tension between "I Am" and "We Are".

Aries Goddess

Heqet, the Fertility Goddess of the early dynastic period of Egypt, is often depicted on the amulets of pregnant women as a frog sitting on a lotus. Associated with germination of corn following the flooding of the Nile (when frogs were most prolific), and with the final stages of childbirth, she is said to breathe the "breath of life" into the bodies of newborn children who are formed on the potter's wheel of her partner Khnum. It was she who breathed life into Horus, in the myth of Isis and Osiris.

The moonlight is now shining on you as you take your self-confidence and self-awareness to a new level. Is it time for you to take on a new role within your community? Have you developed new knowledge, skills, and qualities that you're ready to try out? Ask Heqet to assist you through the stages from tadpole to adult, as you lose your tail and develop your sea legs.

Build Your Altar

Colors Red, black, coral

Numerology 4 – Generosity is practical in nature

Tarot Card Tower – Release from a stuck place, a major breakthrough

Gemstones Diamond, red jasper, coral, obsidian

Plant remedy Oak, pomegranate – Planting new life and rooting new life

Fragrance Ginger – The ability to ingest and digest life

Clearing the Slate

Remember a time when you experienced the following trigger points.
Write down what happened and perform Ho'oponopono, the Hawaiian forgiveness ritual.

Anger

- I'm Sorry
- Please Forgive Me
- Thank You
- I Love You

The Need to Be First

- I'm Sorry
- Please Forgive Me
- Thank You
- I Love You

Arrogance

- I'm Sorry
- Please Forgive Me
- Thank You
- I Love You

Impatient

- I'm Sorry
- Please Forgive Me
- Thank You
- I Love You

Forceful

- I'm Sorry
- Please Forgive Me
- Thank You
- I Love You

October 15th
9:24 PM

Full Moon in Aries

Aries Challenges and Victories

Say all of the statements in this section out loud. Then, underline the phrase that means the most to you. Use the phrase as your special affirmation for recalibrating throughout this phase of the moon.

Today, I let go. I trust that whatever breaks down or breaks through is a blessing in disguise for me. I make a commitment to allow myself to be spontaneous and live in the moment. I know the unexpected is a blessing for me and a way for me to make a breakthrough out of my limitations. I am aware that I am resistant to change. I know I must make changes and am too stubborn to take the appropriate action myself to change. I have built many walls of false protection around me, guarding me and blocking me from the reality that change is a constant. I have freeze-framed my life and desire support to update myself. I have allowed my fear of change to become my false motto and my life is at a standstill. I am unwilling to use any more energy to perpetuate my resistance. I know that continuing to cling to the past is a waste of my energy. I can no longer put things off that delay my process. I feel the breaking down of form. I trust that all changes are in my favor. All changes lead me to golden opportunities. I release false pride. I release false foundations. I release false authorities. In so doing, I allow for everything to crumble around me so I can see that my true strength is within and I will build my life from the inside out.

I am ready for new experiences. I am ready for the unexpected. I am willing to have an event occur so I can become activated towards my breakthrough. I am ready for the power of now. I know being spontaneous will bring me to true joy. I know if I ride this carrier wave it will take me to a place far beyond my scope of limited thinking. I know the will of God works in my favor and knows more than I do in any given moment.

Aries Homework

Now you are ready to take a personal inventory on behaviors such as impatience, talking over people, brat attacks, and starting every sentence with "I."

This is a time when the light becomes a prisoner of polarized forces. This diminishing light begins its yearly sojourn beneath the surface, asking us to balance light and dark by mastering the concept of equilibrium. Equilibrium is the Law of Harmony, where we attempt to reach a state of achievement by combining paradoxical fields that break the crystallization of polarity. Spend time looking for increasing and decreasing fields of light around you.

Recalibrating List

Say this statement out loud three times before writing your recalibrating list!

I am a free spiritual being and it is my desire to be free to think and to express myself fully.

From this day forward I resolve to be true – first to myself and my highest self, and then to the highest self in me which is the Source of Love That I Am.

Aries Recalibrating Ideas

Now is the time to activate a game change in my life, and give up anger as a default, competition and comparison, irritation and struggle, the need to be first, overdoing it and not resting, impatience, impulsiveness, and hostility.

October 15th
9:24 PM

Full Moon in Aries

How to Use the Moon Book With Your Chart

Fill in the blanks on the Cosmic Check-In page. Then look up the degree of the Moon on the chart below. Take note of the "I" statement on the outside of the wheel where the Moon is located. Now, locate the same degree on your own chart and make a note of the house and corresponding "I" statement. Go back to the Cosmic Check-In page and circle the two statements from the charts and read what you wrote. This will give you an idea about what to expect from this moon phase on a personal level.

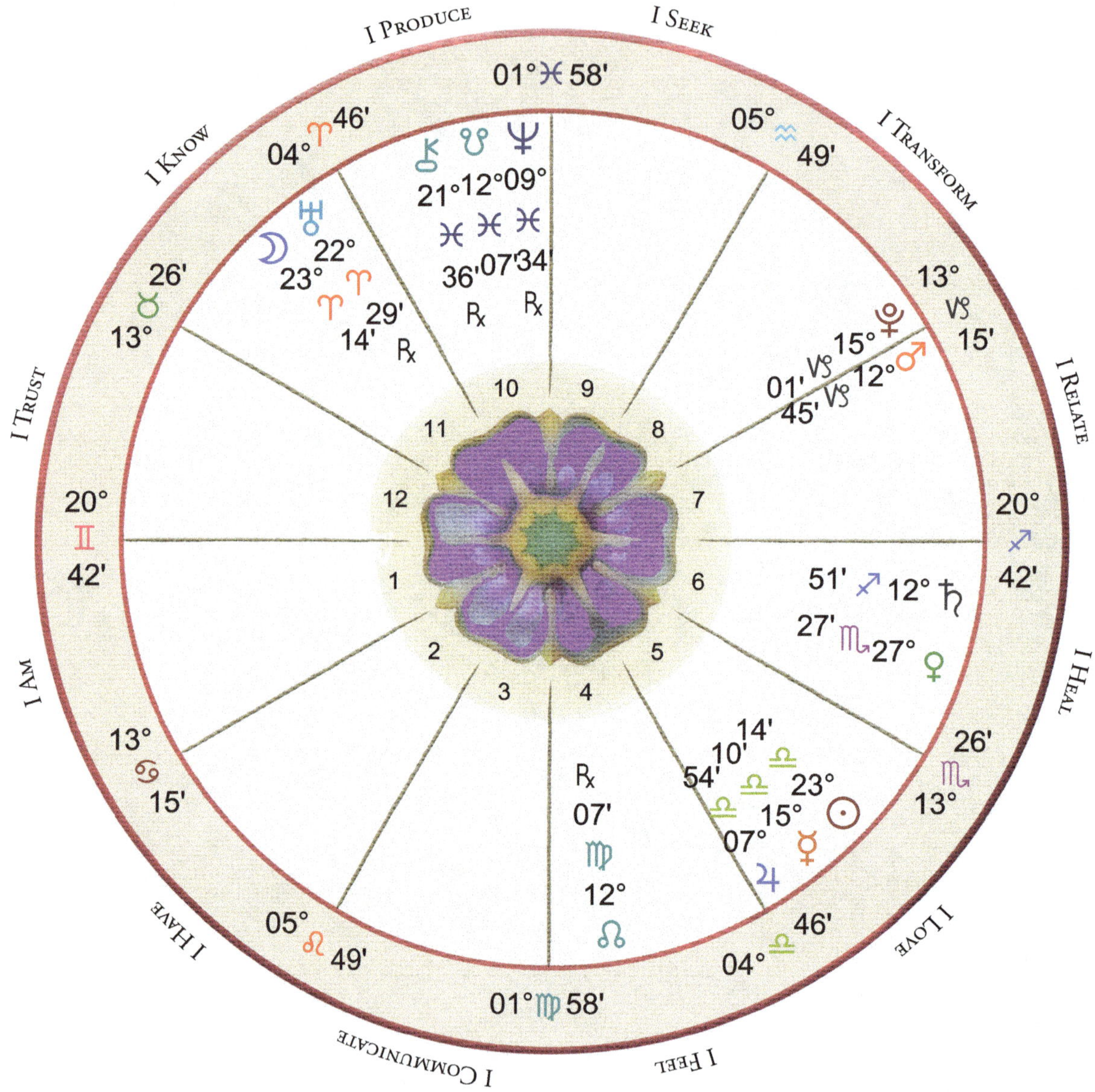

♈ Aries	♋ Cancer	♐ Sagittarius	☽ Moon	♄ Saturn	☊ North Node	V/C Void-of-Course
♉ Taurus	♌ Leo	♑ Capricorn	☿ Mercury	♅ Uranus	☋ South Node	▲ Super-Sensitivity
♊ Gemini	♍ Virgo	♒ Aquarius	♀ Venus	♆ Neptune	➡ Enters	▼ Low-Vitality
♎ Libra	♓ Pisces	♂ Mars	♇ Pluto	℞ Retrograde		
♏ Scorpio	☉ Sun	♃ Jupiter	⚷ Chiron	S/D Stationary Direct		

Cosmic Check-In

Take a moment to write a brief phrase for each "I" statement.
This activates all areas of your life for this creative cycle.

♈ I Am

♉ I Have

♊ I Communicate

♋ I Feel

♌ I Love

♍ I Heal

♎ I Relate

♏ I Transform

♐ I Seek

♑ I Produce

♒ I Know

♓ I Trust

October 30th
10:39 AM

New Moon in Scorpio

Degree Choice Points
7° Scorpio 44'

Light   Willingness to Dive Deep

Shadow   Getting Off-track

Wisdom   Prepare and purify a space – adjust your attitude in order to manifest a dream.

Statement   I Transform
    Body   Reproductive Organs
    Mind   Investigation
    Spirit   Transformation

Element
Water – Intense, passionate, sexual, powerful, focused, controlling, deep, driven, and secretive.

Eleventh House Moon
6° Scorpio 14'

Eleventh House Umbrella Theme
I Know/I Transform – Your approach to friends, social consciousness, teamwork, community service, and the future.

Light   Profound Insights

Shadow   Isolation

Wisdom   Change your vision to change your reality.

Karmic Awakening

Leo/Aquarius – Restriction occurs when devotion is not available on an intimate level due to distractions happening in the outer world.

Karmic stress will appear when attention is going to the group rather than to your loved one. This can bring about an imbalance of choices between a mystical vision and obvious beneficial choices.

When the Sun is in Scorpio

Scorpio is the symbol of darkness which heralds the decline of the Sun in Autumn. Scorpio embodies the Law of Nature, which decrees that even the strongest will must bow to the body's mortality. As we watch all of nature going through a slow death, we begin to recognize the qualities of Scorpio's subtlety and depth, and the hidden forces that threaten those who live only on the surface. Scorpio rules all of the things that you try to keep hidden: death, taxes, power, money, sex, resentment, revenge, ambition, pride, and fear. When you face these self-imposed limits on yourself, you take on the true power of transformation. Transformation establishes pathways for you to decentralize the ego in the interest of higher humanitarian work.

Scorpio Goddess

Scorpio moons ask you to delve deep into your Soul. There's no better companion in this process than Inanna, who journeyed to the Underworld and relinquished her power and possessions, one-at-a-time at each of seven gates, until she was stripped bare to her essential self, without any trappings or embellishments.

Ask your soul sister Inanna to accompany you in a candle-lit meditation to release that which you no longer need to carry in each of your seven chakras. Let go of anything encumbering your essential self, anything weighing you down. Connect with the dark, cool Earth and tune into anything that you feel like you've put behind you, but might not have completely released. Allow Inanna to empty your backpack and lighten your load, so you can rise and be reborn anew.

Build Your Altar

Colors   Deep red, black, deep purple

Numerology   11 – The possibilities are endless

Tarot Card   Death – The ability to transform, transmute, and transcend

Gemstones   Topaz, smoky quartz, obsidian, jet, onyx

Plant Remedy   Manzanita – Being open to transforming cycles

Fragrance   Sandalwood – Awakens your sensuality

Manifesting List

This or something better than this comes to me in an easy and pleasurable way, for the good of all concerned. Thank you, Universe!

Scorpio Manifesting Ideas

Now is the time to focus on manifesting transformation on all levels, bringing light to the dark, knowing and living cycles, knowing trust as an option, accepting change, accepting my sexuality, knowing sex is natural, knowing sex as good, and knowing sex as creative.

October 30th
10:39 AM

New Moon in Scorpio

Scorpio Challenges and Victories

Say all of the statements in this section out loud. Then, underline the phrase that means the most to you. Use the phrase as your special affirmation for manifesting throughout this phase of the moon.

"When the student needs to learn, the teacher appears." Today, I recognize that the Law of Reflection is in operation. I have become aware of this through my over-indulgence of judgment and criticism of other people. I am aware that when my judgment is running rampant, I am in need of a teacher who can interpret this judgment as reflection, so I can see my judgments as my teachers and use them to re-interpret myself. I seek counsel with someone who has the ability to listen to me, hear me, and give me the space I need to see myself. I have become confused by spending too much time looking outside of myself for the answers. Perhaps my authority systems, like my religion or my family traditions, no longer serve me and I need to use this confusion to become aware of a new, more self-reliant way to live my life.

The Law of Reflection

Whatever I judge is what I am, what I fear, or what I lack. I make a list of my judgments:

I rewrite each judgment in the form of a question:
Am I _____? Do I fear _____? Do I lack _____?

Example 1: I judge Mary's wealth. Do I fear wealth? Do I lack wealth? Am I wealthy in my own way and forgetting to acknowledge my own ability to manifest?

Example 2: I judge John's "be perfect" attitude. Do I fear perfection? Do I lack perfection? Have I forgotten to recognize my own perfection?

In moving through this process, I reconnect to myself and find my own authority today. I send blessings to others whose reflection has so beautifully shown me myself today. I now know and cherish my judgments as my greatest teachers and set myself free today.

Scorpio Homework

Scorpios manifest best by being a private investigator, detective, probate attorney, mystery writer, mythologist, Tarot reader, symbolist, hospice worker, transition counselor, mortician, sex surrogate, or in forensic medicine.

The Scorpio moon cycle asks you to transform. In order to do this you must transmute sex drive into creativity, physical comfort into serving the greater good, money into higher value, fear into light, animosity into understanding, ambition into service to beauty, pride into humility, separation into unity, control into harmony, and power into empowerment.

Without Acknowledgment Progress Cannot Occur

Acknowledgement creates space for victory and gratitude, which automatically brings you to a level of completion so a new cycle of opportunity can occur in your life. When you celebrate your wins and acknowledge your victories with gratitude, you update your cells so that your ability to move forward is not hindered by a cellular holographic pattern that is stuck in the past. Cellular lag creates resistance and makes moving forward most difficult. The key is to stay continuously updated by acknowledging yourself for what you did do at the end of each day, rather than heading off to sleep thinking about what you did not do. By acknowledging what you did not do, you play into your karmic storage bank and keep your progress at bay. When you acknowledge yourself and your manifestations you are complete, and more cycles of opportunity become available to you in each new day. Be prepared for miracles!

Victory List

When a creation result is acknowledged it seals the deal. This makes room for more magnificence to expand into your life and increases your abundance factor adding to your ability to receive. As each aspect of your manifesting list arrives in your life, spend time allowing, acknowledging, and accepting it with the true gusto of gratitude! Keep your victory list active here.

Gratitude List

This fulfills the relationship between the giver and the receiver, which completes the cycle with the Universe so that a new beginning can be established.

October 30th
10:39 AM

New Moon in Scorpio

How to Use the Moon Book With Your Chart

Fill in the blanks on the Cosmic Check-In page. Then look up the degree of the Moon on the chart below. Take note of the "I" statement on the outside of the wheel where the Moon is located. Now, locate the same degree on your own chart and make a note of the house and corresponding "I" statement. Go back to the Cosmic Check-In page and circle the two statements from the charts and read what you wrote. This will give you an idea about what to expect from this moon phase on a personal level.

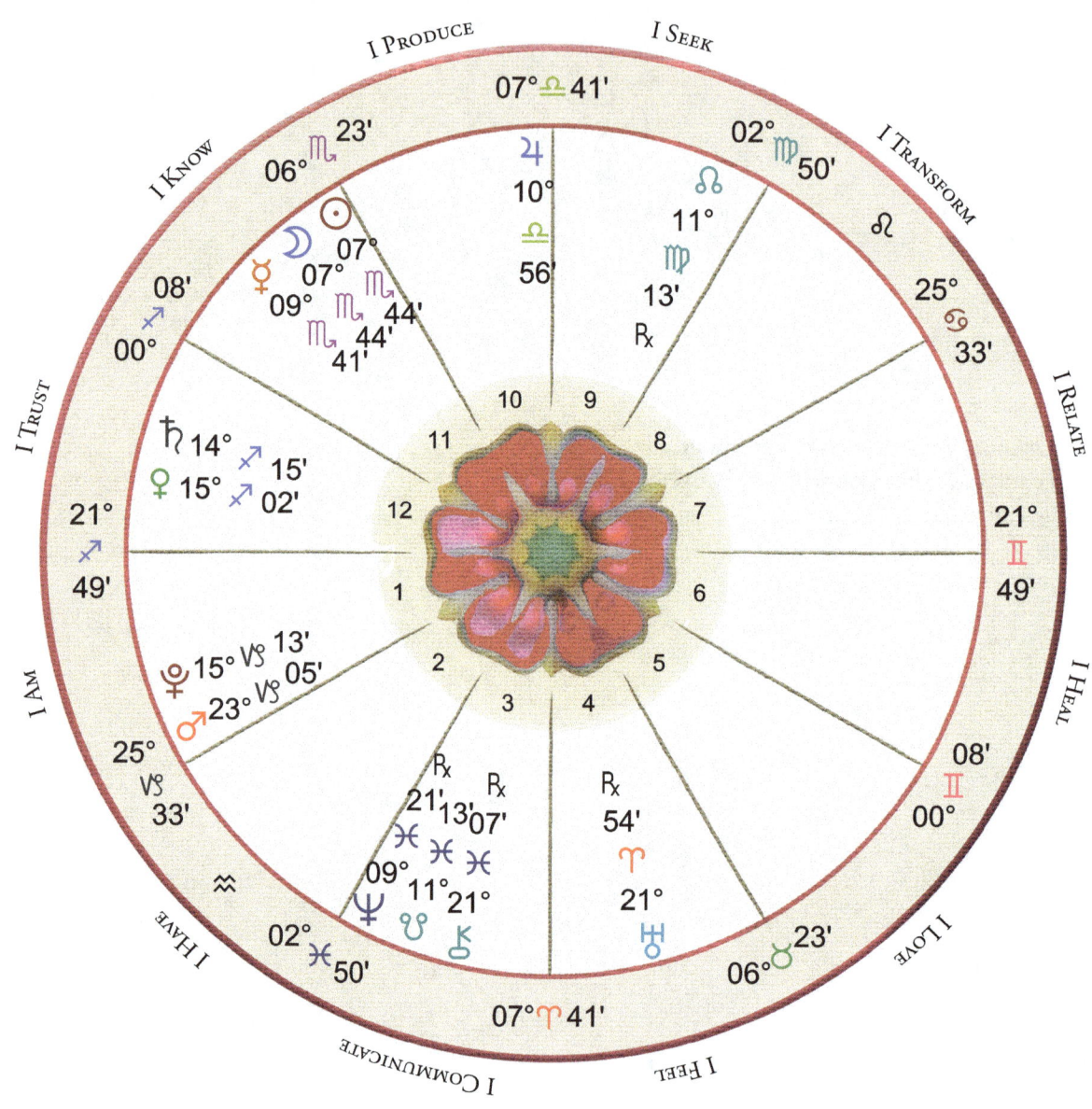

♈ Aries	♋ Cancer	♐ Sagittarius	☽ Moon	♄ Saturn	☊ North Node	V/C Void-of-Course
♉ Taurus	♌ Leo	♑ Capricorn	☿ Mercury	♅ Uranus	☋ South Node	▲ Super-Sensitivity
♊ Gemini	♍ Virgo	♒ Aquarius	♀ Venus	♆ Neptune	➡ Enters	• Low-Vitality
	♎ Libra	♓ Pisces	♂ Mars	♇ Pluto	℞ Retrograde	
	♏ Scorpio	☉ Sun	♃ Jupiter	⚷ Chiron	S/D Stationary Direct	

196

Cosmic Check-In

Take a moment to write a brief phrase for each "I" statement.
This activates all areas of your life for this creative cycle.

♏ I Transform

♐ I Seek

♑ I Produce

♒ I Know

♓ I Trust

♈ I Am

♉ I Have

♊ I Communicate

♋ I Feel

♌ I Love

♍ I Heal

♎ I Relate

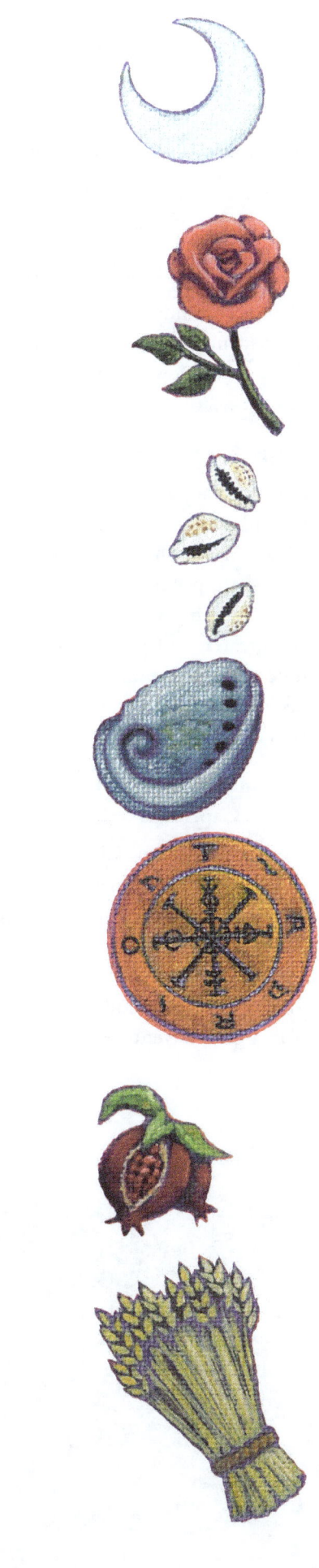

November Planetary Highlights

Neptune is Retrograde in Pisces Until November 19

Get clear around what you owe and who you owe. Now is the true test of your conscious choices regarding money.

Uranus is Retrograde in Aries Until 2017

Uranus continues to hound Aries about creating a future self beyond old illusions. Ride the dragon into the fog and blow it out of the way so you can see clearly.

November 8 – Mars Enters Aquarius

Expect an accelerated mind to take off with a multitude of ideas. Make sure you have an assistant with sharp pencils and a yellow pad – or better yet, the latest and greatest tablet computer – following you around to take notes, so that manifestation can occur.

November 11 – Venus Enters Capricorn

It's time to face the "old man," so that the lessons of being practical can actualize without too many brat attacks.

November 12 – Mercury Enters Sagittarius

These two travel buddies come together to plan a great adventure!

November 21 – The Sun Enters Sagittarius

It's time to celebrate adventure. Be the inspiration you know you are and share what you know.

Neptune and the South Node Conjunct All Month

Really see how far you can extend your energy. Vastness is where it is right now and going for the broad stroke gives you the joy.

November 20 – Venus and Pluto Connect

Sensuality and sexuality meet……….let it be.

Uranus and Jupiter Opposing Each Other Throughout the Month

Two major egos are facing each other, looking right into each other's eyes. It's time to blend the power, not separate it, by feeling like a choice is necessary. Look carefully and ask yourself, "How can I make the best of these two power sources?"

November 29 – Saturn and Mercury Coupled

Research is in order. The best parts of your minds are joined. Use this transit wisely.

Super-Sensitivity – November 2-3, 29-30

Slow down and avoid chaos.

Low-Vitality – November 15-16

Get rest and accept endings.

Sunday	Monday	Tuesday	Wednesday	Thursday	Friday	Saturday
		1 ♅♉♆℞ All Saint's Day ☽→♐ 7:42am 4. If the parts are solid, it's easy.	**2** ♅♉♆℞▲ 5. Change the method, it's refreshing.	**3** ♅♉♆℞▲ ☽ V/C 3:34am ☽→♑ 8:05pm 6. Kindness is spiritual love in action.	**4** ♅♉♆℞ 7. Having to be right is boring.	**5** ♅♉♆℞ 8. A heart filled with love is generous.
6 ♅♉♆℞ PST ☽ V/C 1:56am ☽→♒ 5:55am 9. Compassion fills the Spirit.	**7** ♅♉♆℞ 10. The future is now. Enjoy!	**8** ♅♉♆℞ ♂→♒ 9:53pm ☽ V/C 5:54am ☽→♓ 1:45pm 11. The Universe abounds in magic.	**9** ♅♉♆℞ 3. Play time is as important as work.	**10** ♅♉♆℞ ☽ V/C 3:16pm ☽→♈ 5:44pm 4. Loyalty is a true sign of friendship.	**11** ♅♉♆℞ Veteran's Day ♀→♑ 8:55pm 5. If it's not working, change it.	**12** ♅♉♆℞ ☿→♐ 6:41am ☽ V/C 4:44am ☽→♉ 6:23pm 6. A healthy body is a happy body.
13 ♅♉♆℞ 7. Wait until asked.	**14** ♅♉♆℞ ☽ V/C 5:51am ☽→♊ 5:22pm ○ 22°♉38′ 5:53am 8. Success requires patience.	**15** ♅♉♆℞▼ 9. Acknowledge the God-Self in all.	**16** ♅♉♆℞▼ ☽ V/C 2:57am ☽→♋ 4:56pm 10. Envision a bright future.	**17** ♅♉♆℞ 11. There is an inexhaustible supply.	**18** ♅♉♆℞ ☽ V/C 2:02pm ☽→♌ 7:14pm 3. Go for a new experience.	**19** ♅♉℞ ♆S/D - 9°♓14′ 8:40pm 4. Feel the strength of the foundation.
20 ♅♉℞ 5. Change to a more appealing path.	**21** ♅♉℞ ☉→♐ 1:24pm ☽ V/C 12:33am ☽→♍ 1:33am 6. Create sustainable friendships.	**22** ♅♉℞ ☽ V/C 9:41am 7. Open to new possibilities.	**23** ♅♉℞ ☽→♎ 11:41am 8. A good manager listens.	**24** ♅♉℞ Thanksgiving Day 9. Pray for someone's good.	**25** ♅♉℞ ☽ V/C 5:52am 10. Be open to a new approach.	**26** ♅♉℞ ☽→♏ 12:01am 2. Find balance today.
27 ♅♉℞ ☽ V/C 1:47pm 3. Control stifles creativity.	**28** ♅♉℞ ☽→♐ 12:45pm 4. "Foursquare "is solid and forthright.	**29** ♅♉℞▲ ● 7°♐43′ 4:19am 5. Avoid stagnation, keep things moving.	**30** ♅♉℞▲ ☽ V/C 8:07pm 6. Not all relationships are forever.			

♈ Aries	♎ Libra	☉ Sun	♄ Saturn	☊ North Node	▲ Super Sensitivity	6. Love
♉ Taurus	♏ Scorpio	☽ Moon	♅ Uranus	☋ South Node	▼ Low Vitality	7. Learning
♊ Gemini	♐ Sagittarius	☿ Mercury	♆ Neptune	➡ Enters	2. Balance	8. Money
♋ Cancer	♑ Capricorn	♀ Venus	♇ Pluto	℞ Retrograde	3. Fun	9. Spirituality
♌ Leo	♒ Aquarius	♂ Mars	⚷ Chiron	S/D Stationary Direct	4. Structure	10. Visionary
♍ Virgo	♓ Pisces	♃ Jupiter		V/C Void-of-Course	5. Action	11. Completion

November 14th
5:53 AM

Full Moon in Taurus

Degree Choice Points
22° Taurus 38'

Light	Natural Beauty
Shadow	Superfluous
Wisdom	You are a stabilizing force.
Statement	I Have
Body	Neck
Mind	Collector
Spirit	Accumulation

Element
Earth – Self-value, abundance, aesthetics, business, sensuality, art, beauty, flowers, gardens, collector, and shopper.

Seventh House Moon
16° Taurus 30'

Seventh House Umbrella Theme
I Relate/I Have – One-on-one relationships, defines your people attraction, and how you work in relationships with the people you attract.

Light	Purpose
Shadow	Necessity versus Desire
Wisdom	Accept that others' values are genuine.

The Sun is Opposite the Moon

Full moons are always in opposition to the Sun. This creates a feeling of tension between where you want to shine and how your feelings are flowing on a sensory level about the Sun's directive. The two forces seem like they are working against each other, yet they are on the same team displaying different techniques to obtain the same mission. The Taurus/Scorpio polarity creates tension between "my" money and "our" money.

Taurus Goddess

The Roman Goddess of Abundance and Opportunity, Copia, invites you to drink deeply from her overflowing horn of plenty. As you harvest the bounties of your desires from the seeds you planted last Spring, thank Copia for the increase in your abundance factor! There is no greater prayer than the act of giving thanks.

During this Taurus moon, let receptivity and gratitude be in your attitude and actions! With open hands and heart, ask for Copia's presence at your table, and allow her to fill your cup with blessings. Encourage your gratitude to expand and generously influence all with whom you interact.

Build Your Altar

Colors Scarlet, earth tones

Numerology 8 – Success requires patience

Tarot Card Hierophant – Spiritual authority

Gemstones Red coral, red agate, garnet

Plant remedy Angelica – Connecting Heaven and Earth

Fragrance Rose – Opening the heart

Clearing the Slate

Remember a time when you experienced the following trigger points.
Write down what happened and perform Ho'oponopono, the Hawaiian forgiveness ritual.

Hoarding

- I'm Sorry
- Please Forgive Me
- Thank You
- I Love You

Stubborn

- I'm Sorry
- Please Forgive Me
- Thank You
- I Love You

Greedy

- I'm Sorry
- Please Forgive Me
- Thank You
- I Love You

Irresponsible Stewardship

- I'm Sorry
- Please Forgive Me
- Thank You
- I Love You

Wasteful

- I'm Sorry
- Please Forgive Me
- Thank You
- I Love You

November 14th
5:53 AM

Full Moon in Taurus

Taurus Challenges and Victories

Say all of the statements in this section out loud. Then, underline the phrase that means the most to you. Use the phrase as your special affirmation for recalibrating throughout this phase of the moon.

Everything is possible for me today. My possibilities are endless. I have the power within me to make all of my dreams come true. I have the tools to make my talent a reality. I have the power to identify with my talent. Today, I focus my attention and intention on manifesting with my talent and, in so doing, I transform my ideas into reality. I recognize the part of me that is connected to the cosmic source of ideas, and I express that source within me to manifest my creative power. I see my possibilities and act on them today. I am the creative power. I am all-knowing. I am an individual. There is no one else like me. I can manifest anything I desire. I intend it. I allow it. So be it.

Rules for Manifesting … know what you want, write it down, and say it out loud. Recognize that because you thought it, it can be so. Release your limiting beliefs. Override your limiting beliefs with power statements. Act as if you have already manifested your idea. Lastly, value yourself!

Taurus Homework

Newsflash for the Taurus recalibrating process … consumerism is not practicing abundance. Take a look at what you have accumulated over the last few days, months, and years. Eliminate what no longer resonates to the beauty of the now. Take some of these items to a charity of your choice or give gifts to admiring friends. Take the Taurus recalibration test and go to the store where you made your last purchase and return the items. Do not buy anything else. Remember, quality not quantity, and take the pledge to become a wise steward of your resources.

It's time to transform priorities from the external world of the centralized self, into the depth and subtlety of the hidden forces below the surface that connect us to the vastness of existence.

Recalibrating List

Say this statement out loud three times before writing your recalibrating list!

I am a free spiritual being and it is my desire to be free to think and to express myself fully.

From this day forward I resolve to be true – first to myself and my highest self, and then to the highest self in me which is the Source of Love That I Am.

Taurus Recalibrating Ideas

Now is the time to activate a game change in my life, and give up envy, financial insecurity, being stubborn, hoarding, addictive spending, not feeling valuable, and fear of change.

November 14th
5:53 AM

Full Moon in Taurus

How to Use the Moon Book With Your Chart

Fill in the blanks on the Cosmic Check-In page. Then look up the degree of the Moon on the chart below. Take note of the "I" statement on the outside of the wheel where the Moon is located. Now, locate the same degree on your own chart and make a note of the house and corresponding "I" statement. Go back to the Cosmic Check-In page and circle the two statements from the charts and read what you wrote. This will give you an idea about what to expect from this moon phase on a personal level.

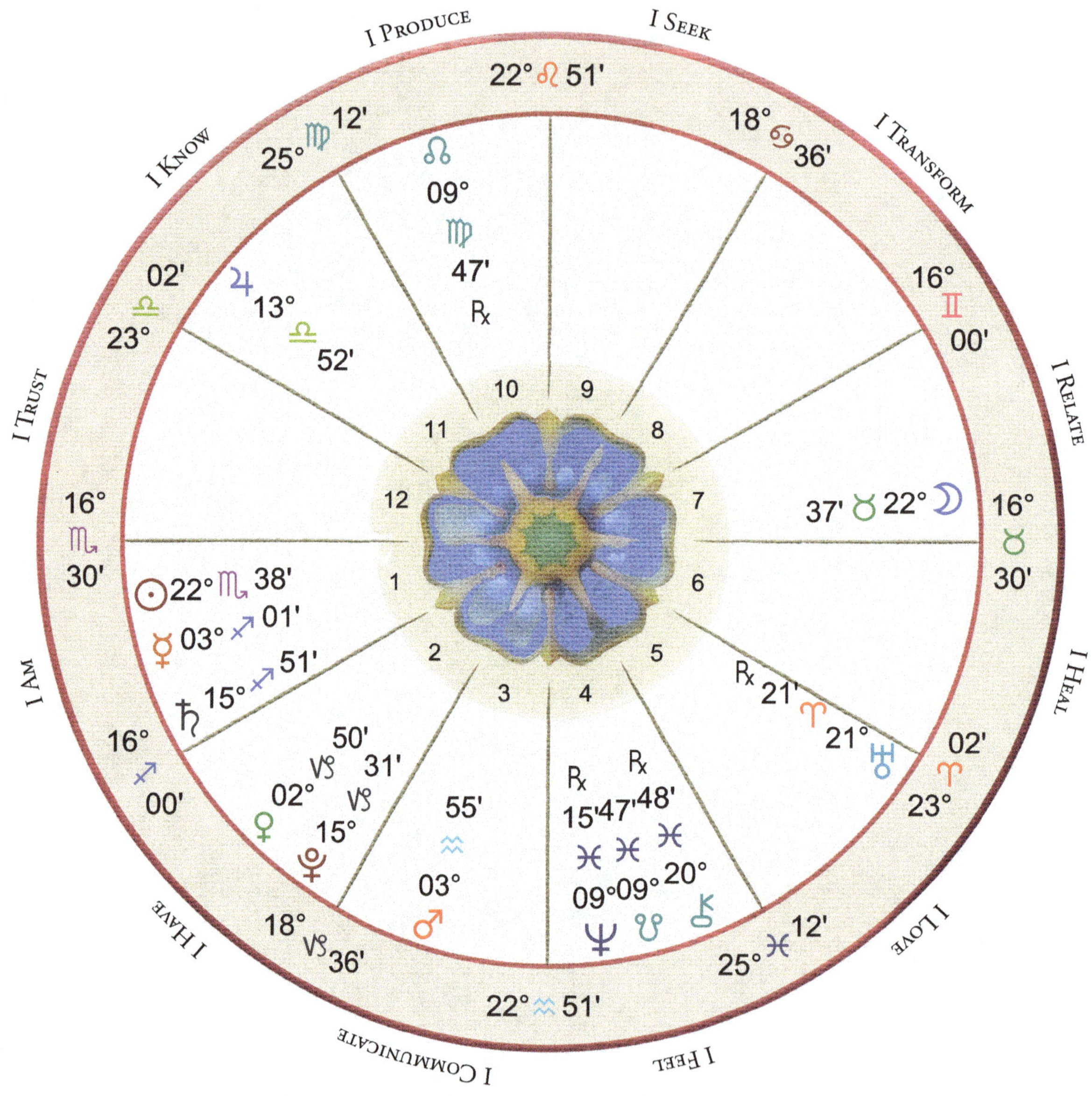

♈ Aries	♋ Cancer	♐ Sagittarius	☽ Moon	♄ Saturn	☊ North Node	V/C Void-of-Course
♉ Taurus	♌ Leo	♑ Capricorn	☿ Mercury	♅ Uranus	☋ South Node	▲ Super-Sensitivity
♊ Gemini	♍ Virgo	♒ Aquarius	♀ Venus	♆ Neptune	➔ Enters	▼ Low-Vitality
	♎ Libra	♓ Pisces	♂ Mars	♇ Pluto	℞ Retrograde	
	♏ Scorpio	☉ Sun	♃ Jupiter	⚷ Chiron	S/D Stationary Direct	

Cosmic Check-In

Take a moment to write a brief phrase for each "I" statement.
This activates all areas of your life for this creative cycle.

♉ I Have

♊ I Communicate

♋ I Feel

♌ I Love

♍ I Heal

♎ I Relate

♏ I Transform

♐ I Seek

♑ I Produce

♒ I Know

♓ I Trust

♈ I Am

New Moon in Sagittarius

November 29th
4:19 AM

Degree Choice Points
7° Sagittarius 43'

Light New Potentials
Shadow Unhealthy Growth
Wisdom Expansion doesn't require suffering.
Statement I Seek
 Body Thighs
 Mind Philosophical
 Spirit Inspiration

Element
Fire – Inspiring, leadership, charisma, igniting, adventure.

First House Moon
9° Scorpio 12'

First House Umbrella Theme
I Am/I Transform – Your outer appearance, the way you present yourself, the way you dress, the way you enter a room, and what you leave behind when you leave a room.

Light Enjoyable Bonding
Shadow Revealed Secrets
Wisdom Scattered energies (yours or someone else's) cause a need for rest.

When the Sun is in Sagittarius

Now is the time for greater expansion of consciousness. Sagittarius is about exterminating all of the man-eating symbols of our illusions, harmful thoughts, inertia, prejudices, and superstitions that hide behind our excuses. It is truth time, so that the Soul Goal of the Sagittarius can come into being and direct its light toward greater aspiration. Questions to ask yourself at this time are: What is my goal for myself? What is my goal for my nation? What is my goal for humanity? All goals get stimulated during this time.

Sagittarius Goddess

Let Persephone, who chose to stay in the Underworld half of the year and became the Queen of Death, be your guide as you enter the dark time of the year. Harvest is over and you now allow the land to become fallow – plowed, but unseeded. Persephone, in the version of the myth unspoiled by patriarchy, hears the cries of those stuck in purgatory, and is moved to voluntarily guide the anguished toward the completion of their spiritual journeys.

Of Persephone, also known as the maiden Kore, Plato wrote, "She is wise and touches that which is in motion." Where might you be stuck and how can Persephone get you moving in the right direction? What in your life do you seek to transform? Who do you wish to become?

Build Your Altar

Colors Deep purple, deep blue, turquoise
Numerology 5 – Avoid stagnation, keep things moving
Tarot Card Temperance – Blending physical and spiritual
Gemstones Turquoise, lapis
Plant Remedy Madia – Seeing the target and hitting it
Fragrance Magnolia – Expanded beauty

Manifesting List

This or something better than this comes to me in an easy and pleasurable way, for the good of all concerned. Thank you, Universe!

Sagittarius Manifesting Ideas

Now is the time to focus on manifesting truth, teaching and study, understanding advanced ideas, optimism and inspiration, bliss, goals, travel and adventure, and philosophy and culture.

November 29th
4:19 AM

New Moon in Sagittarius

Sagittarius Challenges and Victories

Say all of the statements in this section out loud. Then, underline the phrase that means the most to you. Use the phrase as your special affirmation for manifesting throughout this phase of the moon.

Destiny is in my favor today. I know, without a doubt, that I cannot make a wrong turn today. I access my blueprint to ensure perfect timing for all opportunities to be open to me today. I promise to be open to these opportunities, knowing full well that today is my day. I am on time and in time today. My destiny is here and working in my favor. I see all that is available to me today and claim my pathway to success. I pay attention to what comes my way today and know that it is an opening for good fortune to be my reality. I am ready to accept my good fortune now. All I have to do is move in the direction of my truth. I know that my truth is my good fortune. I trust in coincidence and synchronicity to provide me with direction to my destiny. All points of action lead me to my true expression. I can see clearly into my future today with great optimism. I intend it. I allow it. So be it. All is in Divine Order.

Mantra during this Time *(repeat this 10 times out loud)*

"My truth is my good fortune. My timing is perfect. I trust that all that comes to me today is in my highest and best good. I am open to optimism. The drum of destiny beats in my favor. So be it!"

Sagittarius Homework

Sagittarians manifest best through teaching, publishing and writing, travel, spiritual adventures, and as tour group leaders, airline and cruise ship personnel, evangelical ministers, philosophers, anthropologists, linguists, and translators.

The Sagittarius moon cycle creates a magnetic matrix that stimulates us to take direction towards becoming one with a goal and then sheds light on the path. In the ancient mystery schools, Sagittarius moons were used to set the stage for candidates to reach higher levels of awareness by inspiring their desire to reach a goal and then to step toward the goal. It is time now to become one with your goal.

Without Acknowledgment Progress Cannot Occur

Acknowledgement creates space for victory and gratitude, which automatically brings you to a level of completion so a new cycle of opportunity can occur in your life. When you celebrate your wins and acknowledge your victories with gratitude, you update your cells so that your ability to move forward is not hindered by a cellular holographic pattern that is stuck in the past. Cellular lag creates resistance and makes moving forward most difficult. The key is to stay continuously updated by acknowledging yourself for what you did do at the end of each day, rather than heading off to sleep thinking about what you did not do. By acknowledging what you did not do, you play into your karmic storage bank and keep your progress at bay. When you acknowledge yourself and your manifestations you are complete, and more cycles of opportunity become available to you in each new day. Be prepared for miracles!

Victory List

When a creation result is acknowledged it seals the deal. This makes room for more magnificence to expand into your life and increases your abundance factor adding to your ability to receive. As each aspect of your manifesting list arrives in your life, spend time allowing, acknowledging, and accepting it with the true gusto of gratitude! Keep your victory list active here.

This fulfills the relationship between the giver and the receiver, which completes the cycle with the Universe so that a new beginning can be established.

Gratitude List

November 29th
4:19 AM

New Moon in Sagittarius

How to Use the Moon Book With Your Chart

Fill in the blanks on the Cosmic Check-In page. Then look up the degree of the Moon on the chart below. Take note of the "I" statement on the outside of the wheel where the Moon is located. Now, locate the same degree on your own chart and make a note of the house and corresponding "I" statement. Go back to the Cosmic Check-In page and circle the two statements from the charts and read what you wrote. This will give you an idea about what to expect from this moon phase on a personal level.

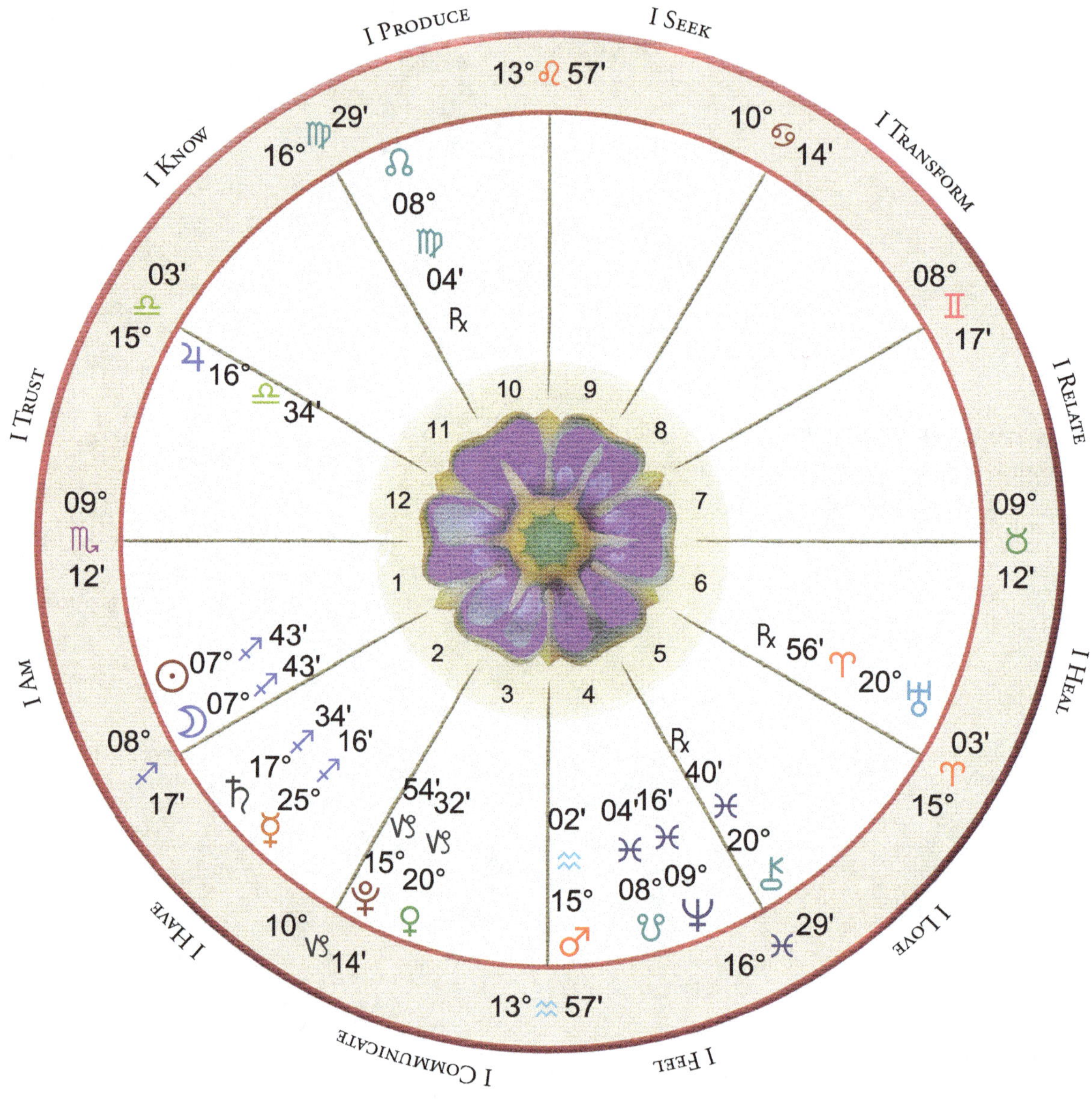

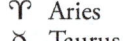

♈ Aries	♋ Cancer	♐ Sagittarius	☽ Moon	♄ Saturn	☊ North Node	V/C Void-of-Course
♉ Taurus	♌ Leo	♑ Capricorn	☿ Mercury	♅ Uranus	☋ South Node	▲ Super-Sensitivity
♊ Gemini	♍ Virgo	♒ Aquarius	♀ Venus	♆ Neptune	➡ Enters	• Low-Vitality
	♎ Libra	♓ Pisces	♂ Mars	♇ Pluto	℞ Retrograde	
	♏ Scorpio	☉ Sun	♃ Jupiter	⚷ Chiron	S/D Stationary Direct	

214

Cosmic Check-In

Take a moment to write a brief phrase for each "I" statement.
This activates all areas of your life for this creative cycle.

♐ I Seek

♑ I Produce

♒ I Know

♓ I Trust

♈ I Am

♉ I Have

♊ I Communicate

♋ I Feel

♌ I Love

♍ I Heal

♎ I Relate

♏ I Transform

December Planetary Highlights

Uranus is Retrograde in Aries until December 29

Know that the independent version of you is ready to live in truth in order to let the new you break through into freedom.

Mercury goes Retrograde in Capricorn on December 19 – Ending on January 8, 2017

Expect to be called into a situation that will require a re-write or a new level of research. Let the retrograde take you to the inner landscape of things, so that a great job can be done from this point of view. What seems like extra work is actually extra money coming your way.

December 2 – Mercury Enters Capricorn

The broad view of your business will incorporate new ways to market your ideas. The results will take you far beyond your former way of doing business.

December 7 – Venus Moves into Aquarius

You can fall in love with your mind right now. It's best to use your mind for creative innovation. Expect to be active in the fun zone. A trip to Disneyland could be very inspiring!

December 10 – Pluto and Mercury are Coupled in Capricorn

Now is the time to do that sales promotion. You have the right words and you have the right focus. You will be unstoppable ... GO FOR IT!

December 19 – Mars Enters Pisces

Sizzling hot emotional issues will be flying. Try to iron them out all at once, so you can be free at last. Face reality and all will be good. Ignoring it will slow you down and keep you from working the best angles. Remember the generous rewards will come to those who let go.

Neptune and the South Node Coupled Ongoing

Pay attention to this karmic situation and allow yourself to see beyond the box and enter the astral world. Be aware of a possible deep need for cosmic nurturing, while advancing beyond religious beliefs. Learn to trust that this is the way to go.

Jupiter and Uranus Opposition Ongoing

Expect sudden windfalls. Be spontaneous – a lot can happen when you turn on a dime.

Mars, Neptune, and the South Node Tripled in Pisces

Here is a difficult space for the ego, when it thinks it is right about holding on to the past. The extreme focus and drive to forge forward can get in the way if Neptune decides to influence with illusion. Beware – this could lead you down a road where there is no u-turn available.

Super-Sensitivity – December 27-28

Chaos is in the air. Do not engage.

Low-Vitality – December 13-14

Get rest and nurture yourself.

Sunday	Monday	Tuesday	Wednesday	Thursday	Friday	Saturday
				1 ♅℞ ☽→♑ 12:52am 7. Heartfelt energy brightens the mind.	**2** ♅℞ ♀→♑ 1:19pm 8. Strength of will knows courage.	**3** ♅℞ ☽ V/C 2:16am ☽→♒ 11:43am 9. Compassion is a caring heart.
4 ♅℞ 10. Be an adventurous spirit today.	**5** ♅℞ ☽ V/C 3:22am ☽→♓ 8:30pm 11. Life challenges us to be all we can.	**6** ♅℞ 3. To optimistic people, living is play.	**7** ♅℞ ♀→♒ 6:52am ☽ V/C 6:05am 4. Create a plan to enjoy the holidays.	**8** ♅℞ ☽→♈ 2:15am 5. Chaos precedes a positive shift.	**9** ♅℞ ☽ V/C 5:06pm 6. Give your living space a lift.	**10** ♅℞ ☽→♉ 4:40am 7. Our mind has Divine direction.
11 ♅℞ ☽ V/C 8:04pm 8. Good fortune is there for the asking.	**12** ♅℞ ☽→♊ 4:41am 9. Integrity is in the soul of beingness.	**13** ♅℞ ▼ ☽ V/C 9:57pm ○ 22°♊26′ 4:07pm 10. At the heart of growth is a new you.	**14** ♅℞ ▼ ☽→♋ 4:08am 11. Universal knowledge is yours.	**15** ♅℞ ☽ V/C 1:36pm 3. Creativity flows spontaneously.	**16** ♅℞ ☽→♌ 5:14am 4. The power of teamwork is infinite.	**17** ♅℞ 5. Stimulate your senses and thrive.
18 ♅℞ ☽ V/C 8:55am ☽→♍ 9:51am 6. Respect your body-temple.	**19** ♅℞ ☿℞ ♂→♓ 1:24am ☿℞ 15°♑07′ 3:56 am 7. There is always more to know.	**20** ♅℞ ☿℞ ☽ V/C 5:55pm ☽→♎ 6:39pm 8. Strive to be a generous leader.	**21** ♅℞ ☿℞ ☉→♑ 2:45am Winter Solstice 9. Spiritual satisfaction is in the now.	**22** ♅℞ ☿℞ ☽ V/C 11:31am 10. Use each rung of the success ladder.	**23** ♅℞ ☿℞ ☽→♏ 6:32am 11. Share your innovative thoughts.	**24** ♅℞ ☿℞ ☽ V/C 11:21pm 3. Your beliefs are truly yours.
25 ♅℞ ☿℞ Christmas Day Hanukkah ☽→♐ 7:18pm 4.You are important to the world.	**26** ♅℞ ☿℞ 5. Know when the direction is right.	**27** ♅℞ ☿℞ ▲ ☽ V/C 5:44pm 6. Meditation is the road to the Soul.	**28** ♅℞ ☿℞ ▲ ☽→♑ 7:11am ● 7°♑59′ 10:54pm 7. Listen quietly, answers are there.	**29** ☿℞ ♅SD -20°♈33′ 2:30am 8. Help others to be themselves.	**30** ☿℞ ☽ V/C 12:06am ☽→♒5:28pm 9. Enlightenment requires discretion.	**31** ☿℞ 10. At years end, a new cycle begins.

♈ Aries	♎ Libra	☉ Sun	♄ Saturn	☊ North Node	▲ Super Sensitivity	6. Love
♉ Taurus	♏ Scorpio	☽ Moon	♅ Uranus	☋ South Node	▼ Low Vitality	7. Learning
♊ Gemini	♐ Sagittarius	☿ Mercury	♆ Neptune	➡ Enters	2. Balance	8. Money
♋ Cancer	♑ Capricorn	♀ Venus	♇ Pluto	℞ Retrograde	3. Fun	9. Spirituality
♌ Leo	♒ Aquarius	♂ Mars	⚷ Chiron	SD Stationary Direct	4. Structure	10. Visionary
♍ Virgo	♓ Pisces	♃ Jupiter		V/C Void-of-Course	5. Action	11. Completion

December 13th
4:07 PM

Full Moon in Gemini

Degree Choice Points
22° Gemini 26'

Light	Spiritual Growth
Shadow	Creative Unrest
Wisdom	You are a champion at living in the moment.
Statement	I Communicate
Body	Lungs and Hands
Mind	Academic
Spirit	Intelligence

Element
  Air – Brings change, promotes curiosity, insight, and concepts.

First House Moon
  14° Gemini 28'

First House Umbrella Theme
  I Am/I Communicate – Your outer appearance, the way you present yourself, the way you dress, the way you enter a room, and what you leave behind when you leave a room.

Light	Like-mindedness
Shadow	Pipe Dreams
Wisdom	Give with an unbiased heart.

Karmic Awakening

Aries/Libra – Karma lives between the "I am" and the "We are."

Karma arises when the feeling of love is being overridden by the mind. Added karma can occur by making a choice for yourself alone and not considering your relationship or by making a choice for your partner without considering her vote.

The Sun is Opposite the Moon

Full moons are always in opposition to the Sun. This creates a feeling of tension between where you want to shine and how your feelings are flowing on a sensory level about the Sun's directive. The two forces seem like they are working against each other, yet they are on the same team displaying different techniques to obtain the same mission. The Gemini/Sagittarius polarity creates tension between community ideas and global thinking.

Gemini Goddess

Saraswati beckons you to withdraw from the party scene and into the quiet, contemplative process to dream your finest creations into being. Goddess of all creative endeavors: writing, art, dance, and music, Saraswati can assist you in your waking hours and in the dreamtime.

Get out your crayons, markers, paints, and pastels, and create a massive mind map with your happiness and fulfillment at the core (your new seedpod). What sprouts from the center? What branches off? Trust the process to generate ideas to rebirth you into joyful action! Post the map where you will see it often so it can serve as an active reminder of who you are and where you're headed!

Build Your Altar

Colors Bright yellow, orange, multi-colors

Numerology 10 – At the heart of growth is a new you

Tarot Card Lovers – Connecting to wholeness

Gemstones Yellow diamond, citrine, yellow jade, yellow topaz

Plant remedy Morning Glory – Thinking with your heart, not your head

Fragrance Iris – The ability to focus the mind

Clearing the Slate

Remember a time when you experienced the following trigger points.
Write down what happened and perform Ho'oponopono, the Hawaiian forgiveness ritual.

Gossiping

- I'm Sorry
- Please Forgive Me
- Thank You
- I Love You

Omitting the Truth

- I'm Sorry
- Please Forgive Me
- Thank You
- I Love You

Not Listening/Talking Too Much

- I'm Sorry
- Please Forgive Me
- Thank You
- I Love You

Hyperactivity

- I'm Sorry
- Please Forgive Me
- Thank You
- I Love You

Over-marketing

- I'm Sorry
- Please Forgive Me
- Thank You
- I Love You

December 13th
4:07 PM

Full Moon in Gemini

Gemini Challenges and Victories

Say all of the statements in this section out loud. Then, underline the phrase that means the most to you. Use the phrase as your special affirmation for recalibrating throughout this phase of the moon.

Today, I blend my old self with my new self, my physical reality with my spiritual awareness, my positive thoughts with my negative thoughts, my past with my present, my feminine with my masculine, my rewards with my losses, my ups with my downs, and my higher self with my lower self. It is a day for me to refine and fine tune my life by looking at my extremes. I recognize what inspires me and what keeps me stuck. I find my center today by acknowledging my extremes. I am aware that balance comes to those who are able to locate the space in the center of these opposite energy fields.

When I am in my center, my polarities are in motion. Healing cannot occur unless my polarities are moving and I know that healing is motion. I am ready for a healing today. I know that by visiting my opposites, and determining their vast opposition to each other, I can find the paradoxes that I have chosen for myself and begin to heal. I am willing to experiment with this blending of opposites and become the alchemist of my own life. When I blend all aspects of myself, rather than separating them, I can truly become whole. Today is a day to integrate, rather than separate, in order to release the spark of light that stays prisoner when my polarities are in operation. When I find balance, motion occurs and the Law of Harmony takes over, putting paradoxical energies to rest, thus breaking the crystallization of polarity. The Law of Harmony is beauty in motion and promotes the flow of color, light, sound, and movement into form. Balance is a condition that keeps my spark in motion. I become the vertical line in the center of polarity today and carry the secret of balance. Balance cannot be my goal; motion is my goal today. When I am in motion, I can take action to evolve and to express all of myself freely.

Gemini Homework

Sit still and invite silence into your space. Stay quiet and still for at least 5 minutes. During this time take an inventory and see where you have interrupted people in the middle of their sentences. Now is the time to make a conscious effort to allow others the space to express their thoughts. Keep sitting in silence and feel the frustration, while embracing the power of silence.

Recalibrating List

Say this statement out loud three times before writing your recalibrating list!

I am a free spiritual being and it is my desire to be free to think and to express myself fully.

From this day forward I resolve to be true – first to myself and my highest self, and then to the highest self in me which is the Source of Love That I Am.

Gemini Recalibrating Ideas

Now is the time to activate a game change in my life, and give up my attitude about unfinished business, shallow communication, old files and office clutter, broken communication devices, lies I tell myself, temptation to gossip, restlessness, over-thinking, and vacillation.

December 13th
4:07 PM

Full Moon in Gemini

How to Use the Moon Book With Your Chart

Fill in the blanks on the Cosmic Check-In page. Then look up the degree of the Moon on the chart below. Take note of the "I" statement on the outside of the wheel where the Moon is located. Now, locate the same degree on your own chart and make a note of the house and corresponding "I" statement. Go back to the Cosmic Check-In page and circle the two statements from the charts and read what you wrote. This will give you an idea about what to expect from this moon phase on a personal level.

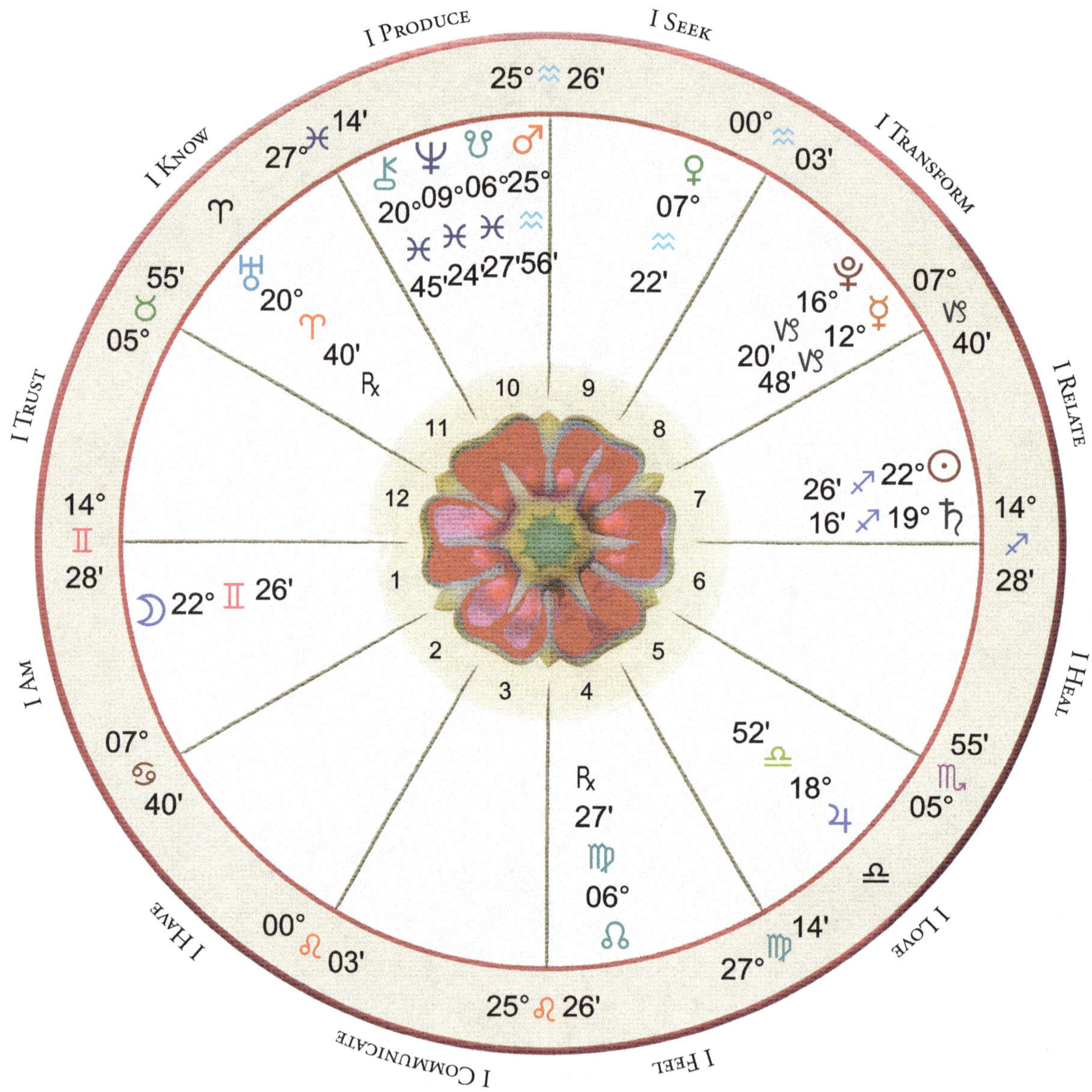

♈ Aries	♋ Cancer	♐ Sagittarius	☽ Moon	♄ Saturn	☊ North Node	V/C Void-of-Course
♉ Taurus	♌ Leo	♑ Capricorn	☿ Mercury	♅ Uranus	☋ South Node	▲ Super-Sensitivity
♊ Gemini	♍ Virgo	♒ Aquarius	♀ Venus	♆ Neptune	➡ Enters	● Low-Vitality
♎ Libra		♓ Pisces	♂ Mars	♇ Pluto	⚷ Chiron	℞ Retrograde
♏ Scorpio			☉ Sun			S/D Stationary Direct

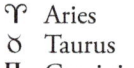

Cosmic Check-In

Take a moment to write a brief phrase for each "I" statement.
This activates all areas of your life for this creative cycle.

♊ I Communicate

♋ I Feel

♌ I Love

♍ I Heal

♎ I Relate

♏ I Transform

♐ I Seek

♑ I Produce

♒ I Know

♓ I Trust

♈ I Am

♉ I Have

December 28th
10:54 PM

New Moon in Capricorn

Degree Choice Points
7° Capricorn 59'

Light   Traditional

Shadow   Dogmatic

Wisdom   Accept the shadows, or fragments, of yourself and others.

Statement   I Produce
    Body   Knees
    Mind   Authority Issues
    Spirit   Self-reliance

Element
Earth – Unveiling the truth about you, security, patience, endurance, determination.

Fourth House Moon
24° Sagittarius 57'

Fourth House Umbrella Theme
I Feel/I Seek – The way your early environmental training was, how that set your foundation for living, and why you chose your mother.

Light   Innate Power

Shadow   Disappointment

Wisdom   You've ignited an internal quest for knowledge and self-renewal.

When the Sun is in Capricorn

When the Sun is in Capricorn, we are given opportunities to receive the blessings of abundance and prosperity on a concrete level. Material satisfaction is at the top of the priority list for Capricorns. This is why they are known to be ambitious. Let integrity and goodwill set the standard for your recognition and accomplishments. Now is the time to take advantage of the energy by being useful and productive with a higher purpose. Capricorn is going through the most difficult times right now as the "old guard" is being swept away and creating space for the opening of the human heart. The presence of Pluto in this constellation is transforming all of the systems and structures that are so familiar and placing the Capricorn on unstable ground. Authority symbols and traditions are dissolving and opening new pathways for self-reliance to emerge as a reality, so that the idea of elitism can diminish and synergy will be the new status quo.

Capricorn Goddess

Employing the mind map you generated last moon, take flight with winged Eos into a new beginning. Eos (known as Aurora by the Romans) awakes each morning to open the gates of heaven with her rosy fingers, so that her brother, Helios, can ride his chariot across the sky each day. She represents the hope of each brand-new dawn, and her strength is unbridled passion.

Instead of writing New Year's resolutions, allow Eos to infuse your world with bright, shimmering possibilities. She can gift you with a new daily mantra to live by, to amplify your dreams and take your desires to new heights. Allow the sparkling lights, glitter, and candlelight all around you remind you of how you can awaken to each new day and shine!

Build Your Altar

Colors   Forest green, tan, earth tones, deep red

Numerology   7 – Listen quietly, answers are there

Tarot Card   The Devil – Being a prisoner of a choice-less reality

Gemstones   Topaz, carnelian, amber, smoky quartz, jasper

Plant Remedy   Rosemary – The power of memory

Fragrance   Frankincense – Opens the gateway for the Soul to enter the body

Manifesting List

This or something better than this comes to me in an easy and pleasurable way, for the good of all concerned. Thank you, Universe!

Capricorn Manifesting Ideas

Now is the time to focus on manifesting flexibility, productivity, authenticity, timing, new paradigms, transmuting, transformation, and re-translating structure.

December 28th
10:54 PM

New Moon in Capricorn

Capricorn Challenges and Victories

Say all of the statements in this section out loud. Then, underline the phrase that means the most to you. Use the phrase as your special affirmation for manifesting throughout this phase of the moon.

Ultimate fulfillment is mine today! My willingness to live my life to the fullest, each day, is making all of my dreams come true. I am fulfilling the promise of my destiny, and, in so doing, I make my mark on the world. I have completed my commitment to the Earth and to the cosmos by being all that I can be in the cycles of time on the inner and outer planes of awareness. All four seasons have been activated within me, so that I am in alignment and in motion with the cycles of releasing, rebirthing, planting, and harvesting. I can now claim my citizenship in all four worlds. I am open and ready for the inspiration that the spirit world brings me. I am ready to conquer the mental world by using thought, rather than thinking. I am open to the expression of my heart and the magnetic field of love that is ever-present in my experience. I am open to receive abundance from Nature and I contribute to the physical world by actively manifesting my ideas into reality. I am in harmony with the four elements and keep them active within me, as well as contribute to them externally. The element of air is within me as I breathe in the miracle of life. The element of earth is within me as I honor my body and use all of its senses to enhance the quality of life. I honor the Earth as my home and take complete stewardship of my home and property on this Earth. I honor the water, the wellspring of life eternal, and allow for the flow of my feelings and emotions to be a creative influence on the unconscious and conscious planes. I honor the fire within me as the spark of light that is a source of inspiration in my experience, and, in so doing, I have fulfilled the promise of my destiny to live fully, freely, and passionately on all levels and on all dimensions with my Earth-Cosmos connection.

Capricorn Homework

The Capricorn moon is the reincarnation of Spirit, emerging from the dark waters of our past emotions and releasing us from our fears of change and loss. Awaken your powerful and positive spiritual connection to be open to new possibilities. Ask yourself to move beyond your emotional loyalty to the past in order to manifest. We are reminded of our need for material and emotional security at this time. In order to ensure this, we must learn to build a foundation for ourselves that is lit from within, and made from the materials of love, goodwill, and intelligence. Give yourself permission to throw away your watch and celebrate living in the moment.

Without Acknowledgment Progress Cannot Occur

Acknowledgement creates space for victory and gratitude, which automatically brings you to a level of completion so a new cycle of opportunity can occur in your life. When you celebrate your wins and acknowledge your victories with gratitude, you update your cells so that your ability to move forward is not hindered by a cellular holographic pattern that is stuck in the past. Cellular lag creates resistance and makes moving forward most difficult. The key is to stay continuously updated by acknowledging yourself for what you did do at the end of each day, rather than heading off to sleep thinking about what you did not do. By acknowledging what you did not do, you play into your karmic storage bank and keep your progress at bay. When you acknowledge yourself and your manifestations you are complete, and more cycles of opportunity become available to you in each new day. Be prepared for miracles!

Victory List

When a creation result is acknowledged it seals the deal. This makes room for more magnificence to expand into your life and increases your abundance factor adding to your ability to receive. As each aspect of your manifesting list arrives in your life, spend time allowing, acknowledging, and accepting it with the true gusto of gratitude! Keep your victory list active here.

This fulfills the relationship between the giver and the receiver, which completes the cycle with the Universe so that a new beginning can be established.

Gratitude List

December 28th
10:54 PM

New Moon in Capricorn

How to Use the Moon Book With Your Chart

Fill in the blanks on the Cosmic Check-In page. Then look up the degree of the Moon on the chart below. Take note of the "I" statement on the outside of the wheel where the Moon is located. Now, locate the same degree on your own chart and make a note of the house and corresponding "I" statement. Go back to the Cosmic Check-In page and circle the two statements from the charts and read what you wrote. This will give you an idea about what to expect from this moon phase on a personal level.

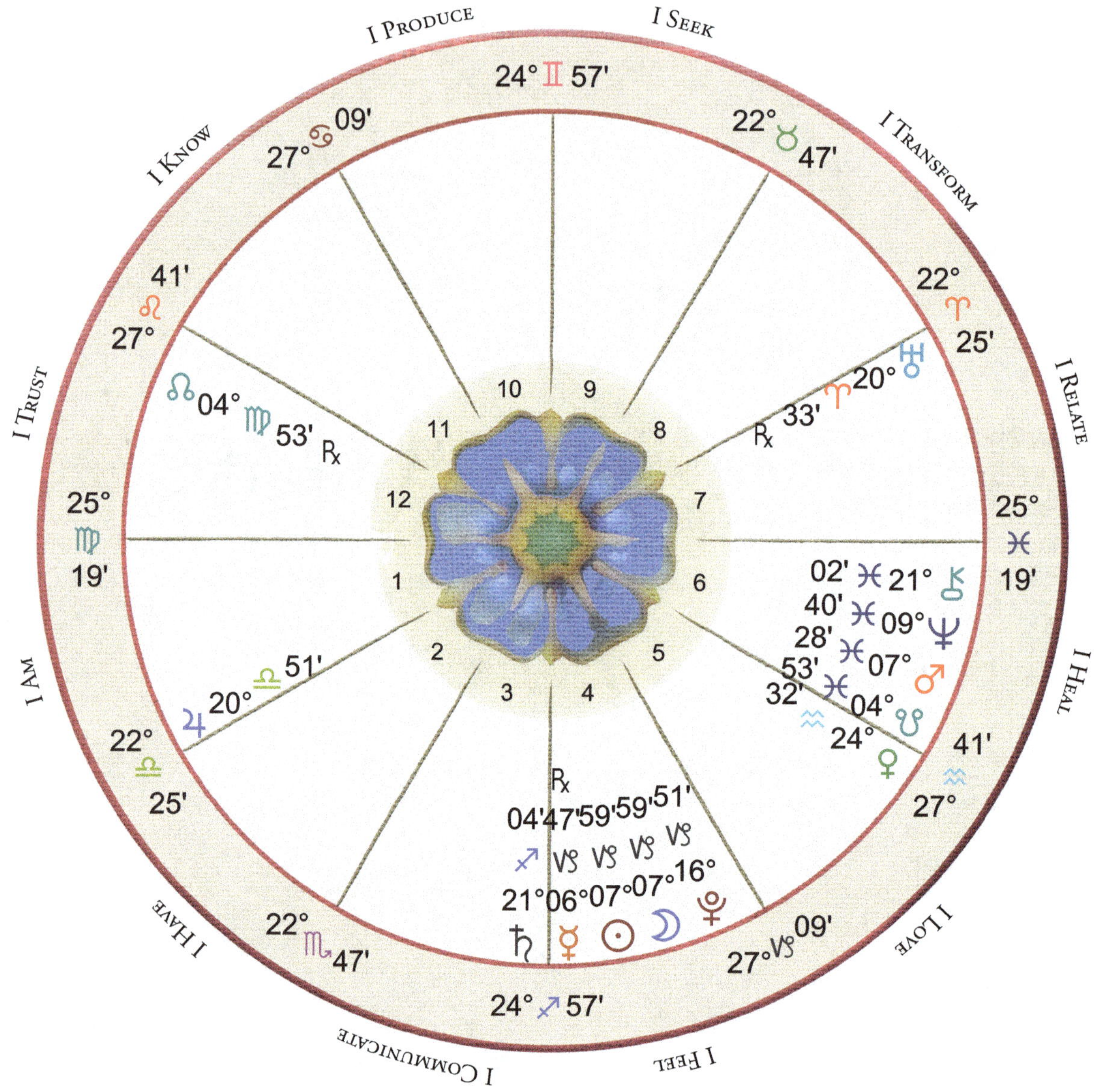

♈ Aries	♋ Cancer	♐ Sagittarius	☽ Moon	♄ Saturn	☊ North Node	V/C Void-of-Course
♉ Taurus	♌ Leo	♑ Capricorn	☿ Mercury	♅ Uranus	☋ South Node	▲ Super-Sensitivity
♊ Gemini	♍ Virgo	♒ Aquarius	♀ Venus	♆ Neptune	➧ Enters	▼ Low-Vitality
	♎ Libra	♓ Pisces	♂ Mars	♇ Pluto	℞ Retrograde	
	♏ Scorpio	☉ Sun	♃ Jupiter	⚷ Chiron	S/D Stationary Direct	

232

Cosmic Check-In

Take a moment to write a brief phrase for each "I" statement.
This activates all areas of your life for this creative cycle.

♑ I Produce

♒ I Know

♓ I Trust

♈ I Am

♉ I Have

♊ I Communicate

♋ I Feel

♌ I Love

♍ I Heal

♎ I Relate

♏ I Transform

♐ I Seek

About the Author

Interested in ongoing Moon Classes and workshops with Beatrex?

Contact her at beatrex@cox.net or visit www.beatrex.com

For Moon-related products created by Beatrex, visit

www.MyMoonBook.com

Beatrex Quntanna

Tarot expert, published author, symbolist, poet, lecturer—Beatrex is one of the luminaries of our time. Synthesizing 40 years of spiritual teachings, intuitive skills, and conventional counseling, she translates this wealth of wisdom into practical language making it accessible to all and applicable in today's world. Known for being "the teacher's teacher," her experience and advice has served as an invaluable support for many of today's spiritual teachers and professional psychics. She guides with profound insight, compassion for the human experience, and humor; inspiring personal growth and activating an inner-knowing in her students that sparks a self-confidence to walk tall in this world as a spiritual being.

Her life's work is showing how to Live Love Every Day by *living* astrology, not just intellectualizing it—teaching others how to ebb and flow with the natural cycles of the Moon and the cosmos, rather than working against them. She teaches this through Moon Classes held regularly throughout the year, and is the creator of *Living by the Light of the Moon*, a popular annual workbook that takes you step-by-step through her process.

Beatrex has written the ultimate book on the Tarot and its symbols, *Tarot: A Universal Language*, which has been reviewed by magazines in Europe as well as in the United States. She is the creator and co-presenter of the popular Annual Tarot Workshop with Michael Makay, designed as a complete support system to enhance your understanding of how best to work with the transformative energies of the upcoming year.

Beatrex's many print credits, as well as numerous radio, TV, and video appearances include:

- Regular guest blogger for Satiama.com and True Nature Healing Arts
- Contributing author to two anthologies by Maria Yracébûrû – *Prophetic Voices* and *Ah-Kine Remembrance*
- Monthly guest on *Spirit Seeker Hour* with host Cynde Meyer – tune in to *Spirit Seeker Magazine's* internet radio show on the first Tuesday of each month to get a free psychic mini-reading
- *Cosmic Check-In with Beatrex Quntanna* – a monthly YouTube show produced by Janet Blessings of The Lightstone Academy of Psychic Arts

Beatrex teaches ongoing astrology classes, facilitates a regular meditation group, and continues to be available for private group workshops in Encinitas, California.

2016 The Year of Generosity

Wall Calendar

Presented by

Beatrex Quntanna ☙ Michael Makay ☙ Katherine Sale

It is generosity that keeps prosperity alive.

Generosity was born out of the heart of compassion. According to Buddhist mythology, "One day a Yogi was walking through the forest and saw a man starving. The suffering was so severe that the Yogi wanted to cut off his own arm to feed the man to end his suffering. He could see that the suffering was distracting the man from his spiritual path. When suffering is present, one can't experience the bliss created by being spiritual." Hence the Generosity Buddha was born to keep prosperity alive, to awaken bliss in us, and to end suffering for all.

The Year 2016 is a "9" in numerology and rules spirituality. It's guaranteed to bring us to a new form of bliss. One of the leading roles for this year is being played by Jupiter, "The Great Benefactor." It's all about having a great supply of laughter, fun, good fortune, and abundance. Jupiter's guidance leads us to a place where the grass is greener. The other starring role for the year is being played by Neptune, whose assignment is keeping spirituality alive by inspiring new dreams, causes, or consciousness groups. So, concepts like service, unification, humanitarianism, and volunteerism will come into the forefront in our lives.

For the last three years, we've been experiencing subtle, emotional energy and now the Fire element comes into play. You can expect your personality to be more passionate, dynamic, expressive, and right out front. You will succeed by being warm-hearted, giving generously, and allowing yourself to receive.

This calendar is designed as a complete support system to enhance your understanding of how best to work with planetary movements and numerological influences throughout the entire year.

To order, call 1-760-944-6020
or go to www.mymoonbook.com

The 2016 Wall Calendar is packed full of intuitive hints to help you along your way, including:

- Planetary Highlights that explain what's happening with the planetary bodies in an easy-to-understand way

- Daily Intentions based on Tibetan numerology by Michael Makay

- Planetary Retrogrades listed monthly

- Moons (New, Full, and Void) calculated by Katherine Sale and referenced with regard to time, astrological sign, and degree

- Super-Sensitivity and Low-Vitality days

- Ingresses that mark when the Sun enters a new Zodiac Sign

- The art, graphics, and thoughtful creativity of Jennifer Masters

Tarot: A Universal Language

Experiencing the Road of Life Through Symbols

By Beatrex Quntanna

Embark on this fascinating journey through the unfolding Story of Life as told by the Universal Language of the Tarot. This book contains innovative avenues to understand the tarot through the author's in-depth knowledge of symbology.

Learn how to quickly read and interpret the Tarot by following this simple, informative, and illustrated guide. Use the expanded symbology section to understand each symbol depicted on the Minor and Major Arcana cards.

This book includes an interpretation of all 78 Tarot cards, plus readings created by this nationally-known Tarot teacher, reader, and symbolist.

**To order, call 1-760-944-6020
or go to www.Beatrex.com**

"Brilliantly Engineered."

"Amazingly Accurate."

"A refreshing, uncluttered approach to learning the Tarot."

"Her exceptional background in symbology and numerology, as well as her extraordinary psychic insight, make this book unique among Tarot books, and a must-have reference for the Tarot novice and professional alike."